MEDINA IN BIRMINGHAM, NAJAF IN BRENT

INNES BOWEN

Medina in Birmingham, Najaf in Brent

Inside British Islam

HURST & COMPANY, LONDON

First published in the United Kingdom in 2014 by
C. Hurst & Co. (Publishers) Ltd.,
41 Great Russell Street, London, WC1B 3PL
© Innes Bowen, 2014
All rights reserved.
Printed in England

The right of Innes Bowen to be identified as the author
of this publication is asserted by her in accordance with
the Copyright, Designs and Patents Act, 1988.

A Cataloguing-in-Publication data record for this book
is available from the British Library.

ISBN: 978-1849043014

www.hurstpublishers.com

CONTENTS

ACKNOWLEDGEMENTS

This book could not have been completed were it not for the help of those whom it is about: the followers of Britain's most important Islamic networks. I am grateful to the many individuals who made time to be interviewed and trusted me to tell their stories. They are too numerous to mention here by name but most are attributed in the chapters that follow. Some of those I interviewed and who helped me in my research deserve special thanks for their time and patience: the Muslim Brotherhood activist Dr Kamal Helbawy; Abu Khadeejah of Salafi Publications in Birmingham; Mehmood Naqshbandi, creator of the indispensable website muslimsinbritain.org; Faruqe Master; and Yahya Birt.

Writing this book has been a part-time project, undertaken in the evenings, weekends and holidays around my full-time job as a BBC journalist. It has therefore taken a long time to complete—almost seven years, in fact. Thankfully I had a patient and encouraging publisher in Michael Dwyer of Hurst. He made finishing the manuscript feel achievable at a time when I was ready to give up. I am grateful to his team: copyeditor Tim Page and proofreader Hannah Wann, cover designer Fatima Jamadar, and the rest of the team: Jon de Peyer, Rob Pinney and Georgie Williams. They have done a wonderful job in producing and marketing the book.

I have colleagues, friends and family to thank too. First among them is my editor at the BBC, Nicola Meyrick, who encouraged me soon after I arrived in her department in 2002 to develop an interest in this topic. When that interest grew into an extra-curricula obsession she regarded it as an asset rather than a nuisance. This book is not a BBC project but it was prompted by the journalism I did and the radio programmes I

ACKNOWLEDGEMENTS

made under Nicola's editorship. Other early inspiration for this topic came from Dr Aminul Hoque who presented my first BBC programme about Islam in Britain and from my colleague Mukul Devichand who, as ever, was ahead of the game in getting to grips with an important subject that few of us understood. Andrew Bowen urged me to channel my interest into a book and never seemed to doubt that I would complete it. Without his encouragement, I would not have embarked upon such a huge task. Fiona Leach, a fellow BBC journalist, read the whole book in draft form and did much to help me improve the structure and content. Former *Woman's Hour* colleagues Sharmini Selvarajah, Katy Hickman and Jenni Murray read some of the draft chapters and suggested ways of making them more accessible to readers who do not share my preoccupation with the subject. Helen Grady, another BBC journalist, read some of the draft material and suggested people to interview and stories to pursue. Sajid Iqbal from BBC Monitoring was on hand at short notice to translate from Urdu into English and to offer wise advice.

Finally, I wish to thank my mother, Janet. When I have needed time and a lack of distractions to write, she has taken care of all the essential things in life like food and a place to stay and has never uttered a word of complaint about my reclusiveness or expected anything in return. Without her support I might never have finished.

Innes Bowen   February 2014

GLOSSARY

A note on italicisation

Foreign words which are now in common use in the English language (e.g. hijab, jihad and sharia) appear in roman script (without italicization) and an 's' is added to denote the plural. The exception to this is the term *ulema*, which means Islamic scholars, and is in more common use in English than the word for a single scholar which is *alim*.

For less familiar words which are used regularly in this book (e.g. *alima*) in the first instance the word is defined in English and its transliterated foreign form follows italicised in parentheses. Thereafter, I have used either used the English term or the foreign term in roman script.

alim (plural: *ulema*)	Islamic religious scholar (male)
alima	Female Islamic religious scholar
amir	leader
ayatollah	honorific title given to senior shi'ite religious scholar
caliph	ruler of the *caliphate*
caliphate	an Islamic state or empire
bayat	an oath of allegiance
chillah	The group Tablighi Jamaat's term for a trip of forty days to do missionary work.
darul uloom	Islamic seminary.
dawa	Inviting people to practise the Islamic faith.
fatwa	An opinion on an issue of Islamic law, issued by a scholar.

GLOSSARY

hadith	A recorded deed or saying of the Prophet Moham-med or one of his early companions.
hijab	Literally a screen or partition; the term is more commonly used to describe modest clothing for Muslim women, in particular the headscarf.
khalifa	Successor or deputy to a sheikh in *tasawwuf*.
kuffar	Non-believers or non-Muslims.
madhab (plural: *madhahib*)	A traditional school of Islamic law and doctrine. The four major schools of Sunni Islamic law are Hanafi, Maliki, Hanbali and Shafi'i. Most Sunni Muslims follow one of these four *madhahib*.
marja	a leading shi'ite scholar recognised as worthy of emulation
markaz	Term used by the missionary group Tablighi Jamaat to describe one of its main centres.
milad a nabi	Celebration of the Prophet Mohammed's birthday (also known as *mawlid*).
mawlid	Celebration of the Prophet Mohammed's birthday (also known as *milad a nabi*).
mureed	Disciple of a sheikh in *tasawwuf*.
niqab	Face veil.
pir	A sheikh in *tasawwuf*, also sometimes referred to as a *murshid*.
salafism	A branch of Sunni Islam which attempts to emulate the early followers of Islam and defers less to the traditional schools of Sunni Islamic law.
sufism	A branch of Islam which emphasises spirituality and mysticism.
tariqa	A sufi network led by a sheikh in *tasawwuf*.
tasawwuf	The spiritual and mystical aspects of Islam.
ulema (masculine singular: *alim*; feminine singular: *alima*)	Islamic religious scholars
zikr (also *dhikr*)	Spiritual meditation, chanting or more ecstatic forms of worship.

INTRODUCTION

What individual Muslims feel in their hearts about Britain and its people will have a huge impact upon the future of the UK's community relations as well as its national security. Yet the religious trends which inform the thoughts and feelings of Britain's Muslim communities are still poorly understood.

This book aims to fill that gap in understanding. The book is based on extensive interviews with followers from all the mainstream Islamic groups in the UK and is a guide to the way these believers see the world.

There already exists a great deal of sociological research into Britain's Muslim population, including analysis of ethnicity, familial structures, gender roles, educational attainment, employment, migration patterns and experiences of racism.[1] This is useful work. But ideology is important too. The phenomenon of 'home-grown' terrorism in Britain cannot, for example, be explained in purely sociological terms. Those involved in terrorist plots have come from a wide range of ethnic, social and educational backgrounds. The only thing they have had in common is a shared set of ideas and a willingness to act on them.

The motivation for writing this book was the belief that the content of the ideologies that are popular in Muslim Britain matters. The task of researching and explaining those belief systems felt all the more urgent when I realised that the politicians, interfaith groups, police and journalists who interact with these Islamic groups often know shockingly little about them.

In one English city I visited, the police had a relationship with the management committees of just five of the 100 local mosques. A police officer I spoke to despaired at the ignorance of many of his colleagues, yet even he knew little about 95 per cent of the mosques in his patch and was oblivious to the fact that one of his favoured Muslim organisations had played host to a jihadi leader from Pakistan.

A lack of knowledge exists not just at the grassroots level of the British state but at the top as well. In 2006 I met a man who was advising a senior Cabinet minister on relations with Britain's Muslim communities. He told me that a mosque mentioned in an August 2005 edition of the BBC series *Panorama* should have been identified as Shi'ite.[2] He was quite sure about this because the mosque in question was a prominent one in his hometown. But he was wrong. Like the vast majority of mosques in the UK, it was Sunni controlled. The same man also spoke warmly of a prominent British Islamic organisation but was ignorant of its barely concealed links to a foreign political party. He would not have been the minister's only adviser on this topic, but the fact that such an unreliable source of information was relied upon at all says something about the lack of expertise—even five years after 9/11—at the highest level of government.

When I started to research my first programme on Islam in Britain for BBC Radio in 2003 I knew almost nothing about the topic. I was grateful to find a couple of young researchers who had a head start on me and were willing to share what they knew. But I struggled to find reliable sources of information about the bigger picture: the identity, size and beliefs of these different groups across Britain.

In those days I, like most journalists, assumed that the Muslim Council of Britain (MCB) was the true representative body of Islam in Britain. In 2005, shortly after the 7 July bombings in London, that view was corrected by journalist Martin Bright and BBC *Panorama* reporter John Ware. Although they worked independently of each other, Bright and Ware reached the same startling conclusion: far from being representative of Muslims in Britain, the MCB was controlled by a group which manages fewer than 4 per cent of Britain's mosques and which had links to the Jamaat-e-Islami, a political party based in Pakistan and Bangladesh. The Jamaat-e-Islami, we were told by Ware and Bright, was an 'Islamist' political party which sought to turn Muslim-majority countries into states governed by sharia law and united under a single leader called a *caliph*. It was a surprise to be told that the leaders of the group usually described as the voice of 'moderate mainstream' British Muslims might be dreaming of a theocratic state.

The work done by Bright and Ware was followed in 2007 by the publication of *The Islamist*, the memoir of Ed Husain, a former member of one of the Jamaat-e-Islami's British youth organisations. Husain identified Islamism—which he defined as an ideology preoccupied with creating Islamic states—as the principal cause of Muslim radicalisation in Britain and a source of hostility towards secular Britain and its people.

Ed Husain's book and the journalism of Bright and Ware provided essential background for any layperson trying to understand Islamic politics in Britain at the time. But their work gave rise to another mistaken assumption: that all the activists of Britain's Jamaat-e-Islami spin-offs still adhered to the party's original vision of establishing an Islamic state. In reality, the British groups and organisations which were set up with the help of Jamaat-e-Islami elders have evolved in diverse ways, with some even supporting secularism and holding relatively liberal views on the role of women.

However, by 2006, the tide against the MCB had begun to turn. Key government ministers, perhaps influenced by the revelations of Bright and Ware, began to look for other Muslim groups with which they could do business—and they settled on the Sufis.

Sufism tends to emphasise the spiritual aspects of religion, often through ecstatic forms of meditation and chanting. It was seen as the 'love and peace' alternative to Islamism because, although Sufis tend to believe that Muslims will one day live in an Islamic state, they trust that this will be brought about by the grace of God rather than political action.

In Britain, the Sufis managed only belatedly to gain political recognition at a national level. Between 2005 and 2006, they launched two umbrella organisations: the British Muslim Forum (BMF) and the Sufi Muslim Council (SMC).

Sufism is the dominant form of Islam among British Muslims of Pakistani origin, which is easily the largest Muslim ethnic group in Britain.

Sufism in Britain is dominated by two rival South Asian religious movements: the Barelwis and the Deobandis. Only the Barelwis were represented by the Sufi Muslim Council and the British Muslim Forum.

The Barelwi movement was established in nineteenth-century India to defend certain types of Sufi practices against ideological attack from the Deobandis. The Barelwis and Deobandis are both mainstream Sunni Muslim movements but they express their religious devotion in different ways. Thus, whereas the Barelwis celebrate the birthday of the Prophet Muhammad, the Deobandis regard the way in which these celebrations are marked with festivities as wrongful innovation. The Barelwis emphasise love and spirituality while the Deobandis are more puritanical, putting more stress on orthodoxy and knowledge of Islamic texts. Most Muslims follow one of four main Sunni Islamic legal schools of thought (each one known as a *madhab*): Hanafi, Maliki, Hanbali and Shafi'i. Both Barelwis and Deobandis tend to adhere to the Hanafi school, so in a sense they subscribe to the same laws but have somehow evolved different religious cultures.

Neither the SMC nor the BMF could credibly claim to represent a majority of British Muslims as neither had managed to attract support from the Deobandis. Deobandi organisations run most of the UK-based training of Islamic scholars and control 44 per cent of Britain's mosques and nearly 40 per cent of mosque capacity. Barelwis control around one-quarter of the UK's mosques and nearly 36 per cent of UK mosque capacity.[3] These figures probably underestimate Deobandi influence: Barelwi mosques are far more likely than Deobandi mosques to provide prayer facilities for both the men and women in their communities, so the capacity of Barelwi mosques is large relative to the number of families they serve.[4]

It is perhaps the austere style of many Deobandis which leads some outsiders to jump to the conclusion that they are a spin-off of Saudi Arabia's puritanical Wahhabi movement. In the Deobandi-dominated districts of Britain such as Savile Town in Dewsbury and Highfields in Leicester, for example, women wearing Saudi-style black gowns and face veils are a common sight. A briefing prepared for President Barack Obama's adviser on Muslim engagement even stated that the Highfields district of Leicester was dominated by Wahhabi influenced Muslims.[5] Yet as this book explains, the similarities between the Deobandis and the Wahhabis are largely superficial and the doctrinal differences are deep.

The real Wahhabis of Britain prefer to call themselves Salafis, a term which literally means predecessors but in the Islamic context means those who follow the practices of the first generations of Muslims. Salafis feel that to call someone a 'Wahhabi' is to suggest that the person in question is a follower of Mohammed ibn Abd al-Wahhab rather than a follower of 'the true Islam'. To complicate things further, not even all Salafis agree with the Islamic interpretations of Mohammed ibn Abd al-Wahhab.

Britain's Salafis are as much misunderstood as the Deobandis. The fact that many follow the dominant religious ideology of Saudi Arabia has meant, with some justification, that they have long been suspected of intolerance towards other religions and other branches of their own faith. In the aftermath of 9/11 it was noted that Osama bin Laden and fifteen of the nineteen airline hijackers had been brought up in Saudi Arabia. 'Wahhabi' ideology was widely blamed for creating Islam's terrorist fringe. Many wanted to know what influence it had in Britain.

Saudi Arabians have never made up more than a tiny fraction of the UK's Muslim population. The small South Asian Salafi movement, known as the Ahl-e-Hadith, has been active in the UK since the 1960s. From the 1990s the Salafi presence in Britain grew more rapidly as North African veterans of the Afghan jihad—many of whom regarded themselves as Salafis—sought exile in the UK, as did some of their leading ideologues, such as the preacher Abu Qatada. By this time Salafism was also starting to find a receptive audience among some of the sons and daughters of Britain's first generation of South Asian Muslim immigrants and was attracting British converts to Islam too. Some of the most dedicated young Salafis were recruited with Saudi-funded scholarships to study at the Kingdom's international university in Medina. They returned home as preachers, setting up mosques and bookshops and spreading the Salafi message in English to another generation of potential recruits.

When it became clear that a small element within Britain's Muslim population posed a terrorist threat to the wider community, the growing Wahhabi–Salafi presence was blamed. Like many people, I found the claim easy to believe on the basis that the most prominent radical preachers in Britain—Abu Qatada, Abu Hamza, Abdullah al Faisal and Sheikh Omar Bakri—called themselves Salafis.

But conflating Salafi doctrine with the ideology of al-Qaeda was a mistake, as I discovered when a colleague and I visited a Salafi bookshop in Birmingham in 2004. 'Osama bin Laden is a Muslim yes, but he's a Muslim who's evil and every single Muslim should be united in opposing him,' we were told by Abu Khadeejah, a prominent British Salafi. He gave a pithy explanation of why in Islamic terms the 9/11 attacks were wrong: 'Salafis don't deny jihad. But for a jihad you need to have a leader and that leader needs to have a land. Osama bin Laden has no land. He is no leader of the Muslims. He is just an ignorant individual with a lot of money.'

Abu Khadeejah's explanation of what constitutes a lawful jihad follows that of some senior Salafi scholars in the Middle East. Their basic conclusion sounds similar to traditional Western distinctions between war and terrorism—governments can declare war but individuals and insurgent groups cannot. It is a view that Abu Khadeejah and his colleagues have been arguing in British Salafi circles since the mid-1990s and that they have spread to an English-speaking audience worldwide via the Salafi Publications website.

The Metropolitan Police's Special Branch understood these nuances. It was one of the few public sector organisations that had the resources and inclination to develop in-depth knowledge about the ideological make-up of the Islamic population. Through its Muslim Contact Unit, the Met sent officers into the community to engage openly with members of London's diverse Muslim population. The aim was to get to know and understand the local Muslim communities in all of their complexity.

This book is likewise largely based on research at grassroots level, albeit on a more modest scale. Since 2007 I have interviewed over eighty Muslims from the most important Islamic groups in Britain.

To help identify which groups might be worth researching, I looked for data on the ideological affiliations of mosques in Britain. I found that the most detailed, publicly available research had not been carried out in a university or government department, but in the spare bedroom of a terraced house in South London. The man who has done all of this (unpaid) research is Mehmood Naqshbandi, an English convert to Islam who works full time in IT. For many years his job took him to different parts of Britain, and wherever he went he sought out a local mosque in which to worship. He started to share his knowledge of mosque locations, size and affiliation on a website.[6] The number of visitors to the site grew rapidly. Naqshbandi estimated that the site was receiving over 120,000 unique users per month by March 2013. The site's popularity has brought with it the opportunity to 'crowd source' information as users contact Naqshbandi with updates and corrections. After the UK Census, the site is the single most useful dataset on Islam in Britain.

In April 2013 Mehmood Naqshbandi kindly did some calculations for me based on the extensive data he had collected.

Mehmood Naqshbandi gives this caveat: he has no information regarding the capacity of around 40 per cent of the places of worship on his database. In these cases he has assumed a capacity of 200 people on the basis that this is the average for smaller mosques. Furthermore, the school of thought to which those controlling the mosque belong is not necessarily the school of thought to which the whole congregation subscribes.

Mosque type	Number of mosques in UK	Mosque capacity in the UK	Percentage of total number of mosques in UK	Percentage of total mosque capacity in the UK
Deobandi	738	330,502	44.4	39.5
Barelwi	428	299,725	25.7	35.8
Other Sufi	49	25,330	2.9	3.0
Maududi inspired [Jamaat-e-Islami]	51	26,900	3.1	3.2
Salafi	98	44,994	5.9	5.4
Arab and African mainstream	43	27,521	2.6	3.3
Muslim Brotherhood	7	4,870	0.4	0.6
Shia Twelvers and Ismailis*	70	38,955	4.2	4.7
Modernist	2	600	0.1	0.1
Ahmadiyya movement	22	8,130	1.3	1.0
Non-denominational Muslim prayer rooms etc.	156	29,291	9.4	3.5
Total	1,664	836,818	100.0	100.0

*Mehmood Naqshbandi cautions that his figures on the Shia are less authoritative than his figures on other groups. The figure of seventy Shi'ite mosques and places of worship is probably an underestimate. Shia community sources indicate that the true figure is around 110.

This book looks at all the larger groups listed in Mehmood Naqshbandi's table, as well as some of the smaller ones. The UK's Ismaili Muslim population, which estimates its size to be no more than 50,000, is the subject of a chapter on the basis that, although it is small, it has influential links with the British establishment and internationally. Likewise, the Muslim Brotherhood controls just seven mosques in Britain but, on account of its importance in the Middle East, it is the subject of a separate chapter too.

Some minor groups are not included in this book. I have not for example researched the Ahmadiyya movement (also called the 'Qadianis' by their detractors). Many Muslims do not regard the Ahmadis as true followers of Islam, but, the omission of a chapter on the Ahmadiyya movement is purely due to their size rather than their interpretation of Islam.

Nor does this book reflect the increasing ethnic diversity of Britain's Muslim population. It instead concentrates on the Islamic trends followed by the most influential Muslim ethnic groups in Britain. The South Asian (Pakistani, Indian and Bangladeshi) Muslims of Britain are the dominant group. According to the 2011 Census, Muslims who identified themselves as of Pakistani, Indian or Bangladeshi ethnicity made up 60 per cent of the Muslim population of England and Wales. Of the 2.7 million Muslims living in England and Wales in 2011, 38 per cent described themselves as of Pakistani origin, 15 per cent as Bangladeshi and 7 per cent as Indian. The book also draws on interviews with many Arab immigrants as they have had a significant role within Shia and Islamist circles in Britain.

There is not much in this book about the Islamic groups with links to Britain's smaller minorities, or those which have come to the UK in large numbers only recently. As some of these communities—such as the Hazara Shia or the Somalis—establish more of their own institutions they will no doubt warrant inclusion in any sequel.

Even as a study of Islamic belief systems, this book is not a comprehensive guide but a basic framework. It is designed to help the reader understand the most important groupings in Britain and be able to guess where any mosque or Islamic organisation sits in the bigger picture. In doing so it perhaps overemphasises the ideological divisions in Muslim Britain and gives the false impression that every Muslim fits neatly into a sectarian box. I have met many people who manage to be Muslim in a non-sectarian way and some who are not even conscious of internal rivalries. But what has been more striking is the grip that sectarian groups with overseas origins continue to have even over Muslims born and raised in the UK.

If the number of Muslims in Britain was small and declining then the task of getting to know how its communities think might not be worth the effort. But this is not the case—the Muslim population of Britain is growing in both its size and religiosity, creating more opportunities for

Islamic leaders to run mosques and organisations which divide along sectarian as well as ethnic lines. This book, I hope, makes it possible for interested outsiders to understand who British Muslims are and what they think.

THE DEOBANDIS

THE MARKET LEADERS

Sheikh Ibrahim Mogra is the sort of imam with whom the British establishment feels relatively comfortable. He is involved in interfaith work; he gives talks that are sufficiently uncontroversial to appear on BBC Radio 4's *Thought for the Day*; and during the World Cup he drives round his adopted home of Leicester with a St George flag adorning his car.

Elsewhere in Leicester another scholar, Mufti Muhammad ibn Adam al-Kawthari, warns against excessive integration by advising followers to be polite to non-Muslims but not to take them as close friends.[1]

Both men are the product of the Deobandi school of Islam and of its most important British institution, Darul Uloom al Arabiya al Islamiya, an Islamic seminary near Bury in Lancashire.

Deobandi Islam is the dominant branch of Islam in the UK, with 44 per cent of British mosques following its teachings.[2] Perhaps because of its size, it is a school of thought which incorporates a diverse range of views, practices and sub-groups. It cannot be pigeonholed into any neat category marked 'extreme' or 'moderate'. It has its own jihadi offshoots, based in Pakistan but with links to Britain. Yet the leading scholars at its founding seminary in India issued a fatwa denouncing suicide bombing and the killing of innocents, and organised a series of public rallies in India to condemn terrorism as un-Islamic. What most Deobandi scholars have in common is a conservative interpretation of Islamic law: television and music for the purposes of entertainment, for example, are frowned upon if not banned; attitudes towards women are deeply conservative with, for example, some scholars advising Muslim women that their religion does not permit them to travel any distance unless accompanied by a close male relative. That this description of such an austere brand of Islam sounds similar to that propagated by the Taliban in Afghanistan should not be surprising—the Taliban movement grew out of the Deobandi madrassas of Pakistan.

The origins and principles of the Deobandi movement

The movement has its origins in nineteenth-century colonial India. Both of its founding scholars, Mohammed Qasim Nanaotawi and Rashid Ahmad Gangohi, fought against the troops of the British East India Company during the mass rebellion of Muslims and Hindus in 1857. The failure of the uprising to overthrow British dominance in India prompted these two Islamic scholars to retreat from military struggle and to concentrate instead on protecting the religious practices and the identity of Muslims in India. To that end they founded an Islamic seminary called Darul Uloom—meaning house of knowledge— in the village of Deoband about 130 miles north of Delhi in the state of Uttar Pradesh. Darul Uloom soon gained a reputation as a centre for religious scholarship, with other seminaries modelled on Deoband starting up in the same region.

Deoband's founders wanted to protect Indian Muslim identity against British influence, but they also sought to steer the faithful away from what they saw as sinful, innovative local practices. Many of these practices were associated with Sufism, a strand of Islam which stresses mysticism. The Sufi traditions which some Deobandi scholars opposed included the celebration of the Prophet Muhammad's birthday as a festival (*milad al-nabi*), the commemoration of the deaths of Sufi saints (*urs*) and worshipping at the graves of Sufi saints.

The Deobandis' stress on avoiding any form of worship that might be interpreted as idolatrous or a deviation from strict monotheism has led many to deduce that the Deobandis reject Sufism. But that is not the case. The early Deobandi scholars may have rejected some Sufi practices but they did not reject Sufism per se. In fact the school's founders were Sufis and initiated their followers into their Sufi orders (each one known as a *tariqa*).[3]

THE DEOBANDIS

The Silk Letter Conspiracy

While there was agreement within the original school of Deoband on the basic spiritual and theological principles, there was a split over the permissibility of violent jihad against the British colonial government of India. At the turn of the century, Mohammed Qasim Nanaotawi, one of the school's founders, thought that jihad against the British was inapplicable.[4] However, other leading Deobandi scholars—notably the head teacher of Darul Uloom Deoband, Sheikh Mahmud al Hasan—believed that jihad against the British was necessary for the betterment of the religion. To achieve that aim, Sheikh Hasan and his supporters became involved in a plot, known as the Silk Letter Conspiracy, to support Britain's First World War enemies in order to overthrow British rule.

The plotters made plans to form an Islamic army to support the Turkish Ottoman sultan who had sided with Germany during the First World War. They hoped that a victorious Ottoman *caliphate*, together with the *amir* (leader) of Afghanistan, would help them eject the British from India. However, letters that the conspirators had written on yellow silk which detailed their plans were intercepted by British intelligence in India. Over 200 Islamic scholars, many of them Deobandi, were arrested.[5] Sheikh Mahmud Hasan, the former head teacher of Deoband who was behind the plot, was interned by the British on Malta for the rest of the war. The school of Deoband managed to distance itself from the plotters by convincing the British authorities that it had severed its links with the conspirators before the First World War.[6] As if to emphasise its disapproval of the conspiracy, one plotter was even expelled from the school as an 'infidel'.[7] But once the war was over, support within the school shifted from the apolitical quietists back to the pro-jihad faction. The Deobandi religious scholars (*ulema*) had been politicised by various issues, including the defeat and abolition of the Ottoman caliphate at the hands of the British. On his release from Malta, Sheikh Mahmud Hasan emphasised non-violent struggle against British rule rather than military jihad. To that end, in 1919 he set up a political party: the Jamiat Ulama-Hind (JuH), meaning the Party of Indian Islamic Scholars.

The Madani/Thanawi split

When Sheikh Mahmud died in 1920, his former student Husain Ahmad Madani took over as the figurehead for the political activist faction. The

JuH designated Madani as Sheikh ul Islam, implying leadership of all Muslims in India, in 1921.[8] By 1922, the JuH was in effect the political wing of the Deobandi movement, even sharing branch offices around India with the Deoband seminary.[9]

The JuH adopted a position of non-violent opposition to British rule. Its vision for a post-colonial India was one in which Muslims would live peacefully as a religious minority, albeit one governed by a parallel Islamic legal system.[10]

In the years leading up to Indian independence in 1947, Muslim opinion was split on the issue of whether Muslims should have their own separate state or should live as a minority in a united India. The JuH being firmly in favour of the latter, struck a deal with the Congress Party to ensure that Muslims in India would be governed by sharia law, thus giving the ulema enhanced influence.[11]

The anti-Pakistan stance of the JuH led to a further split within the Deobandi ulema and the creation in 1945 of the pro-Pakistan party, Jamiat Ulama ul Islam (JuI).[12]

The Jamiat Ulama e Britain

The JuI has a British offshoot: the Jamiat Ulama e Britain (JuB). Founded in 1975, the JuB is a network of Pakistani Deobandi scholars based in the UK. Indian Deobandi scholars in Britain have their own equivalent body: the Hizbul Ulema.

According to Maulana Islam Ali Shah, one of the JuB's executive committee members, the organisation's main purposes are to educate Muslims in Britain; to provide chaplaincy services to Muslims in prison or hospital; to give Muslims information about such things as the dates of religious festivals; to ensure that mosques know how to comply with UK laws and regulations; and to advise Muslims about what is and what is not permissible. The organisation's leaders have also been involved in some interfaith meetings.[13]

Mr Shah was trained at Pakistan's leading Deobandi seminary, Jamia Uloom Islamia in Binori Town, Karachi. He follows the traditional Hanafi school of Islamic jurisprudence. Unlike the original Deobandis he does not regard himself as a Sufi. He takes an uncompromising line on what is and is not permissible for Muslim women living in Britain, believing that they are not permitted by their religion to work in mixed-sex environments unless working in their family's own business. He also believes that it is a religious obligation for Muslim women to wear the face veil (*niqab*), although he says that women must not be forced to wear it.

When the then Labour Cabinet Minister Jack Straw triggered a national debate in 2006 about the niqab by writing an article in which he said he would rather that women did not wear it, representatives of the JuB had a meeting with Straw in his Blackburn constituency in an attempt to change his views.[14]

The organisation has a leadership council of twelve scholars, a general committee of forty scholars and a governing committee of twenty-three scholars. Most of the scholars are of Pakistani descent.

According to Shah, on questions of Islamic law their ultimate source of scholarly advice is the Jamia Uloom Islamia in Binori Town. However, they have such a large network of scholars in the UK that they rarely need to seek guidance from overseas.

The JuB has an annual conference, usually held at Wakefield Central Mosque, where Shah works as imam. Although Mr Shah insists that the JuB is not formally affiliated to any overseas political party, the leader of one the JuI's factions in Pakistan, Maulana Fazlur Rehman, has been one of their previous conference speakers.

The JuB has scholars on its committees from towns and cities throughout the UK. However, the JuB is not the most important Deobandi organisation in Britain. The two most influential Deobandi networks in the UK are: (i) the Deobandi seminaries, in particular Darul Uloom Bury and its offshoots; and (ii) the missionary group Tablighi Jamaat (discussed in the next chapter).

These three networks overlap to some extent, with leading JuB figures having strong connections with both the Bury Darul Uloom and the Tablighi Jamaat.[15] However, the Bury network and the Tablighi Jamaat in Britain have their own power structures and within both it is Muslims of Gujarati Indian rather than Pakistani origin who occupy most of the leadership roles.[16] According to one Deobandi scholar this is perhaps because Muslims of Gujarati origin in Britain are more likely to have come from religiously conservative backgrounds than those of Pakistani origin.[17] Furthermore, those Gujaratis who came to the UK from former British colonies in East Africa often had commercial backgrounds, relatively high levels of education and the managerial skills to run successful voluntary organisations.

The seminaries

The first and most important Islamic seminary in the UK is Darul Uloom al-Arabiya al-Islamiya, more commonly known as Darul Uloom Bury. It has on its roll around 350 male students aged between thirteen and twenty-five who study GCSEs and A levels alongside a traditional seminary course. Those who pass the course of religious education at a darul uloom qualify as an Islamic scholar (*alim*). Opened in 1979, Darul Uloom Bury is housed on the site of a former hospital on the edge of the small Lancashire town of Holcombe near Bury. Its founder and long-serving principal, Sheikh Yusuf Motala, was sent to the UK from India by his teacher and spiritual guide Sheikh Mohammad Zakariya (1898–1982), a prominent sheikh in the history of the Deobandi movement and a man revered by many Gujarati Muslims in Britain.

Zakariya taught at a Deobandi seminary in the Indian city of Saharanpur and was a Sufi sheikh, claiming a line of spiritual authority going back to the Prophet Muhammad.[18] As a Sufi he encouraged the practice of silent recitation of the names of God, accepted oaths of allegiance (*bayat*) from disciples (each one known as a *mureed*) and, in the case of his most important followers such as Motala, conferred authority to act as his deputy (*khalifa*) and to initiate new adherents.

Another important British seminary was opened in 1982. The Institute of Islamic Education is a full-time boarding school and seminary run by the Deobandis' missionary wing, the Tablighi Jamaat. It is based on the same site as the Tablighi Jamaat's UK headquarters in Dewsbury. Hafiz Mushfiq Uddin, an Islamic educationalist based in East London, studied at the school for four years from 1986. Although discipline was strict according to Mushfiq Uddin, it was not considered a serious matter if a pupil failed to perform well in GCSE and A level exams—the emphasis was on Islamic rather than secular education.[19]

The founders of the original Darul Uloom Deoband in India shunned the pursuit of secular qualifications on the basis that it is preferable to acquire knowledge for its own sake rather than worldly gain. However, in the twenty-first century such attitudes changed in both Deoband and its British offshoots. While the focus on religious subjects remained, the Darul Uloom Deoband in India began teaching English, journalism and modern sciences. In England, some of the changes to the darul ulooms were prompted by the tougher registration requirements that the government began to impose from 2002 onwards. All full-time educational institutions teaching school-age children are inspected by the Office for Standards in Education, Children's Services and Skills (Ofsted) or another recognised inspection body.[20] While independent schools in England are not obliged to follow the National Curriculum, they must be registered with the Department for Education; teach maths, science, technology, PE and 'aesthetic and creative subjects'; and provide lessons in written and spoken English (although English does not have to be the main medium of communication). Although teachers do not have to be formally qualified, the standard of education provided has to be satisfactory.

Ofsted inspection reports suggest that the mainly fee-paying independent schools run by the Deobandis tend to teach the National Curriculum in addition to the Islamic curriculum, often creating a long working day for their pupils. When a journalist visited the Darul Uloom London (based in Chislehurst, Kent) in the summer of 2010, the pupils' day started with dawn prayers at 3.45 a.m., followed by a rest before breakfast at 7.30 and then lessons in the Islamic curriculum between 8 a.m. and 12.30 p.m. After a break for lunch, pupils studied the National Curriculum subjects from 1.30 p.m. until 4.30 p.m. The evening included two hours of homework and revision and then final prayers at 10.30 before bed at 11 p.m. There were art lessons but no music and drama on the basis that they are un-Islamic activities. Although history was on the timetable, the visiting journalist was denied any information about the periods of history being studied. Despite this relatively broad curriculum, the headmaster's lack of interest in secular qualifications echoed the attitude of Hafiz Mushfiq Uddin's teachers in Dewsbury: 'As Muslims we're not interested in an education that is simply about getting a job. We're not on Earth for this reason. We live on Earth merely with a view to the next life.'[21]

The timetable at Bury follows a similar pattern, with the day split between Islamic studies and a secular curriculum.

Increasingly, there are opportunities for female as well as male students to receive full-time training as an Islamic scholar (*alima*). For example, Jamea al Kauthar, a boarding school for girls near Preston in Lancashire, offered pupils between the ages of eleven and twenty the chance to combine secular and religious education. The school achieved a high GCSE and A level pass rate and an Ofsted inspection in 2010 rated every aspect of the school's educational provision as outstanding.

However, the school's website in that same year created the impression of an austere regime, warning that the following items are forbidden: 'song cassettes, novels, kettles, irons, toasters, heaters, mobile phones, fridges, Walkmans, Mp3 players, Mp4 players, iPods, televisions, radios, make-up, short clothes, indecent nightwear, beat & head banger nazams/nasheeds [songs with an Islamic theme], hairdryers, hair straighteners and chewing gum'. Pupils were warned that such items would be confiscated and that possession may lead to suspension—those caught with a mobile phone could even face permanent expulsion.[22]

Both Darul Uloom Bury and Jamea al Kauthar have allowed older pupils to study additional subjects, such as business studies, at the local further education college.

A 2008 Ofsted inspection at Hafiz Mushfiq Uddin's old school in Dewsbury stated that while the breadth of the school's teaching had improved significantly in recent years, secular education (including GCSE studies in Arabic and Urdu) still took up only 40 per cent of the school's curricular provision and standards were merely 'satisfactory'.

The main difference between the Dewsbury and Bury networks is the influence of Sufism. The head of the Bury Darul Uloom, Sheikh Yusuf Motala, has several deputies (each one known as a *khalifa*) who are authorised to initiate Sufi followers. In common with Deoband's founders, they avoid crossing the line into the more exuberant forms of Sufism: there is no loud chanting (*zikr*), no ecstatic movement and no commemoration of the deaths of Sufi saints (*urs*) or celebration of the Prophet's birthday (*milad-al-nabi*). However, according to one follower, some of the Deobandi Sufi sheikhs authorised by Yusuf Motala are perceived to be 'only one centimetre away from that line'. For example, Maulana Adam ibn Yusuf in Leicester will not celebrate the Prophet's birthday but around the time of it will organise special lectures about the life of Mohammed. 'The word celebration is never used,' observes one local Deobandi, 'but it implies a commemoration.'[23]

By contrast, Dewsbury graduate Hafiz Mushfiq Uddin says of himself and his contemporaries, 'A lot of us don't have sheikhs in that spiritual sense.' According to Mushfiq Uddin, if a Dewsbury graduate were to bind himself to a spiritual sheikh he would not feel obliged to follow one of his Dewsbury teachers. Mushfiq Uddin's perception is that Bury graduates tend to give *bayat* (an oath of allegiance) to those associated with Bury and its parent institute at Saharanpur in India. He believes that Dewsbury graduates are more independent and 'don't all follow the mother-ship'.[24]

Mushfiq Uddin estimates that there are twenty-two Deobandi darul ulooms in Britain, fifteen of which he says are offshoots of Bury.[25] Among the full-time Deobandi educational institutions offering alim courses are:

- Madinatul Uloom Al Islamiya School, Kidderminster. An independent boarding school and seminary for 200 male students aged eleven to twenty-four, established in 1992. The school's original principal was Sheikh Riyadh ul Haq, one of Bury's most influential graduates. It follows a similar syllabus to Bury.
- Darul Uloom Leicester. An Islamic educational institute for around 100 male students aged eleven to twenty-three years. Established in 1992.
- Jameah Riyadul Uloom, Leicester. Established in 1991 by Bury graduate Maulana Saleem Dhorat, it provides boarding facilities and a full-time alim course for male students over the age of sixteen.
- Jamiatul Ilm Wal Huda (the College of Islamic Knowledge and Guidance), Blackburn. A day and boarding school opened in 1997 and registered in 2001. The principal, Mufti Abdus-Samad Ahmed, is a Bury graduate and has also studied at Mazahirul Uloom in Saharanpur. The school has 400 male pupils aged between eleven and nineteen on its roll and provides a secular education alongside the alim course.[26]
- Markazul Uloom, Blackburn. A girls' day school and boys' day and boarding school with around 200 pupils between the ages of eleven and nineteen, providing secular and Islamic education. An emergency inspection by Ofsted in 2012 led to the closure of the school's boarding facilities on health and safety grounds. However, a 2010 inspection of the school found the education provision at the school to be satisfactory and the care of the health and welfare of the pupils to be good.
- Darul Uloom Birmingham. A full-time independent school, established in 1985, with around 130 boys aged between eleven and nineteen on the roll. The staff have studied at a range of Deobandi institutions including Darul Uloom Deoband in India, Bury, Blackburn, Kidderminster, Jameah Islamia Dabhel in Gujarat and Al Azhar University in Egypt.

- Madrasatul Imam Muhammed Zakariya, Bolton. An independent secondary school for girls with around 120 on the roll. Ofsted inspections in 2007 and 2010 rated the school's education provision as outstanding, with pupils achieving high standards at GCSE while also studying for a degree-level course in Islamic theology. The proprietor, Mahmood Chandia, is a Bury graduate with a PhD in Middle Eastern Studies from Manchester University and a lecturing post in Islamic Studies at the University of Central Lancashire.
- Jaamiatul Imaam Muhammed Zakaria School, Bradford. An independent girls' secondary school and seminary for students aged between eleven and twenty-one. There are over 400 pupils, all of whom are boarders. Students combine study for GCSEs with a five-year alima course. One of the trustees is a lecturer at Darul Uloom Bury.

Many of those who graduated from the British darul ulooms continued their studies abroad before returning to the UK. The Deobandi institutions of India and Pakistan were once popular destinations for further study; however, increasingly tight visa restrictions and, in the case of Pakistan, a complete ban on recruitment of foreign students by seminaries since the 7/7 bombings, made this difficult for those with only British nationality. Some students have continued their studies in Saudi Arabia at the University of Medina. One such person is Bury graduate Maulana Rashid Ahmed Ali Seth who went on to become an imam in Bolton. Although the Saudis promote Salafism, as a follower of the Hanafi madhab Maulana Rashid was taught by non-Salafi scholars.[27] According to former Dewsbury darul uloom student Hafiz Mushfiq Uddin, Al Azhar University in Egypt was also once a common destination for darul uloom graduates, but in 2010 Islamic seminaries in Syria were a more popular choice for those wanting to further their religious studies and improve their Arabic.

Hafiz Mushfiq Uddin is chief executive of Ebrahim College, an institution offering an alternative to the traditional darul uloom. He sees his college's connection to Deoband as an academic connection, rather than a sectarian or political one. Based in Whitechapel, Ebrahim College offers an alim course which it hopes will be the first to be accredited by a British university as a degree-level qualification.[28] The college has taken the content of the traditional alim course, translated it into English and applied modern methods of study and examination. For example, students are required to write essays or give presentations rather than being examined via oral assessments. Mushfiq Uddin hopes this will mean that those graduates of the college who do not become full-time imams, chaplains or scholars will easily find employment elsewhere.

Ebrahim College offers full- and part-time alim courses. Among the growing network of institutions offering part-time alim and alima courses in the UK, graduates of Bury and its offshoots also dominate.

One of the most important part-time Islamic colleges in the Deobandi network is Al Kawthar Academy in Leicester. It offers alim-level courses for men and women and less advanced classes at its premises in Highgate, Birmingham, and in Leicester. Its leading scholar is Sheikh Riyadh ul Haq.

Sheikh Riyadh ul Haq

Sheikh Riyadh ul Haq is one of the most high profile Islamic scholars in Britain, and is widely seen as a potential successor to the principal of Darul Uloom Bury, Sheikh Yusuf Motala. He is the Muslim equivalent, therefore, of a bishop tipped to be the next Archbishop of Canterbury.

Born in Gujarat, India in 1971, Sheikh Riyadh ul Haq came to Leicester at the age of three to join his father, an imam at one of the city's mosques. Among pious Muslims in Leicester, his father was revered as an eminent scholar and the family was treated with particular respect. The young Riyadh ul Haq had memorised the entire Quran by the age of 10. Before he was even a teenager he regularly led prayers for Muslim pupils at his state school in Leicester and gave talks about religion. He transferred to Darul Uloom Bury at 13 where he was fast-tracked into adult classes within a year of his arrival. He was not just bright, he was well connected too: Sheikh Yusuf Motala, the head of Bury Darul Uloom, was an old friend of Riyadh ul Haq's father, having shared a dormitory with him at a seminary in Gujarat. In 1992, just one year after his graduation, Riyadh ul Haq was made the first head teacher of Madinatul Uloom Al Islamiya, the Deobandi school and seminary in Kidderminster. He also began lecturing to Muslim audiences across the UK and internationally. At 21 he became the lead imam at Birmingham Central Mosque, recruited not just for his scholarship but his ability to lead Friday prayers in Urdu, English and Arabic. In 2004 he returned to Leicester where he became the leading scholar at Al Kawthar Academy.[29]

The sheikh's lecture tours continued and many of his talks, delivered in English, were made available as podcasts or YouTube videos.

Comments written in response to the sheikh's lectures on YouTube (each one having been viewed thousands of times) give an idea of the esteem in which the sheikh is held by many. Even those Muslims who are not devotees of the man will credit him with an impressive ability to recall hadiths and verses from the Quran.

The image of the sheikh outside Islamic circles however has been overwhelmingly negative. 'The homegrown cleric who loathes the British' was the headline of a piece about him published in *The Times* in September 2007.[30] In a series of articles, journalist Andrew Norfolk portrayed the sheikh as hostile to non-Muslims. The sheikh was quoted as describing Jews as 'all the same' and monopolisers of 'money, interest, usury, the world economy, the media, political institutions... tyranny and oppression.'[31] A 2003 recording of the sheikh aired in a BBC Panorama documentary reinforced the image of a preacher who saw non-Muslims as the enemy.[32] Even Philip Lewis, an interfaith adviser and the author of thoughtful books on Islam in Britain, described a 2002 presentation by the sheikh as portraying reality 'in terms of a familiar binary opposition' of Muslims versus non-believers.[33]

'I've made mistakes,' said the sheikh when he granted me a rare interview in 2014.[34] Stung by *The Times* experience he was wary of talking to a journalist. But having in the past been branded a 'hate preacher', he wanted to address the issue. The comments about Jews, he said, were 'one-off, uncharacteristic comments' made during a period of intense conflict between Palestinians and Israeli forces in 2000. The context, he felt, was mitigation but not an excuse. 'Now I would never say such things,' he told me, 'because I don't believe them.' One of the sheikh's aides was in the final stages of preparing a dossier designed to put the sheikh's 'uncharacteristic comments'—made before 2004—in the context of a career that has involved thousands of hours of public speaking on mainly scholarly and spiritual matters.[35] The aide pointed me to the transcript of a 2001 speech in which the sheikh reminded followers that God commanded Muslims to be just in their views on and treatment of Jews and non-believers. As to the charge of hostility to non-Muslims in general, the aide turned to excerpts from the transcripts of two speeches from 2006 in which the sheikh implored his audience to fight injustice whoever the victims of that injustice may be, Muslim or non-Muslim. In one of those speeches the sheikh told his audience that non-Muslims were doing more than Muslims in the fight against poverty and injustice.

The Times had quoted the sheikh as warning Muslims that taking Christians or Jews as friends made 'a mockery of Allah's religion'.[36] In rebuttal, the dossier prepared by the sheikh's aide quoted a 1997 speech in which the sheikh advised followers that friendship with non-Muslims was permissible but that such relationships should 'not touch the heart'— a view expressed by other Deobandi scholars. How does that advice look in the context of the school playground? What would the sheikh do if one of his sons came home from school full of enthusiasm for a best friend who happened to be a non-Muslim? 'I would not have a problem with that,' the sheikh told me, 'I would never say anything to him to negatively influence his friendship.' It must be possible, the sheikh reasoned, for a Muslim to love a non-Muslim because Muslim men are permitted by the sharia to marry Christian and Jewish women.

The sheikh's aides displayed extreme courtesy, humility, good humour and generosity when I visited their base in Birmingham. It was all very much in keeping with the spiritual teachings of the sheikh about reformation of character and purification of the soul.

But in my two and a half hour meeting with the sheikh there were still flashes of the binary world view about which Philip Lewis complained. The sheikh claimed for example that Muslims sometimes received harsher sentences in British courts than non-Muslims convicted of the same crimes. Pushed on this point he became more nuanced. But the initial statement was a sweeping one, apt to foster a Muslim sense of persecution.

Work and family commitments meant that the sheikh's exposure to the non-Muslim world had mainly been through the media (he was a regular listener to BBC Radio 4). But in an era when the British news agenda is regularly filled with stories about conflict in the Middle East and an anti-terrorism campaign at home, it is easy to see how anyone— Muslim or non-Muslim—might occasionally opt for the 'them and us' narrative instead of the more complicated truth.

Political engagement at local and national level

In Leicestershire, representatives of the Deobandi community control the local Federation of Muslim Organisations (FMO). Non-Deobandi groups play a part in the FMO too, but Deobandi dominance reflects the movement's strength at a community level. Although the chair of the organisation in 2014 was a local Deobandi scholar, Sheikh Ashraf Makadam, laypeople play a leading role. One of the FMO's most prominent figures is executive committee member Suleman Nagdi. Like most Gujarati Muslim immigrants to Leicester, he came to the UK from Africa rather than India itself. Born in Malawi in 1956, he arrived in Britain at the age of nineteen. In Leicester he joined a community of Gujarati Indians who had come as refugees from Idi Amin's Uganda and others who had migrated from Malawi, Tanzania and Kenya.[37] Compared to the smaller Pakistani and Bangladeshi Muslim communities, the Gujarati immigrants to Leicester were well educated and experienced in business. Nagdi ran a fabric pleating business in the city for twenty-six years until the local textile industry that it served collapsed. Since then he has devoted even more of his time to community work. Through the FMO he has helped to educate public bodies and service-providers about the religious requirements of the local Muslim population and encouraged the provision of halal food and prayer facilities in state hospitals and schools. He helps to run the Muslim Burial Council of Leicestershire (MBCOL) and has persuaded Leicester City Council to give MBCOL's funeral service out-of-hours access to the local cemetery to allow burial within twenty-four hours of death, in order to comply with Muslim religious obligations.

While representatives of the Deobandi community are often fully engaged in local Muslim organisations like the Leicestershire Federation of Muslim Organisations, the movement is more reluctant to become directly involved in national intra-faith organisations such as the Muslim Council of Britain (MCB).

Although the Leicestershire Federation of Muslim Organisations is an affiliate of the MCB and was involved in its creation, only 10 per cent of Deobandi mosques are direct affiliates of the MCB. This compares to a direct affiliation rate of 73 per cent among mosques and organisations controlled by the Jamaat-e-Islami.[38]

More significantly, there is no Deobandi representative on the board of trustees of the government-funded watchdog the Mosques and Imams National Advisory Board (MINAB), despite the fact that the Deobandis control 44 per cent of Britain's mosques. (Although Sheikh Ibrahim Mogra of Leicester is one of the vice chairs of its large executive board.) One member of the MINAB board of trustees—a Shia from the Al-Khoei Benevolent Foundation—claims that the Deobandis have been encouraged by him to join.[39]

So why might Deobandi leaders have refused to join MINAB? According to Hafiz Mushfiq Uddin of Ebrahim College, the Deobandis have not been guaranteed representation in proportion to the huge influence they have among the mosques and imams that MINAB aspires to govern. Understandably, the Deobandi scholars wonder what the point would be of giving credence to MINAB only to be outvoted on its board of trustees by those representing less influential Islamic trends.[40] Granting representation to the Deobandis in proportion to their following would allow them to dominate MINAB in coalition with the Muslim Council of Britain. The failure to agree terms which might be conducive to Deobandi participation in MINAB effectively stymied the government's attempt to create a state-friendly 'trade association' for Muslim clergy.

Sheikh Ibrahim Mogra from Leicester and Hafiz Mushfiq Uddin from East London are exceptions to the usual pattern of reluctance to engage with national institutions. Mogra has served as the Muslim Council of Britain's assistant secretary general and has had various inter-faith roles.

Hafiz Mushfiq Uddin of Ebrahim College tried without success to persuade senior Deobandi scholars to meet with British government officials and policy-makers. The scholars, he says, are not hostile to outsiders but are unconvinced that such an engagement would be a good use of their time: 'They say "Tell them to come and visit us instead. We'll have a cup of tea with them and we'll tell them what we do." They don't understand that it doesn't work like that. You have to proactively go out and tell people who you are.'[41]

Yet at grassroots level it is impossible to run mosques and schools in Britain without having some engagement with the local authorities. The ulema tend not to be the ones who deal with local officialdom. So in areas where there is a Deobandi presence, so too is there usually someone like Leicester's Suleman Nagdi to act as the link man between the local Deobandis and organisations like the health authority, police and council. Outsiders' attempts to speak to anyone else about Deobandi community business will often be thwarted—ordinary followers will feel too inhibited to talk and all roads will lead back to the local Suleman Nagdi. These link men generally present a different image to the outside world than that presented by the ulema. The Deobandi ulema wear traditional Islamic clothing and might advise their followers not to 'adopt the dress of the unbelievers',[42] but the Suleman Nagdis will wear a suit to meet outsiders like me. Some leading Deobandi ulema may have warned their congregations against taking non-Muslims as close friends, but the Suleman Nagdis are usually involved in interfaith work. Nagdi regularly gives talks about the Islamic faith to churches in Leicestershire. 'People are frightened and confused,' he says, 'so I usually start by saying, "Don't worry, I'm not wearing a suicide vest. I'm just fat!" People laugh and that helps to break the ice.'[43] In Dewsbury, a local link man, Kaushar Tai, is also heavily involved in the interfaith network. Yet when I met him in Dewsbury in 2010 he recommended to me the lectures of Zakir Naik,[44] a preacher based in India who has told Muslims that Jews are 'our staunchest enemy'. (Tai later told me that he was unaware of Naik's controversial reputation.) Darul Uloom Deoband had issued a fatwa against Naik noting that he was 'free of mind and does not wear Islamic dress' and advising that his speeches should not be relied upon.[45]

Tai talks the equal opportunities language of the public sector with ease, yet when pressed he admits that the new mosque which he helped to found and manage does not admit women.[46] He says that he would have liked the mosque to provide prayer facilities for women but could not persuade a majority of the management committee to agree.

In Dewsbury, some mosques discriminate not just on gender but on ethnicity too. According to one local Deobandi, a formal system of membership operates in most of the Deobandi mosques in the town, with each mosque restricting eligibility not just to a specific ethnic group but in some cases to ethnic sub-groups. Thus a mosque run by Gujaratis from the district of Surat does not accept Gujaratis from the Bharuch district as members, and vice versa.[47] (In Leicester, according to one local Deobandi, such a system of narrow ethnic membership has now largely been abandoned.)[48]

The Deobandis' link men are often involved in local politics, usually via the Labour Party. Nagdi is not one of those but he does hold a civic position: he is a deputy lieutenant of the county of Leicestershire—a ceremonial role which has required him to lay the wreath on behalf of the war dead on Remembrance Sunday and to take the salute on behalf of the Crown.

Attitude towards integration

Figures like Suleman Nagdi and Kaushar Tai may be fully engaged with the institutions of mainstream society, but their role is not to encourage integration. Rather it is to protect the ability of Muslims to live as a religious minority, fully practising and expressing their faith. The lack of integration of some Muslim communities in Leicester was described as 'striking' by the US State Department's senior adviser for Muslim engagement, Farah Pandith, following her visit to the city in 2007. A confidential cable released via WikiLeaks revealed that Pandith found Leicester's Muslim community to be the most conservative she had seen anywhere in Europe and that, at a local bookshop, she had seen texts in English which 'seemed designed to segregate Muslims from their wider community ... playing up the differences between Islam and other religions ... and feeding hate of Jews to the young'.[49]

The mission to create a community apart is in keeping with that of the Deobandi ulema of colonial India who worked with the Congress Party to ensure that Muslim identity and separateness were reinforced. In India that went as far as applying Islamic law to Muslims who came before the secular courts.[50]

In Leicester, Nagdi does not go as far as campaigning for a parallel legal order for Muslims. But many among the Deobandi population in Leicester will voluntarily submit themselves to the authority of the Deobandi ulema. A local sharia council helps to settle disputes between adherents. The wearing of the face veil, which some Deobandi scholars regard as a religious obligation, was once unusual among Muslim women in Leicester. Now it is the practice of a substantial minority. 'People thought the opposite would happen,' says Nagdi, 'we thought the faith would become more diluted.' The Jameah Girls' Academy, a Deobandi-run girls' school in Leicester, insists that all pupils over the age of eleven wear the niqab on journeys to and from school. Nagdi says that as a layman he does not want to comment on this from a religious point of view. However he will make the case for it politically: he uses the language of human rights and liberalism to defend the freedom of Muslim women to cover their faces in public if they so wish. He extends this to the whole issue of community cohesion, arguing that what some criticise as a failure to integrate is merely an assertion of the right to be different.

Not all leading Deobandis are as relaxed about the lack of social cohesion as Suleman Nagdi. Sheikh Musa Admani, a Deobandi imam in London, says that from a young age Muslim children are subject to a 'subtle demonisation' directed at the wider society. This, he has concluded, is not only a potential cause of violent extremism but goes against

Islamic principles: 'The Muslim community at large have lost the overall concept of humanity at large,' he says. 'Re-inculcating that humanity concept—to be compassionate to all because God is compassionate—is going to take some time.'[51]

The tension between religious expression and integration was further illustrated in the guidelines for hospital staff published by the Muslim Burial Council of Leicestershire (MBCOL) in a printed leaflet and on the organisation's website in 2010: hospital staff were advised that, when dealing with a deceased Muslim patient, menstruating women 'should not appear in the presence or in close proximity of the body'. (Suleman Nagdi later told me that the inclusion of this advice was a 'drafting error' and it was removed from the organisation's website.)

Unwitting politicians sometimes blame radicalisation and any lack of Muslim integration on a shortage of British-born imams. They seem oblivious to the fact the Deobandis' burgeoning network of British seminaries and part-time academies is producing far more scholars than are needed to fill posts as imams, teachers or chaplains. Many of those seminary graduates end up retraining for secular professions or simply taking on menial jobs.

A study published in 2012 found that of the hundreds of Muslim chaplains now employed to work in British hospitals, prisons and universities, many had been trained in Deobandi seminaries.[52] The same study found evidence that Muslim chaplains employed in these secular public institutions were tending to adopt relatively liberal, pragmatic interpretations of Islam.

But the attitude is often quite different among those darul uloom graduates who are not contracted to work within the progressive liberal atmosphere of the British public sector. One Deobandi Muslim told me that the British-trained seminary graduates he saw returning to his community were at least as conservative and anti-integration as their foreign-educated predecessors: 'Many of them advocate a 100 per cent Deobandi lifestyle.' Furthermore, there are now areas of Britain where a high proportion of the population is Deobandi—such as Savile Town in Dewsbury or the Highfields district of Leicester—where the '100 per cent lifestyle' is more easy to achieve. 'It's possible to go out in these areas and hardly ever see a woman who is not in hijab,' says my source. He says the influence of these young ulema on their families is often profound: 'I know a Muslim family which was fairly relaxed and integrated. But then one of the sons became an alim and it completely changed the way the family lived. The son married a woman who wears the niqab and he told me I would never see her face.'53

The most popular scholars, like Riyadh ul Haq, have their own websites offering online lectures and fatwas. The questions put to the scholars via their websites indicate the extent to which some followers are concerned about adhering to the sharia in the fine detail of their lives. For example, among the issues dealt with by Mufti Muhammed ibn Adam al-Kawthari, another Bury graduate based in Leicester,54 via his www.daruliftaa.com website are:

- Is it permissible to wear teeth braces? Answer: only to correct a defect but not if purely for reasons of beautification.
- Is it permissible to wear a football club jersey upon which is printed the logo of the club's sponsor, a beer manufacturer? Answer: no, it is not permitted for a Muslim to wear anything that advertises and promotes alcohol.
- If only boar bristle paint brushes are available, can they be used? Answer: yes, so long as one ensures that stray bristles do not become attached to the wall and that one is sure the bristles have been scientifically dried so moisture from the animal does not mix with the paint.
- Is it permissible to wear a tie to work if asked to do so by one's employer? Answer: yes, but it is better to 'avoid the dress of the unbelievers' and one should confine the wearing of the tie to work as many scholars have declared it to be impermissible.
- Is it necessary for a man to grow a beard? Answer: yes, although scholars differ on the required length.

Similar questions and answers can be found on other Deobandi sites such as muftisays.com (run by scholars at Darul Uloom London) and the site of Darul Uloom Deoband itself.

Mufti Muhammed ibn Adam's advice on women's issues is, typically for a Deobandi scholar, conservative. This is among the advice on his website:

- It is necessary for a woman to cover her face in 'normal' situations, unless she fears physical or extreme verbal abuse, or harm to herself when walking in a crowded area.
- A female is encouraged to remain within the confines of her home unless there is a need for her to emerge outside.

- It is generally impermissible for a woman to travel a distance of more than 48 miles unless accompanied by a male relative, even if the purpose is to attend a religious gathering.[55]

Despite the efforts being put into girls' and women's education by Deobandi scholars in Britain, over 40 per cent of Deobandi mosques in the UK do not admit women.[56] The reasons usually given for this are: there is no obligation on women to pray in congregation; women should be encouraged to offer their prayers at home instead as this allows them to more easily fulfil their domestic obligations; and a lack of demand from the women themselves. Mufti Muhammad ibn Adam takes a relatively liberal stance by Deobandi standards, recommending on his website that mosques should offer prayer facilities for women 'so that if a sister is traveling she is able to make Wudu [ablutions] and offer her prayers without having to miss her prayers altogether'.[57]

Do many Muslims of Deobandi background really live by these kinds of restrictive guidelines? 'I would say 30–40 per cent of Deobandis try to live by the rules in a pretty thorough way,' says one insider who knows Britain's main Deobandi communities well, 'But then you have other people who might only follow parts of what the ulema say: for example, you might have a guy who watches a Bollywood movie on his widescreen television before going to Friday prayers and then on the way home listens to music in the car. Or you might have a woman who does the five daily prayers but does not wear hijab. Sometimes people think that they will get round to living the 100 per cent Muslim lifestyle one day but not yet. Sometimes people will give up the things they think they shouldn't do, like going to the cinema, for Ramadan.'[58] According to another Muslim from Deobandi-dominated Leicester, very few adhere to the 100 per cent lifestyle: they have a pious code of conduct for the mosque and a more pragmatic mode of being for day-to-day life.

It is not surprising that the rules Deobandis in Britain are told to live up to sound similar to those laid down by the Taliban in Afghanistan. The Taliban movement is effectively a Deobandi offshoot, having grown out of the Deobandi madrassas in Pakistan where many Afghan refugees were educated during the 1980s and 1990s. When the Taliban established an Islamic emirate in Afghanistan in 1997, they did so in close consultation with Deobandi groups in Pakistan who advised them on their religious policies.[59]

Taliban links

In the 1990s, there were direct links between Deobandi followers in Britain and the Taliban in Afghanistan. Taliban representatives collected money in Britain to build schools and hospitals.[60] Some members of the Taliban were even visiting Leicester in the hope of setting up trade deals with local businessmen, according to another local Muslim resident. *Dharb-e-Momin* (Shield of the Believer), an English-language version of the Taliban's newsletter, used to be openly available in the UK's Deobandi mosques until 9/11. But after 9/11 it apparently disappeared overnight. The need for the community to be seen as law-abiding and loyal to Britain trumped any desire to garner support for the Deobandi brethren in Afghanistan.

Ahead of the post-9/11 invasion of Afghanistan, Prime Minister Tony Blair said that he did not believe that anyone would want to live under a Taliban regime.[61] But Nagdi says of the Deobandi population in Leicester that 'the majority don't have a problem with the Taliban'. He feels that Western governments failed to understand the distinction between the Taliban and al-Qaeda.[62] A former deputy head of MI6 agrees: 'if we had known in 1998, 1999 what we know now,' said Nigel Inkster in 2008, 'it would have been possible to foment dissent between them ... the Afghan Arabs did not view the Taliban as constituting a genuine emirate.'[63] Islam Ali Shah of the JuB believes that the post-9/11 invasion of Afghanistan was unjustified: he thinks that the Taliban should have been given evidence of bin Laden's guilt and the option to hand Osama bin Laden over to the government of another Islamic country for trial in an Islamic court.[64]

Kashmiri jihadi groups

The Taliban movement is not the Deobandis' only link with al-Qaeda. Two of the most prominent Kashmiri jihadi groups, Jaish-e-Mohammed (JeM) and Harakat-ul-Mujahideen (HuM), have strong Deobandi ties, yet are thought to have aligned themselves with the ideology of Osama bin Laden. HuM was one of several jihadi groups encouraged and funded by the Pakistani intelligence service (ISI) from the late 1980s.[65] In 1998 HuM's then leader, Maulana Fazlur Rehman Khalil, appears to have signed Osama bin Laden's declaration of 'jihad against the Jews and Crusaders'.[66]

The Kashmiri issue had originally been framed as a nationalist struggle, with the leading armed group, the secular Jammu and Kashmir
Liberation Front (JKLF), fighting for an independent Kashmiri state.
However, the ISI-funded fighters were formed out of the jihadi groups
which had fought in the 1980s against the Soviets in Afghanistan. The
goal of the campaign became the incorporation of Indian-held Kashmir
into Pakistan, an objective described as a jihad which Muslims should
support as a matter of religious obligation.

In the early 1990s, HuM sent its top fundraiser and orator, Masood
Azhar, to Britain to garner support. He was hosted by a scholar from East
London but travelled extensively, preaching to packed audiences in
mosques across Britain and raising both funds and recruits. Azhar also
acquired in Britain a stolen Portuguese passport for use on under cover
missions.[67] He targeted working-class Pakistani expatriates[68] but he
visited Gujarati-run Deobandi mosques as well. By the time of Azhar's
UK tour he was already a close associate of Osama bin Laden and was
involved in militant operations in Somalia as well as Kashmir.[69] Yet in
Britain Azhar visited mainstream rather than militant institutions. In
one town at least, the scholar organising Azhar's engagements was a man
with strong links to the apolitical, pietistic school of Deobandi thought.
Local legend in that town has it that, after one of Azhar's sermons, giving
was so enthusiastic that the donations created a mountain of cash.[70] One
British Muslim who heard about Masood Azhar's call to jihad was Omar
Saeed Ahmed Sheikh, then a student at the London School of Economics
but now infamous as the man guilty of the kidnap and murder of
American journalist Daniel Pearl. Sheikh is thought to have met Azhar
for the first time at a HuM training camp in Pakistan in 1993.[71] The
following year Sheikh was sent on an undercover mission to India.
Masood Azhar had been imprisoned by the Indian authorities after
entering India on the false Portuguese passport he had acquired in the
UK and trying to foment an uprising in Indian-controlled Kashmir.
Sheikh had been ordered to kidnap four Westerners who would be held
as hostages until the Indian government agreed to release Azhar. Sheikh
captured one American and three British tourists but was caught by the
Indian police. He remained in an Indian prison until December 1999
when he, Masood Azhar and one other were flown to Afghanistan. They
were exchanged by the Indian government for passengers being held on
a hijacked plane at Kandahar airport. Azhar and Sheikh apparently went

on to meet Osama bin Laden and the head of the Taliban government Mullah Omar before returning to Pakistan. In January 2000, Masood Azhar formed his own group, Jaish-e-Mohammed (JeM). Around 10,000 armed followers attended the launch at a mosque in Karachi where Azhar declared they should not rest until they had destroyed America and India.[72]

Jaish has been implicated in various terrorist attacks in India, including a suicide attack against an Indian army barracks carried out by a British student from Birmingham in December 2000.[73] In 2006, Jaish was suspected of involvement in a plot by British Muslims to smuggle explosives through airport security in the UK. The convicted men were thought to have links to Rashid Rauf, an alleged JeM operative who fled Britain for Pakistan following the murder of his uncle.[74]

In 2008 a journalist working undercover in Britain infiltrated a group raising funds for JeM. The local group's leader told the journalist that he had fought for Jaish in Kashmir before being ordered by Masood Azhar to return to Britain as a fundraiser. However, it seems unlikely that there was much support for JeM among the local Muslim population in the English town where they were based, as those collecting money door to door were instructed to pretend they were raising funds for an orphanage rather than a jihad group.[75]

Jaish-e-Mohammed's association with al-Qaeda means it is not endorsed by the mainstream Deobandi ulema in Britain.

Senior Deobandi ulema in Britain have given a clear condemnation of al-Qaeda's methods. Following the 2005 bombings in London, for example, Mufti Muhammad ibn Adam in Leicester wrote on his website: 'If Muslims feel that the UK and US governments are killing innocent civilians in Iraq and elsewhere, it does not give them the right to kill innocent citizens in London or New York.' He set out in detail the main religious edicts that the bombers had broken: the obligation to obey the law of the land in which one is living; the prohibition on taking the lives of women, children, the old and the meek, the sick and those that are worshipping; and the command not to damage or destroy the wealth of others.

Darul Uloom Deoband in India issued a worldwide fatwa against terrorism in 2008, declaring that the 'Killing of innocents is not compatible with Islam. It is anti-Islamic.'[76] A few months later the seminary's vice rector sought publicly to distinguish the Indian seminary from

Deobandis involved in terrorist activities in Pakistan, and a former vice rector of Deoband criticised the Deobandi clerics in Pakistan for not coming out against the killing of innocents.[77]

In Britain, some leading Deobandis have gone further than mere condemnation of the terrorist attacks of 9/11 and 7/7. Sheikh Musa Admani,[78] a London-based Deobandi scholar, helped to set up the Luqman Institute, an organisation which used Islamic theology to argue with young people attracted to the ideas of al-Qaeda. Following his appointment as Muslim chaplain of London Metropolitan University in 2001, Sheikh Musa soon became so concerned about the problem of radicalisation on university campuses that he tried to persuade the government to back a plan to send in a task force of moderate imams to debate theology with the extremists.[79]

Conclusion

The Deobandis' ascendancy in Britain has gone largely unnoticed. Few outsiders are aware that the Deobandis control almost half of Britain's mosques and have overwhelming dominance in Islamic education in Britain. The only obvious threat to their future success is their failure to incorporate newer immigrant groups such as the Somalis, North Africans and Kurds (perhaps due to the Deobandis' continued use of Urdu). But with an abundance of British-trained imams, the Deobandis are probably in a stronger position than any other Islamic group to adopt English as the main language of the sermon. Furthermore, the Deobandis' emphasis on the core tenets of religious practice allows them to run what appear to be generic mosques, free of rituals which other trends might find alienating.

So what implications does continued Deobandi success have? If the success of Deobandi Islam raises any issues for wider society, it is one of social cohesion rather than violent extremism. The flirtation with jihadi groups in the 1990s can now be seen as an aberration for a network dominated by the apolitical, pietistic strand of Islam. But much of Deobandi teaching still fosters a sense that to embrace non-Muslim society too warmly risks contaminating one's Islamic values. With a plentiful supply of British-trained imams and a growing network of Muslim schools, the Deobandis appear unlikely to change that message or lose their position as Islamic Britain's most influential players.

2

THE TABLIGHI JAMAAT

MISSIONARIES AND A MEGA MOSQUE

Most evenings after the sunset prayer, groups of young Muslim men across Britain set out from their mosques in parties of ten. Often dressed in the traditional shalwar kameez, they knock on the doors of Sunni Muslims who have not been seen in the mosque much of late.

The Tablighi Jamaat (TJ) is a Deobandi missionary movement and one of the largest Islamic groups in the UK. Its emphasis on door-to-door recruitment means it is often described as the Islamic equivalent of the Jehovah's Witnesses. But unlike Jehovah's Witnesses, the tablighis are not out to make converts. Rather, they aim to shepherd less committed Muslims back into the fold and to join in the group's missionary work.

The Tablighi Jamaat sent its first missionaries to the UK from India in 1945. Since then it has quietly grown into one of Britain's most successful Islamic movements. Vast numbers of British Muslims have spent time in its ranks. Yet, for the first sixty years of its presence in Britain, few non-Muslims were even aware it existed.

All that changed in 2005. Shortly after the 7/7 bombings, it emerged that several of the men involved had spent time in the Tablighi Jamaat. Then it was revealed that the TJ had plans to build a 'mega mosque' on land it had acquired near what would be London's Olympic village. Suddenly lots of people were asking, 'Who are the Tablighi Jamaat and should we be worried?'

They received few answers from the Tablighi Jamaat itself, which held fast to its tradition of keeping itself to itself. Rumours, confusion and gross oversimplifications filled much of the information vacuum.

Through talking to those who have come into contact with the Tablighi Jamaat as followers, potential recruits or sympathisers, and by drawing on the research of those who have studied the organisation's history and ideology, the following pages should put paid to some concerns about the TJ—but will raise others too.

Modus operandi

As a young British Muslim growing up in Blackburn, Faruqe Master was one of those Muslims who experienced the Tablighi Jamaat missionaries' knock at the door. 'They try to appeal to one's sense of guilt and if they manage to do that they will then try to persuade you to come to their gathering on Thursday nights at the mosque.' Master recalls the occasions when he has been persuaded to do just that: 'They give you tea and biscuits then you listen to someone who reads from the hadiths. Then that person gives a powerful and emotional speech in Urdu.'[1]

Although Master's family spoke Gujarati at home, he had no difficulty understanding Urdu and he says most second-generation South Asians would be the same. At some Tablighi Jamaat gatherings, speeches in Urdu are now translated for the benefit of converts and the growing third generation of British Muslims, some of whom speak only English. In the main tablighi centre in London, there will be interpreters capable of translating into other languages such as Arabic and Somali for an increasingly diverse Muslim population.

Master says that, after the main speech, a youth will stand up and ask in English 'Who is ready now to go on jamaat for three days?' Going 'on jamaat' means leaving home for a period to join in the Tablighi Jamaat's missionary work.

'Once again they will appeal to your sense of guilt and obligation,' says Master. 'Usually someone will then stand up and say "I'm ready for three days." Then they'll say, "Who is ready for ten days?" Again, someone will stand up and volunteer. Then they'll say "Who is ready for forty days?" (which is known as a *chillah*) and someone will usually volunteer for that too.'

Master has never answered the call to leave his home and go 'on jamaat'. But what would he have been getting himself into if he had?

Some of those who agree to go on jamaat will set a date some weeks or months away for their trip. Others will rush home straight away to pack, returning to the mosque that night with a sleeping bag and rucksack. From the mosque, they will leave in minibuses and cars for one of the Tablighi Jamaat's main centres (known as a *markaz*). In Blackburn, those who agree to go on jamaat for three days will simply gather at the Blackburn Markaz, from where they will be dispatched to mosques around the north-west of England. The TJ also has markazes in Dewsbury, London, Leicester, Birmingham and Glasgow.[2]

Some of those who volunteer for the shortest period on jamaat will in fact do only two days of missionary work, as the Tablighi Jamaat in Britain has decided it must now offer followers the chance to fit their religious duties into the European weekend.

Volunteers who sign up for longer stints will travel to the Tablighi Jamaat's European headquarters in Dewsbury, West Yorkshire. There they will meet other Muslims who, like them, have travelled from a British mosque after volunteering for a ten-day, forty-day or even year-long mission. But they will almost certainly meet others from much further afield too: Morocco, Indonesia, the Caribbean, France or any other country where Muslims live.

Those who go on jamaat in England will be hosted by a local Deobandi mosque which will provide them with food and allow them to sleep in the mosque overnight. In return, the visiting tablighis will attempt to persuade local Muslims to come to the mosque for a talk.

This method of inviting people to practice the religion (*dawa*) is one that has been followed since the movement was founded in India in the 1920s by Maulana Mohammad Ilyas.

For those British followers who want to volunteer for longer spells of missionary work—periods of up to four months are common—there is the chance to travel abroad. Those who go on international jamaats will usually be expected to pay their own travel expenses, which often means buying a seat on a Tablighi Jamaat-chartered flight.

Time spent on preaching tours is an opportunity to swap the distractions of modern life for a simpler, more spiritual existence. Some will retain a lifelong relationship with the movement, going regularly on jamaat, attending one of the movement's mass gatherings (*ijtima*) on Thursday nights and becoming a member of a mosque controlled by the movement's supporters. Others will simply pass through the TJ in search of some spiritual refreshment.

'Omar', a London-based tablighi, has been on every length of jamaat. He does not want his real name to be used but was happy to talk to me about his experiences.

He explains that his local markaz in Stratford, East London, serves the whole of the south-east of England: 'People come from as far afield as Oxford, Portsmouth and Luton.'[3]

He says the markaz knows where to send people on jamaat because on Tuesday of each week they will get a message from the Tablighi Jamaat's headquarters in India telling them where they should focus 'the effort'.

Born in Britain to Bangladeshi parents in 1977, Omar was brought up in the East London borough of Tower Hamlets—now home to over 80,000 people of Bangladeshi origin.[4] He was introduced to the Tablighi Jamaat by his father. When I met him at the school where he was employed as an educational social worker his appearance was in line with TJ recommendations: he was bearded and wore the traditional clothing of Muslims from the Indian subcontinent, the shalwar kameez. However he often wears Western clothes with an Islamic twist: a track-suit with a prayer cap, for example.

He says that his initial involvement in the Tablighi Jamaat was not motivated by the correct intentions: he simply saw the chance to go on jamaat as an opportunity to get away for the weekend. 'Officially you are not meant to go on jamaat until the age of sixteen but I've been going on three-day jamaats from the age of fourteen.' He recalls the time when he and some friends were sent on jamaat to the seaside town of Southend. 'We sneaked off to the funfair,' he admits.

However, by the age of eighteen, Omar says he had developed a deeper understanding of Islam, having studied at a Deobandi madrassa in Nottinghamshire for two years and memorised the entire Quran. As a more deeply religious teenager he went on a four-month jamaat to Pakistan.

'First of all we went to the Tablighi Jamaat headquarters in Raiwind, Lahore where they sorted us into groups of ten people.'[5] He says that the TJ tries to group together people who are likely to get on well so he was put with other educated people. His group, which was sent via Peshawar to Sawabi and Mardan in the North West Frontier Province, included a Pakistani radar technician and a former Pakistani government minister. The missionary work he engaged in while in Pakistan took the same form as that in the UK—calling on Muslims in their homes and inviting them to come to the mosque for a talk.

He explains why the Tablighi Jamaat's primary aim is to reform those who already call themselves Muslims, rather than gaining converts: 'The Tablighi Jamaat believes that Muslims need to become better Muslims before they can even start thinking about inviting non-Muslims to come to Islam.' This echoes the thinking of the movement's founder Mohammad Ilyas.[6]

The Tablighi Jamaat's approach to being a good Muslim is relatively simple. It promotes six principles (*chhe baten*): (i) the creed of Muslims: there is no god but God and Mohammed is His messenger; (ii) prayer; (iii) the acquisition of knowledge; (iv) respect for other Muslims; (v) the purification of one's intentions and to remain sincere and self-appraising; and (vi) sacrificing time for missionary work.

The Tablighi Jamaat's founder, Maulana Ilyas, originally banned the use of written materials in the movement's work on the basis that if the Tablighi Jamaat's missionaries explained their message directly to potential followers there would be less chance of misunderstanding.[7] However, Ilyas had a change of heart once the group was better established, and he commissioned Maulana Mohammed Zakariya, his son-in-law, to write a series of nine booklets for their followers. The booklets were then amalgamated into two volumes known as the *Tablighi Nisab*, later renamed the *Fazail-e-Amaal* (The Virtues of Actions of Worship).

But face-to-face communication rather than publishing remains the main method of propagating the tablighi message, according to Omar: 'The way that knowledge and understanding is spread through the Tablighi Jamaat is "I will say something to you and you will repeat it ten times to learn it".'

There is no major doctrinal dispute between the TJ and the main-stream Deobandi movement in Britain, just a difference in method when it comes to encouraging religious observance. The emphasis in the TJ is on spreading basic knowledge via laypeople. In the mainstream Deobandi movement the emphasis is on advanced scholarship, delivered through their Islamic seminaries known as darul ulooms.

The Tablighi Jamaat does have some involvement in the formal training of Islamic scholars, operating a darul uloom on the same site as the markaz in Dewsbury. Britain's main network of Deobandi seminaries, headquartered at Darul Uloom Bury, has strong links to the Tablighi Jamaat. The founding head of Darul Uloom Bury, Sheikh Yusuf Motala, was directed to set up the institution by Muhammad Zakariya, the author of the Tablighi Jamaat's core text, the *Fazail-e-Amaal*.[8]

The darul uloom and the markaz in Dewsbury are funded by a Tablighi Jamaat charity called The Anjuman-e-Islah-al-Muslimeen (Madrasa Taleem ul Islam) of United Kingdom. Although the contact address for the charity is the same as the TJ's centre in Dewsbury, the words 'Tablighi Jamaat' appear nowhere in the official framework of the charity nor in its annual report for 2010.[9] This is perhaps because Tablighi Jamaat is simply the name ascribed to the movement rather than its official title. The accounts for TJ's UK charity in 2010 show an annual income of nearly £700,000. Of that, 80 per cent comes from 'parental contributions' (presumably school fees for pupils at the darul uloom). The rest is categorised simply as 'donations and collections'.

Dewsbury became the location of the TJ's European headquarters almost by accident: the man who was to become the leader (*amir*) of the TJ in Britain, Hafiz Yusuf Patel, settled in Dewsbury in the 1960s after he was invited by some Gujarati Muslims in the town to live among them and guide them on religious matters.[10]

Such is the movement's attachment to tradition that even the use of new technology in the group's administrative work is shunned. One Deobandi imam recalls a meeting with the amirs of the Tablighi Jamaat in Dewsbury where the offer of a young follower to set up a computer database of adherents was dismissed by the TJ elders with the comment 'What need have we of computers when pen and paper will do?' London-based tablighi 'Omar' has no objection to the TJ's low-tech methods of operation, but in his life away from the TJ he regularly posts jokes and news on his Facebook page and writes a blog on topics which have nothing to do with religion.

Another aspect of the Tablighi Jamaat's work that may appear strikingly anachronistic is the fact that most of its activities are for men only. Women's jamaats, which are far more unusual than the men's jamaats, tend not to make use of the mosques. Instead, the women will stay in the homes of tablighi women in the area to which they are sent, and the local women will invite others to come to the house for a talk. Using the mosques is often impractical as over 40 per cent of Deobandi mosques do not admit women.[11]

Despite its low-tech and old-fashioned methods, the Tablighi Jamaat has proved highly successful in recruiting Muslims.

A study of the Tablighi Jamaat in Britain published in 1998 observed that the movement was dominated by older, lower-class, first-generation immigrants. The author of the study predicted that the TJ would struggle to recruit younger and more educated Muslims in Britain on account of its simple, traditional teaching and its South Asian character.[12] But this proved not to be the case. Subsequent research, published in 2012, suggested that while older men still made up the majority of attendees, the number of young men was growing and a wider cross section of the Muslim male population had been drawn in.[13]

It is certainly not hard to find young, British-born, middle-class followers like Omar. The TJ's weekly gathering in London is attended by around 3,000 men. According to Omar, visits to the UK by the Tablighi Jamaat's top speakers from India can attract audiences of over 10,000. Internationally, the TJ's annual gathering (*ijtima*) in the Bangladeshi town of Tongi attracts 5 million followers, making it the largest gathering of Muslims in the world, exceeding even the numbers attending the annual pilgrimage to Mecca.[14] All this is achieved without the need for posters, websites, emails or press releases.

Terrorist connections

The Tablighi Jamaat's aversion to publicity meant that it was virtually unknown to non-Muslims before 2001. However, in the years since, it has frequently been the subject of newspaper articles highlighting the fact that, of the dozens of British-born Muslims charged with terrorist offences, many turn out to have something in common: time spent in the Tablighi Jamaat.

Among those UK-based Muslims who have been involved in terrorist plots and who are also said to have spent time in the Tablighi Jamaat are:

- Zacarias Moussaoui: the '20th hijacker', recruited to take part in the 9/11 attacks but arrested on immigration charges before he had the chance.
- Richard Reid: the 'shoe-bomber' who tried unsuccessfully to blow up a flight from Miami to Paris a few weeks after 9/11.
- The 7/7 bombers: at least three of the four bombers regularly attended Tablighi Jamaat mosques.
- The 21/7 plotters: the leader of the would-be bombers, Muktar Ibrahim, is reported to have attended a tablighi mosque in East London. The 'fifth bomber', Manfo Asiedu, was also reported as having attended a tablighi gathering in Dewsbury for three days.[15]

- The airline bomb plot: several of the men accused in 2006 of plotting to blow up transatlantic airliners with liquid bombs had Tablighi Jamaat connections.
- The Glasgow Airport/London nightclub bombers: Kafeel Ahmed, an Indian doctor who was pulled out of a burning jeep after attempting to explode it at Glasgow Airport in 2007, had been involved in the Tablighi Jamaat in Bangalore. So too was his younger brother Sabeel, a doctor charged with attempting to explode a car bomb in London the previous day.[16]
- The 7/7 'missing link', Zeesham Siddiqui: a British Muslim thought to link those involved in various major plots was arrested in Pakistan in 2005. He claimed to be in Pakistan to attend a Tablighi Jamaat conference.
- Associates of the 21/7 bomb plotters: a man who was the subject of a control order was part of a group which trained in Cumbria with the 21/7 would-be bombers and claimed to have been on a Tablighi Jamaat-inspired trip to Somalia.[17]

Are the terrorist accusations fair?

The charge sheet against the Tablighi Jamaat in the UK is a long one. But do the charges stick? The Tablighi Jamaat's leadership, with its traditional reluctance to engage with the media, has failed to offer an increasingly suspicious public anything more than the briefest of statements denying any accusations that it promotes violent extremism.

Speculation about the Tablighi Jamaat's connections were fuelled in 2006, following the arrest of a group of British Muslims accused of plotting to blow up transatlantic aeroplanes using liquid bombs. Some of the accused lived in East London; several others lived over 50 miles away in the Buckinghamshire town of High Wycombe. Within a few days of their arrest, a number of British newspapers ran stories saying that the men were connected through the Tablighi Jamaat.[18] The most prominent of these articles ran on the front page of *The Guardian* and was headlined: 'Inside the Islamic Group Accused by MI5 and FBI'.[19] The article was about an evening the reporter had spent at the Tablighi's Jamaat's main centre in East London where he did not find any evidence of terrorist activity. The implication in the headline that the group had been 'accused' of something sinister by MI5 was not substantiated in the article or in any other articles published by *The Guardian* around that time. In common with several other newspapers, *The Guardian* did quote an FBI official who had told the *New York Times* in 2003, 'We have a significant presence of Tablighi Jamaat in the United States, and we have found that Al Qaeda used them for recruiting, now and in the past.' But the *New York Times* article went on to put the FBI official's statement in context, making it clear that the US authorities did not believe that the Tablighi Jamaat advocated support for terrorism, but rather they thought that the group was susceptible to infiltration by extremists seeking to use it as a hunting ground for new recruits.[20]

This certainly appears to be the explanation for the involvement of Jamal (aka Jermaine) Lindsay, one of the 7/7 bombers, in the Tablighi Jamaat. In an unbroadcast and unpublished research interview conducted by a BBC journalist, a former close associate of Lindsay said that Lindsay regarded himself as a Salafi when he converted to Islam. Lindsay rarely worshipped at his local Salafi mosque but chose instead to go with his Salafi jihadi mentor to a Tablighi Jamaat mosque because, according to his former associate, they had identified it as a place where they might find people who they could convert to their far more radical belief system.[21]

The Tablighi Jamaat is seen as a good recruiting ground for the jihadists not because the TJ preaches a message of violent extremism (it does not) but for the opposite reason: the TJ refuses to address the political issues which fire up so many Muslims. Thus the jihadist recruiters see an opportunity to move in and pick off those who feel the TJ is too passive in the face of Muslim oppression. According to the London-based tablighi Omar and others who have spent time in the Tablighi Jamaat, even when young people ask direct questions about political issues or about military jihad, the elders refuse to get involved in such worldly discussions and merely advise their followers to become more involved in the group's missionary work and to 'Make supplication to God and pray for a good outcome.'

One man who posed as a tablighi to investigate the TJ in Pakistan experienced this refusal to even discuss jihad. Omar Nasiri, a Moroccan who worked undercover for various European intelligence agencies in the 1990s, explains in a book about his experiences that, having gone to the Tablighi Jamaat's Pakistan hub in Raiwind, he received no help with advice about how to link up with the mujahideen. He describes the reaction from other tablighis when he told them that, for him, jihad meant the fight of the mujahideen against the Russians or the Bosnian Muslims against the Serbs: 'they looked horrified. Oh no, brother, they would tell me. Jihad means love. Jihad means bringing the lost to God. Jihad means saving souls.'[22] He was rebuked by one of those in charge of the Tablighi Jamaat centre for even raising the issue of armed jihad on the basis that 'The only true jihad is the jihad of the Tabligh.'[23]

As for some of the former tablighis who have been involved in terrorist plots, it may be that they too decided to look elsewhere for help in linking up with jihadist groups when they discovered that the Tablighi Jamaat really is the non-violent group that it purports to be.

Zacarias Moussaoui, the 9/11 '20th hijacker', is said to have attended a tablighi mosque in Paris, but his radicalisation seems more likely to have occurred later when he moved to London and came under the influence of Salafi-jihadi preachers such as Abu Hamza, Abu Qatada and Abdullah al Faisal. Richard Reid, the shoe-bomber, came under the influence of these non-tablighis too, saying that it was the sermons of Abu Hamza and others that gave him a greater understanding of how to interpret his faith in a way that supported the use of violence.[24]

Two of the 7 July bombers—Mohammed Siddique Khan and Shezhad Tanweer—had strong ties with the Tablighi Jamaat's European headquarters in Dewsbury. However, the true source of Khan's radical ideology is more likely to have been small, informal groups of individuals that operated outside the established religious movements: in the paintballing and outdoor adventure trips which were mixed with radicalising lectures;[25] and in the back room of the Islamic bookshop which Khan and his associates controlled and where they created their own radicalising videos.[26] These environments, rather than that created by the Tablighi Jamaat, would have helped to develop Khan's belief that the 7/7 attacks on civilian travellers could be justified Islamically. (Furthermore, the radicals' use of video and the Internet to spread their message is inconsistent with the Tablighi Jamaat's rejection of the use of modern media and its refusal to be drawn into discussion on the political issues of the day.)

As for the airline bomb plotters, there were clear connections between the accused and the Tablighi Jamaat. One of the men who was subsequently convicted was caught on television doing missionary work with one of the other suspects.[27] But the group had other more obviously radicalising connections, such as their links to Rashid Rauf, a British man based in Pakistan who had become involved in the Kashmiri jihadi group Jaish-e-Mohammed.[28]

London-based tablighi Omar was adamant that nothing in the teachings of the Tablighi Jamaat could be construed as encouraging terrorism, but says he has had to reflect on the possibility that some of those involved in terrorism might have used Tablighi Jamaat activities as a cover when travelling abroad to jihad training camps: 'When I went on jamaat, I was struck by the fact that when we had to go through the customs and passport control at Delhi airport we were just waved through without any checks. They just looked at us and instantly recognised us as tablighis because of the way we were dressed and because we were all carrying bedding rolls.' The freedom of travel afforded to the Tablighi Jamaat is not limited to the Indian subcontinent. Most countries around the world are willing to allow visiting tablighis to go about their business and, according to Omar, 'even going to Israel on jamaat is not a problem'. (Although the movement was banned in Saudi Arabia because of doctrinal differences with the Salafi religious establishment.)

A would-be terrorist in need of a cover story might find that he could avoid any awkward questions from friends, family or the authorities about an extended trip abroad by saying that he was going 'on jamaat'. This appeared to be the case with an associate of the 21/7 plotters who was issued with a control order. The British authorities believed the man had attended a terrorist training camp in Somalia. A High Court judge said there were reasons to be 'highly sceptical' about the man's claim that the visit to Somalia was a preaching mission inspired by his experience of the Tablighi Jamaat.[29]

Is there anything about Tablighi Jamaat ideology which might 'prime' young Muslims for terrorism?

Even if the Tablighi Jamaat's link with those who have committed terrorist acts can be explained by the fact that many people come into the organisation before looking for more radical ideas elsewhere, and by the suggestion that extremists have targeted the group as a source of potential recruits, those who are suspicious of the organisation are still likely to worry that it is something about the Tablighi Jamaat's message which is acting as a 'primer' in the growth of violent extremism.

One man who shares those anxieties was once at the heart of the movement in the UK. 'The Tablighi Jamaat is not a benign movement,' says Leicester businessman Mehboob Kantharia, 'I think there is a subversive core which influences an individual to become very easily radicalised.'[30]

Kantharia was a dedicated tablighi from his teenage years as part of a Gujarati community in the former Rhodesia. He continued his association with the movement in the UK, first when he moved to London as a student in the late 1960s and later in Leicester when he settled there with his family in the 1970s. He says he was once part of the Tablighi Jamaat 'inner circle' in the UK. Now, however, he sees the group as 'the most dangerous movement for the Muslims worldwide'. He is part of a discreet group of like-minded former followers who talk regularly and exchange emails.

A former bond-dealer turned property entrepreneur, the urbane Kantharia resembles James Caan, the entrepreneur and former *Dragons' Den* investor, and drives around Leicester in a luxury car.

His rejection of the Tablighi Jamaat was a process that began in the 1980s. A major turning point was his decision to withdraw his two oldest children from a local madrassa where they went every evening after school for religious instruction classes. He says he did not like to see his children being indoctrinated. When he heard them repeating conservative views about gender segregation and 'men's superiority to women' it offended his egalitarian instincts. (TJ guidance for women states that it is the husband's right that a wife should not leave the home without his permission.)[31] Kantharia shocked his family by announcing that his children were to stop attending the madrassa: 'I told them to come home and watch television instead. They said "What?!" I said, "Yes. You'll get far more out of it."'

Kantharia's alternative to the madrassa was all the more controversial in the context of the Tablighi Jamaat's view that the watching of television should be discouraged: 'and to a disciple,' he says, '"discouraged" is a very strong word'.

Kantharia feels his decision helped to encourage his children—now adults—to become tolerant, integrated citizens: 'They are just wonderful men and women. They do not discriminate on grounds of colour or religion. They are citizens of the world.'

He contrasts these attitudes with those fostered by the Tablighi Jamaat: 'The problem is the issue of a superiority complex.' He says that the Tabligh convinces its followers that as Muslims they have a 'superior ideology and lifestyle and that all else is wrong in the eyes of God'.

Sheikh Musa Admani, a Deobandi scholar and imam in London, does not share Kantharia's liberal approach to Islam but does share his concerns about the Tablighi Jamaat. Sheikh Musa has criticised the segregation from mainstream society and the 'them and us' mentality which Kantharia says the Tablighi Jamaat promotes. Musa says he does not make these comments lightly: his father was the head of the Tablighi Jamaat in Africa and he too was once heavily involved in the movement in the UK.[32]

A study of the Tablighi Jamaat in Britain by academic Yoginder Sikand, published in 1998, suggested that the movement's UK mission sought not just to impart religious knowledge but to promote a sense of paranoia and even disgust of non-Muslim society.[33] Sikand cited correspondence from an early tablighi missionary to Britain who described conditions in the country thus: 'The bazaar of immorality thrives and Satan has set here a wide and tough snare.' Sikand also quoted from a publication, written in the 1990s by a prominent British promoter of the Tablighi Jamaat, which stated: 'a major aim of tabligh is to rescue the ummah [Muslim community] from the culture and civilization of the Jews, Christians and (other) enemies of Islam to create such hatred for their ways as human beings have for urine (*peshab*) and excreta (*paykhana*)'.[34]

A more recent study written by an academic researcher described TJ practices in Britain as still reinforcing 'boundaries of purity' and an 'undoubted separatism' which 'poses issues for community cohesion in Britain'.[35]

Mehboob Kantharia's eventual rejection of the Tablighi Jamaat was based on doctrinal doubts as well as concerns about 'the superiority complex'. While on a forty-day jamaat to Mecca and Medina with the amir of the Tablighi Jamaat in Britain, Yusuf Patel, he started to question some of the more superstitious claims made by the movement. A story that the Prophet Muhammad spoke from beyond the grave to Tablighi Jamaat's founder offended Kantharia's rational instincts. He says he also became increasingly concerned about the movement's practice of persuading those engaged in what he regards as worthwhile, worldly pursuits to give up their careers in favour of missionary work. He gives as an example a school friend who gave up a successful career as a urologist to dedicate the rest of his life to the Tablighi Jamaat.

In Kantharia's view, Muslims as a whole would be better off if more emphasis was put on making the most of life's opportunities. Tablighis, by contrast, according to Kantharia, can often be heard quoting a hadith which says 'this world is but a trial and tribulation for the believers but it is a paradise for those who do not believe'.[36] TJ doctrine encourages followers to focus on the afterlife and to regard earthly life (*donya*) as akin to a toilet: a place of filth where one needs to go but not somewhere one would choose to linger any longer than necessary.[37]

Mehboob Kantharia does not go as far as accusing the Tablighi Jamaat of preaching a jihadist ideology. However, he thinks that the Tablighi Jamaat creates the 'them and us' mindset that he believes is a prerequisite for extremism.

London tablighi 'Omar' does not display any of the hostility towards mainstream British society that Kantharia fears the TJ breeds: his face appeared on posters throughout the London Underground when the Greater London Authority honoured him in 2011 for his unpaid work as a football coach. He involves himself in voluntary work to the benefit of Muslims and non-Muslims alike: for example, running a half marathon to raise money for a children's Christmas party that was about to be cancelled due to lack of funds, and working as an unpaid helper at the 2012 London Olympics.

Mehboob Kantharia has doubts about how typical Omar is of the tablighis. 'The problem is that he may be one in 1000,' he says.

'I imagine that 99 per cent of tablighis felt a sense of elation and victory when those planes hit the World Trade Center on 9/11.' This is a shocking accusation for Kantharia to make. Is he really saying that he knows tablighis who were pleased about the events of 9/11? He says he knows tablighi and non-tablighi Muslims who thought this, 'but mostly tablighis'. Does he think these attitudes were in keeping or at odds with those of the Tablighi Jamaat leadership in Britain? On this Kantharia is less sure, but he says that even though the leadership does not encourage its own followers to become involved in violent jihad, it does generate in its followers a sense that Muslims are in direct confrontation with the non-Muslims of the world.[38]

The way in which an apparently apolitical group might politicise its followers is explained in an academic paper on the group authored by Yoginder Sikand. In it he argues that the idea that the Tablighi Jamaat's message is apolitical is probably an oversimplification of the reality.[39]

The Tablighi Jamaat shares with the overtly political Islamic groups the aim of establishing an Islamic state for Muslims. The only difference between the Tablighi Jamaat and these other groups concerns how such an Islamic state might be established. While the political groups advocate a strategy that involves forming Islamic political parties, raising political consciousness or fighting military jihad, the Tablighi Jamaat believes that political power will be given by God to the Muslim 'nation' as a reward for piety. This they see as a very long-term goal, involving bringing individual Muslims, person by person, back to the correct practice of Islam.

The movement's founder, Maulana Muhammad Ilyas, blamed Muslims' relative political weakness on an insufficient level of practice of the faith. He promised his followers that if they became better Muslims in their personal lives they would 'dominate over non-believers' and would be 'destined to be the masters of each and every thing on earth'.[40]

Sikand says a distinct shift in the TJ's attitude towards the issue of political power can be detected after Ilyas's death in 1944. According to him, the shift was not so much caused by the change of leadership (Ilyas's son Maulana Mohammad Yousuf succeeded him) but by the partition of India in 1947. Although many Indian Muslims migrated to Pakistan, the Tablighi Jamaat continued to base its headquarters in the Indian capital Delhi. This meant operating in an atmosphere of growing Hindu militancy and Muslim insecurity. Sikand says that to survive in this new environment the movement began to be 'characterised by an increasing insularity from not just political involvement, but from other worldly affairs as well. Its claims of having nothing to do with politics now came to be asserted with pride, as if political involvement itself was a grave sin.'[41]

The movement also went as far as condemning the Jamaat-e-Islami (JI), an Islamic political party based in Pakistan. Sikand identifies the publication in the early 1950s of a book which rubbished the ideas of the JI's founder, Maulana Sayyed Abul 'Ala Maududi, as a significant incident. The book, *The Chaos of Maududism*, was written by Maulana Muhammad Zakariya, the tablighi ideologue who wrote the TJ's main core text (and the man who sent the head of Darul Uloom Bury to Britain to establish the Deobandi education network). Zakariya's views contrasted with those of the Tablighi Jamaat's founder, Muhammad Ilyas, who had praised Maududi's work as complementary to that of the TJ.[42]

But even if the post-1947 Tablighi Jamaat was keen to be regarded as unthreateningly apolitical, the Islamist ideals could still be discerned in the pronouncements of the Tablighi Jamaat's leadership. In a speech shortly before his death in 1965, Maulana Mohammad Yousuf told followers, 'The collective community of Islam should be supreme over groups or nations ... The enforcement of Muslim Brotherhood is the greatest social ideal of Islam ... and Islam cannot be completely realized until this idea is achieved.'43

The Tablighi Jamaat should therefore be regarded, according to Sikand, as a group that has enabled Muslims to come to terms with secularism without supporting it.

In Britain today, the attitude of the Tablighi Jamaat towards the political Islamic groups is mixed.

According to Faruqe Master, who was brought up by Deobandi parents in Blackburn in Lancashire, so clear was his local Tablighi Jamaat's opposition to the more politicised Islamic groups that all young adherents leaving home for university were given a talk beforehand, warning them not to get involved in such movements. 'They advise people not to join any Islamic societies. They advise people just to pray in their homes instead.'44

London-based tablighi follower Omar has adopted an attitude more reminiscent of Ilyas's respect for difference. Omar is acutely aware of the divide between the Jamaat-e-Islami groups and the Tablighi Jamaat: 'If I ever go to the East London Mosque, which is controlled by the Islamic Forum Europe [a group associated with the Jamaat-e-Islami] I feel that they look down on me as some kind of poor relation because the teaching we follow is very simple.' Nonetheless, he does not seem to feel there is any prohibition about mixing with Jamaat-e-Islami supporters and has even married into a family where several of the men have been heavily involved in the Jamaat-e-Islami.

Another prominent tablighi follower in London is Abdul Khaliq Mian. He illustrates a further complication in defining the movement's attitude toward politics. Not content with simply praying for a resolution to such matters as the conflicts in Iraq and Afghanistan, Mian stood as a parliamentary candidate for the Respect Party at the 2005 general election.

Born in Karachi in 1952 and brought up in London since the age of eleven, Mian followed his father into the Tablighi Jamaat. However, he did not become heavily involved in the organisation until 1996, when the Tablighi Jamaat in East London asked him if he could help them find new premises. As a businessman, Mian had the knowledge and organisational skills to help. He subsequently became an unofficial link between the Tablighi Jamaat leaders in East London and the wider community, and he was the only person to purport to speak publicly on behalf of the organisation during the initial stages of a controversy over plans for the TJ to build a so-called mega mosque in East London.45

Mian says he got the urge to become involved in politics after 9/11. He was motivated partly by a rise in anti-Muslim prejudice but also by disillusion at the stance of his local Labour MP, Stephen Timms, on issues such as the wars in Afghanistan and Iraq: 'He was too much of a Labour Party loyalist. Anything which was against the Muslims, he voted for it.'

Mian helped to form a local political party of Muslim groups called the Alliance Party. In 2005, the Alliance joined forces with the Respect Coalition—a group supported by Islamic activists, the Socialist Workers' Party and the former Labour MP George Galloway.

When Mian was asked to stand as the Respect Party candidate against the sitting MP Stephen Timms, he sought permission from the Tablighi Jamaat before accepting. Such was Mian's loyalty to the Tablighi Jamaat (and so strongly was his name associated with it) that he said he would only consent to the nomination if it had the blessing of the markaz. Mian says there has never been any prohibition against voting by the Tablighi Jamaat in Britain. However, a prominent tablighi standing for a party that mixed Islam with politics was bound to be controversial. He says he received the TJ's blessing: 'One of the muftis at the markaz said "At the moment, this is the best jihad you can do. Fight with the pen and with the laws."'[46]

Mian failed to defeat Stephen Timms, the MP who he felt had worked against Muslim interests. But Mian is nonetheless proud of attracting 8,000 votes and helping to reduce Labour's majority from 21,000 to 13,000.

The academic Yoginder Sikand points out that the involvement of tablighi followers in secular politics can be seen in other countries where the TJ is active. He cites as examples several followers in the Chechen Cabinet, former Pakistani President Muhammad Rafiq Tarar and a former head of Pakistan's intelligence service, Lt General Javed Nasir. Maulana Muhammad Zakariya, the leading TJ ideologue who denounced the Islamic political party Jamaat-e-Islami, even entered politics to become chief minister of Pakistan's North West Frontier Province.[47]

The London 'mega mosque'

The Tablighi Jamaat leadership's policy of non-engagement with wider society seemed to do it no harm for the first fifty years of its existence in Britain. That changed in 2005 after the TJ's plans for a so-called mega mosque in the East London borough of Newham were the subject of an alarming article in *The Sunday Times*.[48]

The proposal to build a new London markaz might not have attracted much attention had it not come so soon after: (i) the revelation that several of the 7/7 bombers had spent time in the Tablighi Jamaat; and (ii) London's successful bid to host the 2012 Olympics on a nearby site.

An initial flurry of publicity turned into a media storm in August 2006 when a number of former tablighis were arrested in connection with a plot to smuggle explosives through security at Heathrow Airport.

'The media got onto this and thought, "Hang on. Mega mosque—Olympics—TJ—terror." And they made all these connections,' recalls Alan Craig, a former councillor who led a campaign to stop the new markaz being built. 'Suddenly it takes off. I find myself on US television, British radio. Everybody's watching because of the Olympics.'[49]

A great deal was at stake for the Tablighi Jamaat: it had purchased the land upon which the giant mosque would be built but it still required planning permission from the London Borough of Newham.

The man who stepped forward to give a small number of media interviews on the TJ's behalf was Abdul Khaliq Mian, the tablighi who stood against the local Labour MP as a Respect Party candidate.

Mian had been involved in the Tablighi Jamaat's attempt to acquire new London premises since the mid-1990s, and in 1996 he had advised the movement to purchase the 16 and a half acre site for £1.4 million.

The Observer newspaper, among others, claimed that the mosque would be paid for by Islamist groups in Saudi Arabia.[50] But Mian's response to this was that 'No government, let alone the government of Saudi Arabia, will have to fund the mega mosque.' That still leaves open the possibility that donations could come from non-governmental sources in Saudi Arabia. However, Mian claimed that an appeal to TJ sympathisers at other mosques would be sufficient to raise most of the funds. This worked, he told me, when it came to raising money to buy the land: 'Within two weeks we had £1.6 million. Ladies gave jewellery, people gave houses, wage packets, kids gave pocket money. Some people were too generous and we had to give some money back to people who we felt couldn't really afford to give so much.' Most of the money, he says, was given as an interest-free loan.

Even one of the TJ's detractors, former tablighi Mehboob Kantharia, confirms that the movement can rely heavily on domestic financial support: 'One thing that gives strength to Tabligh—and has a snowball effect—is that people dig into their pockets.'[51]

Yet getting planning permission was not as easy as raising funds. The TJ initially flouted planning regulations by erecting a number of unauthorised temporary buildings on the site which it used for its regular gatherings. After receiving retrospective planning permission to allow the temporary buildings to remain as an interim measure, the TJ commissioned architect Ali Mangera to design a permanent centre which would include a mosque capable of accommodating 10,000 worshippers. *The Sunday Times* article which sparked controversy about the mosque claimed the intention was to accommodate up to 70,000 worshippers on the site.[52] However, according to Mian, the idea was that, on special occasions, the new markaz could make room for up to 40,000 worshippers by using the dining hall, lobbies and outside canopies. But even at 10,000 the mosque would have been the largest in the UK.[53]

The Dewsbury markaz holds just 3,000 (male-only) worshippers. The proposed London markaz would therefore be a likely replacement for Dewsbury as the TJ's European headquarters.

The scale of the proposed new building outraged the then councillor Alan Craig who saw the plans at a meeting of the London Thames Gateway, a special authority set up to redevelop parts of East London. Craig, who represented a ward bordering the site and sat on Newham Council as a member of the Christian Peoples Alliance, rang Mian to ask for more details.

Shortly afterwards, a sketch of the proposed structure was published in *The Sunday Times* above an article outlining concerns that the project was so big that it would create what was effectively an Islamic quarter near the site of the 2012 Olympic Games in London.[54]

Mian admits to being taken by surprise: 'I never expected that the size of the mosque would be regarded as a negative.'[55]

Having spent six months researching the Tablighi Jamaat, Alan Craig of the Christian Peoples Alliance issued a press release opposing the plans for a new markaz.

'It's not about security, it's about culture,' Craig told me.[56] He concluded that the TJ did not support acts of terrorism, but he was convinced from his research into the movement that it promoted separatism and hostility towards the wider society. Even without the 'mega mosque', he believed he could detect in his own neighbourhood a growing tendency for Muslims to demonise non-Muslims. He recounted to me by way of example a story about one of his young daughter's Muslim friends: his daughter was told by this Muslim child that 'one day the Christians are going to burn down all the mosques in this country'. He held the TJ largely responsible for the propagation of these sorts of beliefs.[57]

Multicultural Newham—a borough where 77 per cent of births are to foreign-born mothers—is where Craig had lived for thirty years, having chosen to bring up his young family there and to immerse himself in community work. He feared that if plans for the new markaz went ahead, his neighbourhood would lose its diversity and instead become a Deobandi enclave, like the Savile Town district of Dewsbury where the TJ based its European headquarters.

Savile Town is not some impoverished ghetto—one local resident told me that comfortably off Gujarati Muslims have pushed up prices by out-bidding each other to secure a home there. Even Alan Craig, who has visited Savile Town, conceded, 'They are nice, neat streets.' But pious Deobandis now dominate the area so much that it is possible to spend a day in the neighbourhood without meeting a non-Muslim.

Craig was part of a tiny opposition grouping on a solidly Labour council. But opposition to the mosque gathered support beyond Craig's tiny political party, the Christian Peoples Alliance. In 2007, an e-petition against the 'mega mosque' on the 10 Downing Street website attracted 255,000 supporters. The petition claimed that the new markaz would 'cause terrible violence and suffering and more money should go into the NHS' (although there were no known plans to spend public money on the development). Barelwi Muslim groups organised under the banner 'Sunni Friends of Newham' and gathered over 2,500 signatures for a petition which opposed the TJ's exclusive use of such a large mosque on the basis that it would exacerbate community tensions and promote extremism. They proposed that all Muslim groups should be represented at the mosque.[58] Another Sufi group, Minhaj ul Quran, campaigned in favour of the site being used as a centre for all faiths.[59]

With the whole markaz project in jeopardy, the TJ adopted a radical change in strategy in late 2007. The transformation is described by Zacharias Pieri, who observed the group during this period as part of his PhD research. Pieri describes how the TJ took the unprecedented step of appointing a public relations firm, Indigo Public Affairs, to help improve the markaz project's image. A prestigious firm of British architects was appointed and the number of worshippers was capped at 12,000. Indigo Public Affairs helped to create a sense that the movement wanted to engage with the wider public: a website for the project was launched and an open day was held in 2008.[60]

'It was all extremely smoothly done,' said Craig of the open day, 'But it was a classic English PR exercise. They say it's to consult with the local community. It's nothing of the sort. It's to be seen to be consulting.'[61] The TJ claimed to have put pamphlets advertising the event through every door in the area, but when Craig knocked on doors in the streets around the site the night before the open day he found that none of the residents knew anything about it. Furthermore, when Craig tried to put questions to TJ officials at the event itself, a PR executive told him that his points would not be answered.[62]

By 2012, according to Zacharias Pieri, the TJ leaders in London had 'learnt to use the language that planning officials look for', with one TJ spokesman talking of the movement's wish to 'place the mosque at the heart of the site as a powerful unifying element: a symbol of London's diverse heritage and a celebration of our cultural diversity'.[63]

With its talk of making the mosque a source for unity in a culturally diverse society, the TJ had adapted its public pronouncements to the mood of Newham council's ruling Labour group and mayor, Sir Robin Wales. The council was at the forefront of a new approach to multiculturalism, refusing to give grants to projects aimed at individual ethnic or religious groups and doing what it could to promote cooperation between diverse communities. The council even funded hundreds of street parties to counter what it perceived as a lack of social mixing in some religiously and ethnically diverse neighbourhoods.

But in the end, the TJ's attempts to create a new image for itself were not enough to gain planning consent. In December 2012, Newham councillors voted against the TJ's proposal on the grounds that it went against the council's planning priority, which was to favour developments that would create new homes and jobs. Other reasons for refusal given by the council were: the plans did not include a proposal to demolish the poorly built temporary buildings on the site; such a large mosque would cause traffic and parking problems; and the plans would have an impact on important historic buildings nearby.[64]

In his book on the Tablighi Jamaat, Zacharias Pieri concluded that the TJ's leaders in London had realised that 'if they are to succeed in their ambitions in a liberal democracy, then some modification of their ideologies is necessary'.[65]

Alan Craig, who lost his council seat to the ruling Labour group in 2010, thought Pieri was too optimistic about the TJ. He turned up to the launch of Pieri's book (as did two TJ elders from the London markaz) where he distributed an alternative conclusion to what he thought was an otherwise excellent account of the TJ and the mega mosque saga. According to Craig, the TJ's 'thin programme of engagement with the wider non-Muslim local community' was purely a pragmatic response to the 'existential threat' of planning refusal and the prospect of having to demolish its temporary markaz. Once that fight was over, he predicted, it would revert to type.[66]

But Pieri did not claim in his book that the London TJ's sudden conversion to community engagement was permanent and heartfelt. According to Pieri, the London TJ's change of tack was merely a response to the fact it found itself dealing with constraints from the authorities in London which it had not had to face in Dewsbury.[67]

As an outsider, it is impossible to know whether attitudes have really changed within the TJ; the extent to which there is a range of opinions at the top of the movement in the UK; and whether attitudes among the leaders in London differ from those elsewhere in the UK. One Deobandi scholar suggested to me that the prospect of the TJ's European headquarters moving from Dewsbury to London had caused 'a bit of a split' within the organisation.

The TJ operates largely without the need of help from the British state or local authorities. So it may not find itself facing any pressing need to repeat the adaptation it performed in London. Ordinary members on the ground, however, interact with the wider society on a daily basis. Omar's example shows it is possible to compartmentalise the 'them and us' message to live a life which is pious but nonetheless integrated: raising money for a children's Christmas party, volunteering at the Olympics and sharing his exploits with an eclectic group of friends on Facebook.

The TJ elders might not be applying to Newham council for grants to run diversity street parties any time soon, but the likes of Omar might.

3

THE SALAFIS

'DON'T CALL US WAHHABIS!'

If Hollywood ever produced a film about the life of the founder of the austere branch of Islam known as Wahhabism, the opening scene would surely be this:

The time is the 1740s and the place is a town in the Arabian Peninsula. Surrounded by crowds, the central character Mohammed ibn Abd al-Wahhab is wielding an axe. Some in the crowd are cheering him, others are pleading with him to desist as he chops down a tree, the branches of which are decorated with various objects.

Over 1,000 years after the birth of the Prophet Muhammad, this was ibn Abd al-Wahhab's powerful way of making a point about a central tenet of Islamic doctrine—the oneness of God (*tawhid*). The local Muslim population in his hometown had taken to hanging objects on the branches of several trees in the belief that they could obtain some sort of blessing from the tree, or that the tree could intercede with God on their behalf. Practices like these, ibn Abd al-Wahhab believed, were forbidden innovation (*bida*) because they implied that someone or something other than God had the power to grant blessings.[1] Mohammed Ibn al-Wahhab urged a return to strict monotheism.

According to one British admirer of ibn Abd al-Wahhab's writings, it is a doctrine which has proved particularly attractive to Muslim converts: 'It's simple, it's pure and it's monotheistic in that it calls them to the worship of Allah alone. So that draws in a lot of converts because of the simplicity of the message.'[2]

The term Wahhabi is regarded as derogatory on the basis that it implies that those influenced by ibn Abd al-Wahhab's ideas are followers of the man, rather than followers of Islam in its earliest and purest form. Adherents to this school of thought consequently prefer to be called Salafis. The term *salaf* means predecessors in Arabic, but in this religious context it means 'the pious predecessors' and refers to the Prophet Muhammad and his disciples.

Furthermore, Salafism in Britain is influenced not just by the teachings of Mohammed ibn Abd al-Wahhab but also by a South Asian Salafi movement called the Ahl-e-Hadith, and by more recent Salafi scholars who disagreed with ibn Abd al-Wahhab on certain points of Islamic doctrine.

Mohammed ibn Abd al-Wahhab's teachings emphasised using the Quran and the hadiths (records of the Prophet Muhammad's sayings and actions) as sources of guidance rather than having an unquestioning trust in the judgements that Islamic scholars had handed down over the intervening centuries. The rulings of the madhabs, the traditional schools of Sunni jurisprudence, should be respected, ibn Abd al-Wahhab claimed, but not followed blindly. He himself continued to identify with the Hanbali school.

Some Salafis go further than ibn Abd al-Wahhab in their scepticism about the traditional schools of thought. The founders of the Ahl-e-Hadith movement, for example, refused to follow a madhab altogether.[3]

To call someone a rationalist in Salafi circles is to insult them. Beliefs should be justified by reference to the Quran and hadiths rather than other sources of reasoning. To illustrate this point one Salafi preacher told me that pork would still be forbidden to Muslims even if pigs were bred in laboratories. It is not a matter of proving whether the meat is dirty or clean. It is a matter of accepting that Muslims should never eat pork because it says so in the Quran and to reject that is to put one's mere human intellect above the word of God.[4] By this logic, they also regard secularism as undesirable on the basis that it gives supremacy to man-made laws over divine governance.[5]

The need for beliefs and practices to be textually justified meant that Muslim mystics who claimed to have access to esoteric knowledge were also challenged by Mohammed ibn Abd al-Wahhab.

Ibn Abd al-Wahhab's credibility as a scholar enabled him to question the religious establishment and gather popular support. His most significant breakthrough came in 1744 when he formed an alliance that was to ensure his message was spread not just within eighteenth-century Arabia but around the world for years to come. Ibn Abd al-Wahhab and a local tribal leader, Muhammad ibn Saud, swore an oath of mutual allegiance and agreed that ibn Saud would be the amir (the political leader) and ibn Abd al-Wahhab would be the imam (the religious leader).

That alliance, between the Saud family and the scholars of the Wahhabi doctrine, exists to this day. In the Kingdom of Saudi Arabia a Wahhabi version of Islam dominates daily life.

In the wake of the 9/11 bombings, many viewed the Saudi brand of Islam as the ideology which had inspired the attacks. Fifteen of the nineteen hijackers, as well as Osama bin Laden himself, had been brought up in Saudi Arabia.

But the truth about 'Wahhabism' and Salafism more generally is far more complicated.

What all Salafis have in common is a desire to return to the basic tenets of Islam: they seek to discard the cultural accretions which have become attached to their religion and to imitate what they believe to be the practices of the Prophet Muhammad and his disciples. This desire to emulate the early followers of Islam expresses itself in the routines of daily life. They tend to avoid music, television and photographs of living things. The men often wear trousers or robes which do not cover the ankles and the women often veil their faces when in the presence of males outside their closest family. These practices are not exclusive to the Salafis; nor does every Salafi follow them. But in Britain, those who call themselves Salafis abide by these strictures at least as much as any other Islamic group.

Among the Salafis there are also important divisions. The Salafis can be split into three broad and sometimes overlapping categories: pietistic Salafis who believe that salvation will come through faith, religious ritual and strict adherence to the principles laid down in the Quran and hadiths; political Salafis who believe that Muslims should also strive to establish Islamic states in Muslim-majority countries; and jihadi Salafis who advocate the taking up of arms to overthrow un-Islamic regimes in Muslim lands.[6]

MEDINA IN BIRMINGHAM, NAJAF IN BRENT

JIMAS—Britain's first Salafi youth organisation

In the mid-1990s the tensions and overlaps between pietistic, political and jihadi Salafism could be seen in what was then Britain's main Salafi youth organisation: Jam'iat Ihyaa' Minhaaj al-Sunnah (JIMAS).

I am grateful to some of JIMAS's early leaders who talked to me candidly about the factional divisions and even the jihadi connections of the movement they helped to run in their youth.

JIMAS was a new type of Islamic organisation. Unlike most of Britain's Islamic organisations at the time, it was not the UK offshoot of a larger foreign network. It operated in English and its membership was mainly British-born. JIMAS was founded in 1984 by Manwar Ali,[7] a computer science graduate from London. The son of Bangladeshi immigrants, Manwar Ali's early education in Islam had come from his father, a Deobandi scholar. As a teenager Manwar Ali had started to search for a more 'authentic' version of Islam which appeared to link back directly to the Quran and hadiths—and which deferred less to cultural and scholarly traditions. A charismatic preacher, Manwar Ali toured the university Islamic societies. Within a few years he had built a vibrant youth movement inspired by this mission.

In the early days the leading activists of JIMAS were largely self-taught. Many were converts or Muslims brought up by families which followed traditional Pakistani interpretations of Islam. In JIMAS they learnt to distinguish religion from culture. Manwar Ali describes the membership as modern young men with beards and modern young women in hijab. They were Western-educated but regarded themselves as more authentically Islamic than the older generation of Muslim immigrants. Such was the success of their organisation that by the early 1990s leading Salafis from around the world were competing for JIMAS's loyalty.

Among those who courted Manwar Ali for influence over JIMAS were the Quran wa Sunnah Society of North America (QSS); Salafi scholars from Jordan, Kuwait, Egypt and Saudi Arabia; and the emerging jihadi groups spawned by veterans of the battle against the Soviets in Afghanistan. All JIMAS's ideological suitors regarded themselves as Salafis and all claimed to be returning to the true Islam, yet each had a different interpretation of what that was. There were disputes over such issues as the permissibility of democracy, living in non-Muslim lands and rebelling against unjust Muslim rulers. This in turn caused factionalism within JIMAS.

JIMAS, jihad and Lashkar-e-Taiba

One of the issues over which divisions were particularly intense was that of military jihad.

Encouraged by the victory of the Afghan mujahideen against the Soviet Union, many JIMAS members had a somewhat romantic attachment to the idea of jihad. 'The fashion was army boots, the Afghani hat, the shalwar kameez and the waistcoat,' remembers one former member.[8] There was huge interest in the war in Bosnia too: JIMAS sent over fifty fighters.[9]

The charisma of JIMAS's leader, Manwar Ali, was perhaps enhanced by the fact that he was known to have attended jihad training camps on the Afghanistan–Pakistan border and had spent time on the frontline against the communists in the 1990s. He says he created a route to jihad in Afghanistan from Britain through contacts in Saudi Arabia, Germany and the Netherlands.

JIMAS had been united in its support for the Afghan mujahideen's fight against Soviet invasion. However, in the years following the Soviet withdrawal, the issue of jihad caused division among Salafis worldwide and these were reflected in JIMAS.

Disagreements over this came to a head at the 1995 JIMAS annual conference, to which two leading members of the Kashmiri jihadi group Lashkar-e-Taiba (LeT) had been invited.

LeT was to gain worldwide notoriety over a decade later as the group suspected of plotting the 2008 Mumbai bombings. But back in 1995 two of their most important members had no difficulty travelling to the UK to address large gatherings of Salafis on a fundraising and recruitment tour.[10]

LeT's leader, Hafeez Saeed, and his colleague, Abu Abdel Aziz, were both veterans of the Afghan jihad against the communists. Abu Abdel Aziz had gone on to serve as commander in chief of the Arab–Afghan mujahideen during the Bosnian conflict. By 1995 both men had found a new cause in the disputed territory of Kashmir, a region claimed by both India and Pakistan.

In a speech to hundreds of young British Muslims at the JIMAS conference held at Leicester University, the head of LeT Hafeez Saeed claimed that, as an alternative to years of spiritual and moral training, Muslims could find salvation in a matter of weeks by going to an LeT training camp and then fighting in the insurgency in Kashmir. His lecture appeared to draw on the teachings of a respected medieval Islamic scholar for authority.[11]

Hafeez Saeed and Abu Abdel Aziz also claimed that there was jihad in Bosnia. Furthermore, they claimed that jihad in Bosnia and Kashmir was *fard ayn*, meaning it was an absolute obligation for every able Muslim to take part in jihad in those places.

These claims were regarded with scepticism by a leading group of JIMAS members who followed a more pietistic strand of Salafism. Many of the latter faction followed the guidance of Sheikh al Albani, a Salafi scholar based in Jordan. Sheikh al Albani had stated that there was no jihad in Bosnia. Some other Salafi scholars had said that it was permissible to fight, but only as a member of the official Bosnian army, and not by attending the sort of unofficial camps that those at the conference were being encouraged to attend. Certainly, according to these scholars, there was no obligation to fight.

As for the Indian-controlled part of Kashmir, the pietistic group did not regard incursions from neighbouring Pakistan as permissible unless authorised by a head of government.

Among the other speakers at the conference were some scholars representing the pietistic Sheikh al Albani. Members of JIMAS's anti-jihadi faction went backstage to relate to these visiting scholars what they had heard in the hall from the LeT speakers. Among those in JIMAS's pietistic faction was a preacher from Birmingham known as Abu Khadeejah. According to him, Hafeez Saeed was forced to go back into the hall and make the appropriate retractions: 'But the rectification was not as clear as the original call,' and the audience remained divided.[12] JIMAS had been strongly tied to the pietistic Sheikh al Albani, yet Abu Khadeejah and others now suspected that JIMAS's leader Manwar Ali was attracted to the ideas of the visiting jihadists.

Manwar Ali says that he saw no conflict between giving a platform to the LeT speakers and respecting the teachings of Sheikh al Albani. He was in close touch at the time with scholars claiming to be representatives of the pietistic Albani and they, he says, had never advised him against inviting leading members of LeT to address the conference. He says that he even met the same Albani scholars several times at the main LeT training camp in Pakistan where they were giving talks.[13]

Pietists versus political Islam

According to Manwar Ali the argument within JIMAS over whether to support the Kashmiri jihadi group Lashkar-e-Taiba was not the most important doctrinal division among his Salafi group in the 1990s. From his point of view, a more important split was that between those who supported a quietist, pietistic form of Salafism and those who were drawn to a more political version.

The divisions between these two strands had their origins in the Middle East and they became particularly intense following Iraq's invasion of Kuwait in 1990.

When Saddam's troops invaded Kuwait, Saudi Arabia's ruling family worried that their Kingdom could be the Iraqi army's next target. Osama bin Laden, by then a veteran of the Afghan war against Soviet occupation, offered the services of an international brigade of mujahideen veterans. Bin Laden's offer was turned down and the Saudi government opted instead to allow US troops to set up military bases inside the Kingdom. The controversial decision to allow an infidel army on to Saudi soil was given religious sanction by the Kingdom's most powerful religious scholar: Grand Mufti Sheikh bin Baz. Bin Laden was outraged, not just by the snub to his offer to provide troops, but by what he saw as a convenient misreading of Islamic principle by bin Baz to suit the purposes of the Saudi royal family. In bin Laden's view, the fact that the Saudi government, which had been charged with guarding the holiest sites in Islam, was unable to defend itself without infidel help was humiliating. Furthermore, by entering into an alliance with non-Muslim troops in a fight against other Muslims, bin Laden believed that the Saudi Kingdom was in direct contravention of Islamic law.

There was also dissent within the ranks of the scholars. Two popular Saudi Salafi scholars, Sheikh Safar al-Hawali and Sheik Salman al-Oudah—known as the Awakening Sheikhs—spoke out publicly against bin Baz's ruling. The Awakening Sheikhs also opposed an edict from Grand Mufti Sheikh bin Baz in which he decreed that it was Islamically permissible for Muslim regimes to make peace with Israel by signing a treaty. The Awakening Sheikhs were eventually imprisoned in Saudi Arabia for inciting the population against the Kingdom's rulers.

These divisions in Saudi Arabia were not felt in any significant way within the UK Salafi movement at the time. 'Most of the JIMAS followers were very apolitical,' recalls Usama Hasan, then a leading JIMAS activist. Usama Hasan was well connected through his father Suhaib Hasan with what was then the main Salafi network in Britain: the Ahl-e-Hadith. Founded in nineteenth-century India, the Ahl-e-Hadith rejected the traditional schools of Sunni Islamic law and vehemently opposed Sufism and Shi'ism. It had much in common with Saudi Wahhabism, and in the coming centuries the two groups cooperated and influenced each other's ideologies. In Britain, senior Ahl-e-Hadith members and scholars such as Usama's father had strong connections with Saudi Arabia and may have felt somewhat inhibited about criticising the Kingdom's government over its stance during the First Gulf War.

But some Arab scholars who had settled in Britain were keen to bring the disputed status of bin Baz's ruling to the attention of the UK Salafis.

In Britain, one of the most influential propagandists against the grand mufti's line was Muhammad Suroor Zayn al-Abidin. Suroor had founded an ideological movement which mixed Salafi-style religiosity with the political ideas of the Muslim Brotherhood thinker Sayyid Qutb. An influential disseminator of Suroor's ideology was the Awakening Sheikh Salman al Oudah who had been taught by Suroor in Saudi Arabia.

From 1984 Suroor lived in exile in Birmingham, from where he ran the Centre for Islamic Studies, a think tank established to promote his ideas.[14] Another centre aligned to his ideas—al Muntada in Parson's Green, London—was opened around the same time.

JIMAS's leader Manwar Ali initially followed the advice of the pietistic scholars of the Middle East to preach against the 'Surooris'. But by the mid-1990s Manwar Ali was losing his enthusiasm for this. The more political Islamic activists of Britain dubbed the pietistic sheikhs of Saudi Arabia as the 'scholars for dollars'. The phrase caught on. The activists of JIMAS belatedly became aware of the split between Grand Mufti bin Baz of Saudi Arabia and the Awakening Sheikhs—and Manwar Ali moved towards support for the latter.

As his views changed, Manwar Ali began to lead something of a double life. By day he was a computer programmer at British Telecom's research laboratories in Suffolk. In his spare time he was an increasingly radical preacher, using his annual holidays to visit jihad training camps in Pakistan. Manwar Ali says there was nothing clandestine about his activities: indeed he says that his managers at BT were fully aware of how he spent his holidays, with photographs of his exploits—including one of him holding a gun while standing atop a tank in Afghanistan—even being displayed on the office notice board.

This shift in Manwar Ali's position caused concern among the pietistic faction within JIMAS. The doubts of Abu Khadeejah's faction were reinforced by Dawud Burbank, a British Muslim convert who had studied at the University of Medina in Saudi Arabia.

During his time in Medina, Dawud Burbank had attended lectures given by senior Salafi scholars and had direct access to Arabic texts that were unavailable in the UK. In the pre-Internet era, this was a crucial breakthrough. From 1990, Burbank began translating some of the Arabic texts as well as tapes of lectures by prominent Salafis, including Sheikh al Albani and another pietistic scholar—Sheikh Rabi al Madkhali. Burbank was supported by another prolific translator, Abu Iyad Amjad, a student at Essex University.

Burbank drew his British friends' attention to a book by Sheikh Rabi, a professor at the University of Medina. The book heavily criticised the revolutionary teachings of the Islamist ideologue Sayyid Qutb.[15]

Manwar Ali tried to defend his position against the pietistic faction within JIMAS by calling upon the help of a leading US-based Salafi called Ali al Timimi.[16] Timimi had claimed that Salafi principles were being distorted by some of the pietistic scholars who he said had been manipulated as part of a conspiracy to create a 'New World Order'. In 1996, Manwar Ali arranged for Ali al Timimi to address a meeting of hundreds of JIMAS members at Leytonstone Town Hall in East London. Timimi tried to rally support for Manwar Ali. But while many members remained loyal to their leader, the bulk of JIMAS's most popular preachers had already decided to leave.

A rival group which included the preacher Abu Khadeejah and the former University of Medina student Dawud Burbank was formed in Birmingham. Their group also included Abu Hakim Bilal Davis, an Afro-Caribbean convert who had also studied at the University of Medina, and translator Abu Iyad Amjad. They later established the website Salafi Publications.

At Brixton Mosque in South London, another pietistic group, led by the convert Abdul Haq Baker, cut its ties with JIMAS too.

The arrival of the Salafi-Jihadis

JIMAS under Manwar Ali had to compete not just with the pietistic Salafis but with a new breed of extreme jihadi preachers who were now spreading their message in the UK.

The support of the JIMAS leadership for jihads in places such as Bosnia, Chechnya and Indian-controlled Kashmir was considered radical at the time. So too was their support for the overthrow of autocratic Muslim governments in places such as Saudi Arabia and Egypt.

However, by the early 1990s there were even more radical Salafist groups operating in Britain. A new theory of jihad was being spread by exiled Arab radical Islamists who saw the conflict in more global terms. Western governments, they argued, should be targets too: their recognition and support for Israel and their support for secular, autocratic and corrupt regimes in the Middle East and North Africa had effectively resulted in the occupation of Muslim lands by non-Muslims.

'We came across this reasoning that Britain was a land of war,' remembers Usama Hasan, a Salafi preacher who remained in JIMAS. Usama Hasan heard these new radical preachers claim it was permissible to lie and cheat the non-believers: 'They argued for example that you could lie on tax forms. Some of the really extreme ones used to say that if you can get away with it you can rape women on the street. But as British people we never ever went near that kind of argument because it was just nonsense really. It was devaluing all our moral principles. They would never have been welcome at a JIMAS event.'[17]

Pre-eminent among the 'really extreme ones' that Usama Hasan remembers was Abdullah al Faisal, a Jamaican convert who obtained a degree in Islamic studies while living in Saudi Arabia.[18] Al Fasial was appointed as a teacher at Brixton Mosque in 1991 and Usama Hasan remembers seeing him preach there: 'I took an instant dislike to the guy because he was very arrogant and talking as though he knew everything.'[19]

Another of the newly arrived radical preachers, Abu Qatada, had more scholarly credibility, being a former student of the pietistic Sheikh al Albani. However, some of the Salafis in Britain, such as Usama Hasan, had heard that Sheikh al Albani had disowned Abu Qatada. This did not seem to prevent the Palestinian preacher from attracting plenty of acolytes following his arrival in London in 1993.

While some British-born radicals attended Abu Qatada's lectures, his interactions were mainly with Arabic-speaking Islamist exiles. One of Abu Qatada's most important followers was Abu Hamza, an Egyptian who had spent time in Bosnia and Afghanistan.

Abu Hamza had been injured by explosives and wore a hook where once his right hand had been. By the mid-1990s Abu Hamza had taken the radical message beyond the Arab exiles. He had gathered a substantial following of British-born Muslims, set up his own organisation—the Supporters of Sharia—and had taken control of Finsbury Park Mosque in North London.

As for Abdullah al Faisal, the Jamaican convert and preacher, in 1993 his extremism led to ejection from Brixton Mosque by a pietistic management committee. But he continued to spread his jihadi message. Both he and Abu Hamza gave talks in mosques, on university campuses and in hired halls throughout the UK, while cassette tapes of their lectures were sold in shops in Muslim areas.

'We used to have to battle against them on the campuses,' recalls Usama Hasan. While studying for a PhD at Imperial College London in the mid-1990s, Hasan served as president of the student Islamic Society (ISoc). But even as the ISoc president he felt unable to prevent the society playing host to Abdullah al Faisal and Abu Hamza. 'It wasn't something I could stop because there were other people on the committee who pressed for it and I felt we had to allow them in and challenge them.'[20]

Hasan, who had studied the Quran for twenty years under his Salafi scholar father, felt that al Faisal and Abu Hamza were clearly not well grounded in Islamic theology and had 'just learnt a bit here and there'. But in many of the places that Abu Hamza and Abdullah al Faisal preached, the audience was more credulous. The fact that, unlike most Muslims in Britain, these preachers could speak Arabic gave them a superficial credibility with audiences consisting mainly of converts and Muslims of South Asian origin.

Another leading radical who appeared to have a credible claim to scholarly knowledge was the Syrian-born Omar Bakri Mohammed. Bakri had arrived in Britain in 1986 to take up the role of scholar for the UK branch of the Islamist group Hizb-ut-Tahrir (HT). HT's main policy was the re-establishment of a caliphate—a multinational Islamic government—to unite the Muslim world. Its strategy was to seize power in a Muslim-majority country through a coup d'état, possibly brought about by infiltration of that country's armed forces. But they were neither radical jihadis nor Wahhabis. Cosh Omar, a British Muslim who joined HT and became close to Omar Bakri in the 1990s, recalls that members were not encouraged to fight in foreign jihads in Bosnia or elsewhere but merely to campaign politically. 'And he used go on about how much he detested the Wahhabis,' according to Cosh Omar.[21]

Bakri managed to gain a significant following among British Muslims, particularly students, and in the view of some experts he did more to politicise Muslim youth than anyone else.[22] However, in 1995, after he had declared that Muslims should attempt to establish the caliphate in Britain, he was dismissed by Hizb-ut-Tahrir's worldwide leader.[23] Bakri then established a new group called al Muhajiroun which took up an extreme jihadi position and a Salafi identity. Like Abu Hamza, Omar Bakri now urged British Muslims to fight in conflicts abroad and to attend jihad training camps.

If such a broad range of Muslims—from radical jihadi leaders to their pietistic opponents—could call themselves Salafis and be referred to by others as Wahhabis, which faction is closest to the teachings of the founder of Wahhabism? According to one detailed academic study, the beliefs of the pietistic Salafis are the closest to those of Mohammed ibn Abd al-Wahhab. The huge gap between some of ibn Abd al-Wahhab's interpretations and what has become known as jihadi Salafism suggests that many modern-day Salafists are either unaware of ibn Abd al-Wahhab's teachings or have consciously rejected them.[24]

Saudi influence in Britain

In Britain, the Sufi Muslim groups which found themselves losing their young people to Salafism in the 1990s often attributed the Salafis' success to their ability to obtain funding from Saudi Arabia for mosques and literature. This is an oversimplification.

The Saudis' greatest and most direct influence on Islamic teaching in Britain has probably come through Saudi government scholarships for those who want to study at the University of Medina. Students usually have their fees, airfares and accommodation paid for by the Saudi government and are also given a small grant for living expenses.[25] One expert, Yahya Birt, estimates that hundreds of University of Medina graduates have returned to Britain since the early 1980s. Many of them have trained as preachers.[26] According to Birt, in the early days most of those preachers worked within the Urdu-speaking Ahl-e-Hadith movement on their return to Britain. Some were later involved in setting up JIMAS in an attempt to cater for the English-speaking youth.

Abu Khadeejah of Salafi Publications, a group closely aligned with the pietistic scholars, says his organisation has received no money from Saudi

Arabia and survives purely on donations. To the best of his knowledge, the only Islamic organisations in the UK directly managed by the Saudi government are King Fahd mosque in Edinburgh (also known as Edinburgh Central Mosque) and the World Assembly of Muslim Youth (WAMY).[27]

As far as Wahhabi literature is concerned, Abu Khadeejah says that the only literature he recalls being distributed by the Saudi embassy in the UK during the 1990s was Mohammad ibn Abd al-Wahhab's most famous treatise, *Kitab al Tawhid*. He says that far more literature has been distributed in subsequent years, including a translation of the Quran by Mohsin Khan.[28]

The British Salafi preachers Abdur Raheem Green and Abu Khadeejah say they adopted Salafi ways of thinking before they had even heard of the term Salafi. They were drawn to the rejection of: (i) what they saw as cultural interpretations of Islam; and (ii) the 'blind following' of the traditional schools of Islamic jurisprudence. They preferred to seek textual evidence in the Quran and hadiths. They only started to use the term Salafi when Dawud Burbank returned from the University of Medina in the early 1990s. Before he discovered JIMAS, Green used to carry ibn Abd al-Wahhab's key text *Kitab al Tawhid* around with him: 'It was so brilliant. Simple statements explaining simple concepts around the oneness of God.'[29]

But he and his JIMAS colleagues did not think of their doctrinal interpretation as being distinctively Saudi. According to Abdur Raheem Green, the stronger connection among the early JIMAS members was with Sheikh al Albani, who was born in Albania, raised in Syria and who lived in Jordan until his death in 1999. Albani had pointed out a contradiction in Mohammed ibn Abd al-Wahhab's approach: while rejecting strict adherence to a madhab, one of the traditional Sunni schools of Islamic law, ibn Abd al-Wahhab had in practice continued to adhere to the Hanbali madhab.[30] Albani's call for legal reasoning outside the framework of the Hanbali madhab brought him into conflict with the Saudi religious establishment.[31]

Salafi attitude to women

In Saudi Arabia, the birthplace of Wahhabi Salafism, there are severe restrictions on the lives of women. They are not permitted to drive or to work alongside men. When going out in public, they must wear a black gown and head scarf and be accompanied by a male relative.

In Britain, 94 per cent of Salafi mosques admit women—the highest proportion for any of the main Sunni groups.[32] But this should not be taken as an indication that the Salafis of Britain generally hold liberal attitudes towards gender equality. Much of what is enforced by law and cultural norms in Saudi Arabia is adopted as an act of piety by Salafis in Britain.

When I called at the home of Abu Khadeejah and his family in Birmingham, the door was opened but there was no one standing on the threshold to greet me. Instead, I heard his wife's voice from behind the door inviting me to come in and take my shoes off. Abu Khadeejah's wife does not wish to risk being seen by the neighbours without her hijab. Nor does she want to be known publicly by her birth name, preferring instead to be referred to here as Umm Abdullah, which means mother of Abudullah. Inside the house, Umm Abdullah wears traditional Pakistani clothing without a hijab in the presence of women and children visitors and her family. Male visitors would be met by her husband or one of her sons before being ushered upstairs to her husband's study, thus avoiding contact with the women of the house.[33]

Umm Abdullah, like Abu Khadeejah, was brought up in a traditional Pakistani household. But as a sociology student at Essex University in the 1990s, religion was not a priority, although she prayed and fasted during Ramadan. She enjoyed student life but felt there was always something missing. Her student and academic friends were shocked when she suddenly adopted Salafism during her sixth year at Essex University, while studying for a PhD, and found in it a more fulfilling way of life.

A trip to Mecca with her parents coincided with a sudden conviction that Islam—and the Salafi interpretation of it—was the truth. On her return from Saudi Arabia she started to wear the hijab and gained moral support from a group of British Salafis based at Essex University. She decided it was time for her to get married and asked her parents to help her find a suitable husband.

But the fact that she was now a Salafi made arranging a match difficult as the families in her parents' Pakistani community followed a more traditional and cultural interpretation of Islam, which they feared might be challenged by the zeal of a Salafi convert. She turned down the few suitors introduced to her by her parents. Under Salafi doctrine this was something she was entitled to do, as a woman's consent is necessary for a marriage to be valid. Through the leading Salafi at Essex University she was introduced to Abu Khadeejah, a senior lecturer and teacher in the movement. She decided he would make a suitable husband and a wedding was arranged with celebrations to follow in her hometown of Oxford and her new husband's base in Birmingham.

Over a decade after her marriage, Umm Abdullah's life was largely taken up with family responsibilities when I visited her in Birmingham in 2008. She and Abu Khadeejah had three daughters and two sons. Abu Khadeejah's teenage daughter by his first marriage helped her step-mother look after the younger children. Umm Abdullah taught the children at home using materials from an online college offering mainstream secular courses. Even when she began studying part-time for a PhD at a British university, most of her time was spent inside the house. Umm Abdullah told me she did not feel she had given anything up by adopting such a conservative lifestyle: 'I might be inside my house but my heart is liberated.'[34]

In the UK, Salafi communities emphasise the necessity of the woman's consent for any marriage to be valid. This has sometimes brought them into conflict with the elders of the predominantly South Asian Muslim communities in Britain. Abu Khadeejah says that in cases where parents have tried to force a daughter to marry an irreligious suitor, the group has obtained a fatwa declaring the woman's right to refuse. Occasionally his mosque has even felt compelled by duty to take on the guardianship of young women from families which refuse to permit a valid marriage purely on the basis of race or caste prejudice.[35]

Salafi doctrine, in common with other schools of Islamic thought, recognises the possibility of a husband taking up to four wives concurrently. Ibn Abd al-Wahhab attached certain safeguards to this: the woman can stipulate in the marriage contract that the husband is not to take any co-wives; only the wife can give up some of her days and nights with the husband, otherwise he has to divide his time equally;[36] and plural marriage is only permissible in cases where the husband is able to fulfil his financial and other obligations to all his wives.

Abu Khadeejah defends the practice of taking four wives in countries where it is legal. He resents what he sees as the attempts by some Muslim preachers to make Islam more palatable to Westerners by claiming that such a practice was only permitted in special circumstances: 'Am I going to start saying that this practice was in a time when there was a lot of jihad and a lot of fighting and a surplus of women? No.' Abu Khadeejah believes that the surplus women argument is not supported by the hadiths, which report polygamous marriages entered into by the Prophet himself and his companions to women who were clearly not surplus to need.[37]

In a television documentary about Britain's busiest sharia council, a leading Salafi scholar was shown advising a dissatisfied husband that the solution to his marital difficulties was to take a second wife rather than to divorce.[38]

On the issue of divorce, Usama Hasan believes that the Salafi position has worked to the benefit of Muslim women in Britain. Ibn Abd al-Wahhab regarded as incorrect the idea that a Muslim man could unilaterally divorce his wife simply by repeating 'talaq' ('I divorce you') three times in a row. 'Classically the four schools [madhab] all say that's it, end of marriage,' says Hasan. By contrast, the Salafi-led Islamic Sharia Council concurs with ibn Abd al-Wahhab in stating that the talaq has to be declared on three separate occasions with a waiting period of one month in-between to allow for a possible reconciliation.[39] 'We used to get a lot of flak from people I would describe as narrow-minded madhabists[40] for saying that,' says Usama Hasan. He concurs with Wahhab's advice that if the woman is divorced by talaq then she is entitled to keep her dowry, but if she initiates the divorce she will probably lose the right to financial support from her husband.[41]

A less attractive picture of Salafi attitudes towards women was painted in Channel 4's 'Undercover Mosque' documentary. A Salafi preacher based at an Ahl-e-Hadith mosque in Birmingham was shown in an Internet broadcast saying, 'Allah has created the woman—even if she gets a PhD—deficient. Her intellect is incomplete, deficient. She may be suffering from hormones that will make her emotional. It takes two witnesses of a woman to equal the one witness of the man.'[42]

Salafis and wider society

The strict discipline of Salafism means that many adherents live a life where contact with mainstream society is kept to a minimum. Music is forbidden other than at Eid or wedding celebrations when women are allowed to sing and play the drum. Many Salafis believe that television should be avoided and that they are only permitted to watch programmes that have a clear educational benefit, such as wildlife documentaries. Cartoons for children are acceptable as long as they do not contain music, but entertainment programmes for adults are not allowed. Even photographs of human faces are banned by some. Attending an event where there is music and alcohol, or where men and women mix freely, would be out of the question for many Salafis.

According to Abu Khadeejah, members of his Salafi community try to maintain strong contact with the wider society but with the condition that they do not compromise their faith and religious values. Those who work tend to have jobs in mainstream society. The children who attend the Salafis' primary school make regular day visits to schools that have no Muslim students. But there is a degree of isolation. Abu Khadeejah defends this as an inevitable part of the importance they attach to avoiding what they regard as un-Islamic practices. This extends to the avoidance of religious practices of other Islamic groups like the Sufis. An important part of the Sufi year, for example, is the celebration of the Prophet Muhammad's birthday. Salafis like Abu Khadeejah would never dream of taking part in one of the festive parades or gatherings that take place in the UK every year because, he says, these sort of celebrations were not practised by the Prophet, his disciples or the early generation of Muslims.[43]

Many Salafis even believe that the celebration of any birthday is forbidden.

Abu Khadeejah's group is at the separatist and purist end of the British Salafi spectrum. At the other end of it I have met people who retain a Salafi identity while openly maintaining aspects of a non-Salafi lifestyle, such as smoking, watching entertainment television or mixing with the opposite sex more than is necessary. One man who organised Salafi gatherings told me he was a Hollywood film buff and an aspiring filmmaker. He wore tight jeans and a tight leather jacket and said he loved fashion too much to adopt the usual Salafi garb.

A hostile attitude towards non-Muslim society was revealed in the January 2007 'Undercover Mosque' documentary. A preacher at the Ahl-e-Hadith's Green Lane Mosque in Birmingham was shown telling his audience that all 'kuffar' (i.e. non-Muslims) are liars and that 'No one loves the kuffar, not a single person here loves the kuffar. We hate the kuffar!'[44]

In one of the Green Lane Mosque's regular satellite link ups with the grand mufti of Saudi Arabia, a member of the congregation asked, through a translator, if Muslims should establish good relations and forgiveness between religions. The grand mufti told him that this was 'not true'.[45] This happened at a time when the mosque claimed on its website to be a centre for 'interfaith communication and dialogue'.[46]

By middle age the leaders of JIMAS appeared to have made a sincere commitment to interfaith work. Manwar Ali and Usama Hasan both became involved in interfaith work a few years after 9/11. Usama Hasan says it is one of the things that has transformed him into a more integrated member of society: 'When you become very good friends with priests and rabbis and historians it changes your outlook.' In 2004 he joined Scriptural Reasoning, an interfaith group for Christians, Jews and Muslims based in the City of London. 'We'll take a passage of the Torah and the Quran and the Bible on a similar theme. Each house will present its text and then people will ask questions and interrupt.'[47]

Of the hostile sentiments expressed towards non-Muslims by the Salafi preacher in the 'Undercover Mosque' documentary, Usama Hasan says that he had been asking for years for such sermons to cease. 'I don't approve of the tactics of Undercover Mosque,' says Hasan, 'but there are problems and, embarrassingly, I think it was fairly accurate.'[48]

Part of the documentary that he felt was unfair concerned the portrayal of his father, Suhaib Hasan, who was also filmed at the Green Lane Mosque.[49] Recordings found by the programme makers on the Internet showed Suhaib Hasan giving a talk on how a future Islamic state would operate: he promised his audience that the hands of thieves would be chopped off, drunkards would be flogged and that there would be jihad against the non-Muslims. 'We were furious about the way they portrayed Dad,' says Usama Hasan, pointing out that his father in fact said there would be jihad against 'non-Muslims, the oppressors', a distinction which Usama Hasan feels is important.[50]

He puts his father's fondness for talking about sharia punishments down to a form of idealism that 'does not have much relevance in the real world'. He suggests that his father is perhaps too cut off from the non-Muslim population to realise how alarming his speeches might look to outsiders.

Abu Khadeejah of the pietistic Salafi Publications does not see any necessity to take part in interfaith gatherings, but says he is in favour of good relations between Muslims and others. He lives in a predominantly Muslim area of Birmingham but says that when a non-Muslim man lived next door he got on well with him and they exchanged contact details and kept an eye on each other's houses when either family was away. 'If one of my neighbours is bedridden, I don't mind doing shopping if he's a Muslim or non-Muslim. And also smiling in the face of a non-Muslim, talking to them, communicating with them. But that doesn't necessitate going to the church with them on Good Friday.'[51]

The jihadi Salafi scene in Britain after 7/7

Between 2003 and 2007, the most prominent leaders of the Salafi jihadi groups were jailed or banned from the UK: Abu Hamza was imprisoned in May 2004 and sentenced to seven years for soliciting murder and inciting racial hatred; Abdullah al Faisal was deported to his native Jamaica in 2007 after serving four years of a nine-year prison sentence for inciting followers to murder and race hatred; and Omar Bakri Mohammed, founder of al Muhajiroun, was refused re-entry to Britain after a visit to Lebanon in 2005. When Al Muhajiroun was banned in the following year, Bakri's British followers simply formed new groups such as Islam4UK, Muslims Against Crusades, and al-Ghurabaa. They specialised in provocative demonstrations such as the public burning of Remembrance Day poppies in 2010. While their activities received much publicity, the group appeared marginal.

The Ahl-e-Hadith legacy

The first Salafi movement to establish itself in Britain, the South Asian Ahl-e-Hadith, went into what Usama Hasan described as 'crisis mode' in the mid-2000s, due to its failure to nurture a new generation of leaders to replace the mainly Urdu-speaking elders who migrated to the UK from Pakistan.[52] In March 2005, according to the Ahl-e-Hadith's UK headquarters' website, there were forty-two Ahl-e-Hadith 'branches and circles' in Britain.[53] By March 2011 the organisation no longer had a functioning website.

Even those mosques officially affiliated to the Ahl-e-Hadith vary in the degree to which they have strong organisational and ideological ties with the headquarters in Birmingham. The Ahl-e-Hadith Mosque and Salfia Centre in Dewsbury, for example, appeared in 2010 to be more of a community mosque with those attending mainly attracted to it for reasons of convenience rather than sectarian affiliation.[54]

The headquarters of the Ahl-e-Hadith movement remains at the Green Lane Mosque in the Small Heath district of Birmingham. It is a short walk away from the headquarters of Salafi Publications. Despite the proximity of these two Salafi institutions, there is virtually no contact between them. Abu Khadeejah of Salafi Publications says that while the Ahl-e-Hadith origins in South Asia were good, it has become too close to the ideas of the more politicised Islamic movements.

The JIMAS legacy

Manwar Ali, the man who founded JIMAS as a student in the 1980s, was a grey-bearded grandfather when I met him in 2011. He was still leading JIMAS, but as far as ideology was concerned, both he and the organisation had changed beyond recognition.

JIMAS was no longer regarded as a Salafi group by the wider Salafi movement. Salafi mosques from around the UK used to invite JIMAS speakers to preach. They had ceased to do so. Manwar Ali himself had become a vocal opponent not just of the jihadi tendency but of the political Salafism of the 'Surooris'.

He had a more accepting attitude towards non-Salafi Muslims and was involved in interfaith work with Christians in his hometown of Ipswich. In the 1990s he used to go to his job at British Telecom in robes and a turban; by 2011 he wore a suit unless preaching in a mosque. He still regarded himself as a Salafi but questioned what that means: 'What is this Salafi thing? It's a generic term made up where it's like some people ... gain prominence in religion by mouthing about religion in a very superficial way.'[55]

JIMAS had no branch network and Manwar Ali said that just a small number of supporters helped him to run the organisation. The annual conference was still the most important event of the year but it was inconceivable that the sort of jihadi leaders who addressed the membership in the 1990s would be given a platform even if they could legally enter the UK.

One of Manwar Ali's closest allies in JIMAS, Usama Hasan, underwent a similar transformation after 9/11. In 2008 he served as the director of the City Circle, a liberal Muslim group aimed at young professionals. In the same year Usama Hasan leant his support to the launch of an anti-Islamist think tank, the Quilliam Foundation. This shocked many of his erstwhile allies: Hasan's father, a Salafi scholar, had a good relationship with some of the leading Islamist activists in Britain; and Usama himself had entered into an arranged marriage to the daughter of a prominent Islamist politician from Pakistan.[56] In 2011, Usama Hasan was suspended as imam of a Salafi mosque in East London after publicly stating that Darwin's theory of evolution was compatible with Islam, and saying that he had concluded that the wearing of the headscarf for Muslim women is not a religious obligation but a cultural tradition.[57]

Usama Hasan had decided that JIMAS was mistaken in its attachment to self-segregation, 'idealistic notions of an Islamic state' and being 'very anti-Sufi and anti-Shia'. He was calling himself a 'Wahhabi-Sufi'. He was using the Salafis' freedom from the strictures of the madhab rulings to arrive at interpretations of Islam which are often more liberal than even those who call themselves moderates. On the issue of apostasy, for example, the anti-Salafi traditionalists are bound to concur with the consensus (*ijma*) of the four main schools of Sunni jurisprudence that death is the appropriate penalty for leaving Islam (though many of those traditionalists also say that such a penalty does not apply in certain societies). Most Salafis also think that the death penalty is the appropriate punishment; however, they do at least have the freedom to reject that interpretation if, as Hasan believes he has done, they can show that it contradicts the core Islamic texts.

So what caused Usama Hasan's dramatic transformation? Hasan says that it has been a gradual process, in part brought about by having a professional life which has required him to become more integrated into mainstream British society. After gaining degrees in physics, IT and engineering from elite universities in Britain, he worked in industry and then became a senior lecturer in business information systems at Middlesex University and a fellow of the Royal Astronomical Society. In 2012 he became a full-time researcher at the Quilliam Foundation.

Two incidents during Usama Hasan's period of transition are particularly striking. Shortly after 9/11 an al-Qaeda supporter in Saudi Arabia attempted to recruit him as a translator and disseminator of radical propaganda. After travelling to a meeting in Saudi Arabia, Hasan agreed to help. But after completing his first task—translating the speech of a radical cleric from Arabic into English—he decided he did not agree with its message and wanted no further involvement.[58]

Soon after that, Hasan was shaken by another dramatic event. A member of his congregation returned from a family holiday in Pakistan with the startling news that he had been asked to carry out terrorist attacks in Britain. The man had been attending a meeting of a Kashmiri group called Markaz al-Dawa-wal-Irshad (MDI). His neighbour, like Usama Hasan himself, believed that MDI was a legitimate resistance force, limiting its attacks to Indian military targets. However, the neighbour was approached by somebody from the group who, when he realised the neighbour was a British citizen, asked him 'Are you ready to join the jihad and carry out missions in London?' The neighbour was asked whether he would be prepared to recruit others too. He was in little doubt that he was being asked to take part in suicide bombings.[59]

On his return to London the neighbour related the story to Usama Hasan. 'It was a real eye opener for me,' says Hasan. What must have made the story particularly shocking was that MDI, the group that approached his neighbour, was known to be the political wing of Lashkar-e-Taiba (LeT), the jihadi group whose leaders JIMAS had hosted in Britain back in 1995. LeT's leader, Hafeez Saeed, is the man whose radical rhetoric had helped to split the British Salafi youth in the mid-1990s and who is suspected by the Indian authorities of being the man behind the 2008 Mumbai bombings. He stated after 9/11 that Lashkar's primary focus was still Kashmir but that the organisation was on good terms with al-Qaeda and had some joint recruitment and training.[60] While LeT was not thought to support terrorist attacks in the UK, it had long been suspected of carrying out attacks on civilians in India. Usama Hasan admits he was aware of such accusations but dismissed them: 'Perhaps I was slightly in denial.'[61]

The JIMAS leadership must also have been alarmed by the security crackdown on LeT's Western supporters. In 1997 the Home Office began deportation proceedings against the imam of an Ahl-e-Hadith-affiliated mosque in Oldham, after the man returned from Pakistan having attended a conference of Lashkar-e-Taiba's political arm, MDI. After a series of appeals and counter-appeals, House of Lords judges ruled in October 2001 that Shafiq Ur Rehman, who was said to have raised money for MDI and sent people for military training, should be deported.[62] (Rehman was subsequently allowed to remain in the UK after the Home Office was persuaded that he had severed his links with LeT and no longer posed a threat to national security.)[63]

Ali al Timimi, a regular speaker at JIMAS events until 2002 (and a strong influence on JIMAS's leader Manwar Ali) had been urging his congregation in the United States to go to LeT training camps after 9/11 in order to prepare to fight in Afghanistan on the Taliban side. Under controversial new US legislation introduced after 9/11, Timimi received a mandatory life sentence for his call to action.[64]

The pietistic faction which broke away from Manwar Ali has stuck broadly to its founding ideology and has been far more successful in recruitment terms than JIMAS. Salafi Publications—the pietistic group founded by Abu Khadeejah, the late Dawud Burbank and others—has spread beyond its original Birmingham mosque and bookshop. By 2012 it had a total of eleven affiliated mosques and Islamic centres outside of Birmingham—in Cardiff, Slough, Reading, Cranford, Shepherd's Bush, Walthamstow, Stratford in East London, Bradford, Manchester, Bristol and Stoke on Trent.

Salafi Publications has exerted its influence through its website, salaf.com, which, according to Abu Khadeejah, receives up to 2 million hits per month. It has been proactive in putting forward an Islamic case against al-Qaeda, an issue which it has addressed in numerous lectures and books. In the immediate aftermath of 7/7 the group's preachers embarked on a speaking tour, taking their anti-jihadist message to Muslim communities around Britain.

As well as the Salafi Publications network, there are various independent mosques and bookshops run or inspired by other members of the pietistic faction that broke away from JIMAS. The most noteworthy of these is Brixton Mosque in South London which, after ejecting the jihadi preacher Abdullah al Faisal in 1993, embarked on a policy of banning those who voiced support for violent extremism. After 9/11 the mosque formed a partnership with the Metropolitan Police to promote their anti-radicalisation work. One of the leaders of Brixton mosque, former JIMAS preacher Abdul Haq Baker, explained the deradicalisation programme on a Channel 4 documentary. Rather than condemning violent extremism with woolly generalisations about Islam being a peaceful religion, the Brixton preacher used textual sources to persuade those attracted to violent extremism that their beliefs went against Islamic teachings.[65]

Abdur Raheem Green, the convert preacher who initially threw his support behind the Salafi Publications group, decided he was willing to work with other groups even if his colleagues were not. He remained a Salafi but became a popular speaker at events organised by a wide range of Islamic organisations. From 2007, he became one of the main stars of

Peace TV, a satellite channel based in India which broadcasts Islamic lectures around the world.

The new Salafi scene

The shakiness of JIMAS and the Ahl-e-Hadith in Britain from the mid-2000s onwards is perhaps reflected in the statistics relating to mosque affiliations: fewer than 100 of the UK's 1,700 mosques were under Salafi management in 2013.[66] However, Salafism in Britain has not necessarily passed its peak.

According to Mehmood Naqshbandi—webmaster of MuslimsInBritain.org and collector of the most comprehensive, publicly available data on mosque affiliations—between 2009 and 2013 the number of Salafi mosques in the UK increased by 50 per cent. This made Salafism the fasting growing of the UK's major Islamic trends. Naqshbandi's figures indicated that half of all new mosques opening each year were Salafi controlled.

He attributes much of this growth to the increase in the UK's Somali population. The Salafism which Naqshbandi has observed in predominantly Somali mosques is not, he says, of the 'politically charged' brand, but a version of Salafism which accommodates the more traditional Islam of most Somalis.[67] Despite this accommodation, there are signs that Salafi doctrine is influencing Somali Muslim religious practice: Ismail Einashe, a Somali writer brought up in Britain in the 2000s, has noted that many young Somali women in his community have adopted 'Gulf standards' of dress. Like so many of the British Pakistani youth of the 1990s, the first generation of British-born Somalis are often, says Einashe, attracted to forms of Islam which allow them to avoid the cultural baggage of their parents' generation.[68]

In addition to the growing number of Salafi mosques, a loose but extensive network of independent Salafi bookshops and study circles plays an important role in the UK Salafi scene. Salafis who lack their own mosque often hire venues to host Salafi preachers capable of attracting a crowd.

Among the most popular speakers at these ad hoc gatherings in 2010 were Khalid Yasin, an African American convert based in the UK, and Murtaza Khan, a teacher at an Islamic school in East London. Both Yasin and Khan were featured in a 2007 Channel 4 documentary about Muslim preachers in Britain whose sermons contained anti-Christian and anti-Jewish sentiments. The programme showed an excerpt from a

DVD in which Yasin says: 'We don't need to go to the Christians or the Jews debating with them about the filth which they believe.' Clips from one of Murtaza Khan's DVDs showed him telling an audience: 'Those whom the wrath of Allah is upon, is the Jews, is the Christians.' He also said of Christians and Jews that 'these people are enemies towards us'.[69]

Despite the adverse publicity which resulted from the TV documentary, both Yasin and Khan remained popular enough to be able to charge substantial speaking fees. 'We'd like to get Khalid Yasin but he charges £1000 plus expenses,' said a Reading-based Salafi in 2010, 'But we got Murtaza Khan instead for £600.'[70]

Another popular and controversial Salafi speaker is Sheikh Haitham Haddad, a scholar from al Muntada—the 'Suroori' centre in Parsons Green, London. Haddad is a regular speaker on the student Islamic society scene in London.

The dramatic growth of higher education since the 1980s has led the student Islamic societies to become particularly important sites for the recruitment of British-born Muslims. The Salafis appear to be well represented in the student milieu, managing to take control of some university Islamic societies. In 2009, the president of the Federation of Student Islamic Societies described himself to me as a Salafi.[71]

Mehmood Naqshbandi, a close observer of the whole British Muslim scene, disagrees with the Salafi approach to Islam but can understand why others are drawn to it: 'Its essential nature of opposing received, establishment doctrine and substituting that with re-appraised original sources is a very attractive technique for all manner of anti-establishment persons, from militants to modernists.'[72] The Salafis' willingness to question the older generation's folk wisdom about Islam, and the fact they have been ahead of the game in their adoption of English as the language in which to preach and organise, continues to help them appeal to the younger generation. With students and new generations of British-born Muslim youth in plentiful supply, the market for British Salafism's brand of Islam still looks very healthy.

It is impossible to predict whether the trends seen at the time of writing will continue. But if they do, Mehmood Naqshbandi calculates that half of all UK mosques could be Salafi controlled within a generation.

Whatever the growth rate of Salafism in Britain turns out to be, it looks set to remain a dynamic and diverse movement, and one which is ultimately far more complex than its caricature as the source of modern jihadism.

4

THE JAMAAT-E-ISLAMI

BRITISH ISLAM'S POLITICAL CLASS

From the late 1990s, the Muslim Council of Britain (MCB) was recognised by the government as the representative body of the UK's Muslims. But the truth was that the MCB was dominated by offshoots of a Pakistani political party—the Jamaat-e-Islami (JI)—with which only a minority of British Muslims identified.

The Jamaat-e-Islami's main British network is the UK Islamic Mission (UKIM), which runs forty-two of the country's 1,700 mosques.[1] Among the other institutions which the JI's supporters control are the Markfield Institute of Higher Education and the East London Mosque.

This chapter describes the origins of the Jamaat-e-Islami in Pakistan; the story of its rise to a position of undue prominence in Britain; and the events, following the 2005 London bombings, which led to its marginalisation.

Origins

The Jamaat-e-Islami was founded in 1941 by Sayyid Abul A'la Maududi, a journalist and Islamic revivalist. While living in pre-partition India in the 1930s, Maududi had written of Islam as a political ideology and a tool with which to counter submission to British colonial rule. According to Maududi, serving in the army of a non-Islamic state (as many Muslims living in British India then did) was 'abominable behaviour' and those who did so could not be considered true Muslims. Most importantly, he argued that personal piety was not enough to make a Muslim a true believer. Muslims, he wrote, were obliged to establish the sovereignty of God on earth and to reject secular government: 'If you believe Islam to be true, you have no alternative but to exert your utmost strength to make it prevail on earth: you either establish it or give your lives in this struggle.'[2]

The Jamaat-e-Islami is widely regarded as an 'Islamist' party on the basis that it is on the wide spectrum of movements which use Islam as a political ideology. The label is often rejected by the activists themselves on the basis that what they are following is true Islam, not some politicised variant of the religion.

Maududi led the Jamaat-e-Islami until 1972 and remained its chief ideologue even after his death in 1979. His party was never elected to government in Pakistan but it has had power: its politicians were given ministerial positions in the post-1979 military dictatorship of General Zia, where they helped to implement an Islamising agenda which included the introduction of an Islamic penal code and ensuring all existing laws were compliant with the sharia.

Maududi's followers in the UK

In Britain the ideas of Maududi were first promoted by the UK Islamic Mission (UKIM), founded in 1962. According to the UKIM's website, the organisation was set up by 'a small group of Muslims who used to meet at The East London Mosque in a study circle. They discussed the need of forming an organisation in Britain to convey the message of Islam in the West.'

Although the UKIM leadership in Britain today is coy about its Maududist origins, in the early days these were clearly visible: one of the UKIM's main activities was the promotion of English translations of the works of Maududi and Islamic thinkers of a similar bent. In 1976, Maududi addressed the UKIM conference, praising its members for being 'pioneers of an Islamic movement and resolution in the Western world'.[3]

In the mid- to late 1970s the UKIM's original student founders ceded influence to Pakistani scholars such as Sharif Ahmed and Tufail Hussain Shah, an imam based in Glasgow. With this came a new priority: establishing a network of mosques.[4] From the late 1970s, UKIM centres of worship were established on an ad hoc basis: some were set up by UKIM members who wanted to found a mosque in their local area, while others were set up at the request of Muslims who wrote to the organisation asking for help. The mass migration of Pakistani immigrants to the UK in the 1960s and 1970s provided, on the face of it, a substantial base from which the Maududists of the UKIM could recruit. However, the ideas of Maududi were not as popular among the working-class Pakistani population as they were with the urban, student elite. The bulk of Britain's Pakistani immigrant population came from poor rural areas and lacked the ideological attachments of the UKIM's middle-class founders.

As the UKIM pressed ahead with establishing a network of mosques in the 1970s, another Jamaat-e-Islami inspired organisation, the Islamic Foundation (IF), took its place as the main publisher of Maududist literature. There is no official organisational link between the Islamic Foundation and the UKIM, but there is an overlap in personnel: the general secretary of the UKIM in 2011, Zahid Parvez, was also at that time a trustee of the Islamic Foundation. The Islamic Foundation was established in 1973 by Professor Khurshid Ahmad and Professor Khurram Murad, two close followers of Maududi and high-ranking activists in the JI in Pakistan.

The Islamic Foundation operated out of offices in the city of Leicester until it moved to the site of a former hospital near the village of Markfield in the Leicestershire countryside in 1990. The foundation named its buildings on the 10 acre campus after thinkers who had inspired the Islamist movement: there was a Hassan el-Banna Hall named after the founder of the Egyptian Muslim Brotherhood, a block named after the Islamist ideologue ibn Taimiyya, and a Maududi Hall.[5]

Unlike the UKIM, the Islamic Foundation has no branch structure or membership. However, it has spawned a number of subsidiaries which are also based at its Markfield campus. The most important of these is the Markfield Institute of Higher Education (MIHE), which was established in 2000. MIHE offers courses leading to modern qualifications rather than training as an Islamic scholar. It is an associate college of the University of Gloucestershire. It provides research facilities for postgraduates and its courses include a BA and an MA in Islamic studies and an MA in Islamic finance. Its certificate in Muslim chaplaincy aims to equip students for work as hospital, prison or college chaplains through work placements and a nine-day course. Some of those who attend the course will be darul uloom graduates but, according to the institute's website, students require only 'a basic understanding of theology and religion'.[6]

The Islamic Foundation's first director Professor Khurram Murad, like his colleague Professor Khurshid Ahmad, maintained strong links with the Pakistani Jamaat-e-Islami throughout his time in the UK. However, he is also credited with having the vision to realise that a new generation of British-born Muslims would need their own organisation. So at his instigation Young Muslims UK (YMUK) was established in 1984 to cater to the English-speaking Muslim youth. Its branches operated out of UKIM's mosque network and many of the original group entrusted to lead YMUK had been brought up in families that supported the Jamaat-e-Islami and had been trained in the ideology of Maududism. But the plan was that YMUK should develop a degree of autonomy. Zahid Parvez, a member of the first governing committee of YMUK, recalls, 'The UKIM said, "You can use our mosques but you need to stand on your own two feet."'[7] Activities were run in English and were a mix of religious teaching and social events such as football matches. The annual summer camp was a highlight. 'We had t-shirts printed with the slogan "Putting the fun back into fundamentalism",' remembers one former member from the 1980s.[8] The plan to let the youth go their own way was soon realised as recruits with a less deferential attitude towards the parent organisation joined the YMUK governing committee. The newcomers felt that the UKIM did not provide them with inspiration. When a UKIM president who did not speak English addressed one of YMUK's national gatherings in Urdu they found him boring.[9] They looked elsewhere for mentors, hosting English-speaking preachers such as the African-American convert Siraj Wahaj and the classically trained American Islamic scholar Sheikh Hamza Yusuf. But their mentors were mainly Islamists with an ideology similar to that of Maududi: the Arab Muslim Brotherhood exiles living in the UK and Islamist politicians in Malaysia were particularly strong influences.

The activities of the new generation of YMUK activists in the 1980s were regarded as cutting edge: they promoted modern types of Islamic music; they set up the first Muslim community radio stations which broadcast during Ramadan; and they published a current affairs magazine, *Trends*. According to one former member, activism in the Muslim community had not really adjusted to the British climate until that point.

The emphasis in *Trends* magazine, published between 1990 and 1995, was clearly on Islamic politics rather than spirituality: an interview with a commander of the foreign mujahideen during the war in Bosnia; an account of a visit to an Afghan training camp by two British Muslims; an interview with a Hamas spokesperson; an interview with the Tunisian Islamist leader Rachid Gannouchi; and an article entitled 'Jihad: Offensive or Defensive?' in which liberating lands such as Eritrea, the Philippines, Tashkent, Samarkand, Uzbekistan, Azerbaijan and parts of China from non-Muslim rule is described as an obligation on the world-wide Muslim community. One of the most exciting activities for members in the early 1990s was the trips they went on to meet Islamist politicians abroad. Their expeditions included a seventy-five member delegation to meet Muslim Brotherhood activists in Egypt; a summer vacation trip to Sudan where they were treated as VIPs by the Islamist government of Omar Bashir and his ideologue Hasan Turabi; and a trip to Pakistan.[10]

Running in tandem with YMUK by this time was a new organisation called the Islamic Society of Britain (ISB), which had been formed by those who felt they were outgrowing the youth organisation. Founded in 1990, it was led by former YMUK members and in 1994 it became YMUK's parent organisation.

The ideas of the leading Islamist thinkers which had politicised the ISB members also provided them with justification in Islamic terms for including women in leadership—a controversial move in the eyes of the more conservative Jamaat-e-Islami elders. The YMUK and ISB also operated entirely in English, enabling them to attract members beyond the Pakistani community.

The Jamaat-e-Islami and the Bangladeshi community

The UKIM found it almost impossible to attract Bangladeshi members following the secession of East Pakistan and the founding of the Bangladeshi state in 1971. This was because Bangladesh's split from the rest of Pakistan was preceded by a bitter conflict in which many Bangladeshis were the victims of atrocities committed by Pakistani troops—and the Jamaat-e-Islami had been on the troops' side.

Bangladeshis living in Britain today often have stories of relatives who were killed by Pakistani troops during that time: an uncle who was shot for supporting independence; a grandfather who was executed because his sons were suspected of having left the village to fight on the pro-secession side. Jamaat-e-Islami supporters were suspected of acting as informants for the Pakistani military.

Even those who are too young to remember the conflict feel resentment towards the JI. 'The problem is even to this day, they won't just put their hands up and say sorry. They still justify it and this is why ... it is so bitter,' says one British-born Bangladeshi.

The hostility in the aftermath of the war was not just towards the Jamaat-e-Islami but towards Pakistani institutions generally. The JI's supporters in Britain thought that they would have a better chance of winning Bangladeshi support if they set up an organisation aimed only at Bangladeshis. So in 1978 they set up Dawatul Islam as the Bangladeshi equivalent of the UKIM. A male-only youth wing, the Young Muslims Organisation (YMO), was established in the same year.

The organisation was less successful than the UKIM when it came to establishing a nationwide branch structure. But in the one area where it concentrated its efforts—the Bangladeshi 'quarter' of East London—it was highly effective. According to the 2011 Census there were over 80,000 people of Bangladeshi origin living in the London Borough of Tower Hamlets. The Dawatul Islam managed to gain control of what was to become the most high-profile Islamic institution in the borough: the East London Mosque, which first opened in 1985. This purpose-built mosque on Whitechapel Road, one if the main routes out of the City of London, is a large modern building with minarets. The high-profile site was given to the local Muslim community by the Greater London Council after the buildings which housed an earlier mosque were subject to a compulsory purchase order.

The East London Mosque quickly became a local landmark and was assumed by outsiders to be the leading Muslim institution in the area. The act of naming it the 'East London Mosque', rather than giving it an Arabic, Urdu or Bengali name, made it feel more accessible to non-Muslim outsiders. The mosque was certainly popular enough to be full to overflowing at Friday prayers and in due course require a large extension. But its high profile obscured the fact that the mosques run by the Deobandis and Sufis in the surrounding area combined to provide more capacity for worshippers than the JI institutions.[11]

Even within Jamaat-e-Islami circles there was division. In 1988 another group of Bangladeshi JI supporters set up a rival organisation known as the Islamic Forum Europe (IFE). Dawatul Islam was under the control of Bangladeshis from rural areas of Sylhet. Those behind the IFE came on the whole from more urban and educated backgrounds. Despite the Islamic Forum Europe's grand sounding name it was no more at the head of an extensive network of branches than Dawatul Islam.[12] Instead it fought for control of the same London territory that had been won by Dawatul Islam, not only taking over the management of the East London Mosque but also by becoming the parent organisation for Dawatul Islam's youth wing, the YMO.

The IFE has exerted power and influence beyond the mosque. In 2006, a former president of the IFE, Dr Muhammad Abdul Bari, was elected general secretary of the Muslim Council of Britain. In 2010, Lutfur Rahman became the first directly elected mayor of Tower Hamlets with the help of backing from the IFE. The mayor, Lutfur Rahman, was originally selected to stand as the Labour Party's candidate, but was sacked following an accusation that he was in fact fighting the election on behalf of the IFE.[13] He won the position of mayor by standing as an independent.

The creation of the Muslim Council of Britain

The Maududists' greatest political coup was to take control of the Muslim Council of Britain, which for a while was recognised by the government as the representative body of Muslims in the UK.

The organisation came into being because, by the mid-1990s, there were various bodies claiming to represent Muslims in Britain. Those behind the creation of the MCB argued that as the government would prefer to deal with one organisation, Muslims would have more influence if they united under one umbrella group.

After years of coalition-building, the Muslim Council of Britain was eventually launched in November 1997. The government and the secular media quickly accepted the MCB as a genuine umbrella body representing what was often described as 'moderate, mainstream' British Muslims. At its launch, the MCB was a broad alliance of diverse Muslim groups. However, according to one activist, almost as soon as the organisation was established, a faction linked to the Jamaat-e-Islami took control.[14]

The British Maududists' transformation from publishers and mosque-builders into political activists had taken place during the protests which followed the publication of Salman Rushdie's novel *The Satanic Verses* in 1988. The book provoked protests by a range of Muslim groups but the organisation which emerged as speaking most effectively on behalf of Muslims in Britain was the UK Action Committee on Islamic Affairs (UKACIA). This latter organisation, which was formed in response to the Rushdie issue, was an alliance of campaigners from a wide range of Islamic backgrounds. The UKACIA had a much slicker strategy than those who burnt copies of the book on the street: spokesmen in suits demanded an extension of the blasphemy law so that it would cover Muslims, and the UKACIA collected signatures for a petition to send to the publisher.

In the wake of the Rushdie affair, the UKACIA became one of the organisations behind the formation of the Muslim Council of Britain. The UKACIA's leading spokesman, Iqbal Sacranie, became the MCB's first general secretary. He held the position of general secretary for eight of the first nine years of its existence.

By 2005 the MCB had around 400 affiliates. Superficially, these affiliates appeared to be a diverse bunch—geographically spread and ethnically diverse, with women's groups and youth organisations represented. Furthermore, there were Deobandi, Sufi and Shia organisations among the membership. But the reality was that a majority of mosques in Britain had either boycotted the MCB or had just not bothered to join.

The fact that the MCB was dominated by those aligned to the Jamaat-e-Islami was not obvious to non-Muslim outsiders, and for the first eight years of the MCB's existence few questions were asked about how representative it really was or how apt the 'moderate' label was.

Decline in influence

In the aftermath of the July 2005 London bombings, the Muslim Council of Britain looked set to consolidate its position. The government felt the need to strengthen its links with the Muslim community and the MCB was the most obvious organisation on hand to help. The MCB's leader Sir Iqbal Sacranie, who had been recently knighted,[15] organised the release of a statement by 100 imams and Islamic scholars condemning the attacks in unequivocal terms.

Within a few weeks of the bombings, the government appointed a task force of around 100 mainly Muslim experts and community representatives to investigate the causes of violent extremism. On the group's seven working parties, those with links to Jamaat-e-Islami organisations were disproportionately well represented. According to Ruth Kelly MP—the government minister who had to respond to the working parties' recommendations—civil servants had engaged Muslim organisations without the slightest knowledge of their ideological underpinnings.[16] But if government officials and ministers were still largely oblivious to the existence and ideology of the Jamaat-e-Islami-inspired groups in Britain, they were soon to wake up. A series of exposés in the mainstream media questioned not just how representative the MCB was but how moderate too.

The first prominent public attack on the MCB came from Martin Bright, a centre-left journalist then working for *The Observer*. In an investigative piece published just a few weeks after the 7/7 bombings, Bright wrote that 'far from being moderate, the Muslim Council of Britain has its origins in ... Pakistan's Jamaat-e-Islami, a radical party committed to the establishment of an Islamic state in Pakistan ruled by sharia law'.[17]

In the following week these political links were brought to the attention of an even larger audience by the BBC's *Panorama* programme.[18] The documentary was built around an interview with the MCB's general secretary, Sir Iqbal Sacranie. The reporter, John Ware, subjected Sacranie to the sort of aggressive interrogation frequently experienced by politicians but rarely meted out to religious and community leaders. Unused to this sort of treatment, Sacranie gave evasive answers when he was asked to justify his attendance at a memorial service for Hamas's spiritual guide, Sheikh Yasin, and to explain why the MCB continued to boycott Holocaust Memorial Day. When asked about an MCB affiliate which described on its website the ways of Christians and Jews as 'based on sick or deviant views', Sacranie defended the organisation's continued membership of the MCB on grounds of 'diversity'.[19]

Both Martin Bright's article and John Ware's *Panorama* linked the MCB's leadership to the ideology of Maududi.

The MCB's General Secretary Sir Iqbal Sacranie was in fact from a Deobandi background, but both he and the MCB's media officer defended Maududi and spoke of his inspirational qualities.[20] One of the MCB affiliate organisations identified by the journalists as doing much to promote the ideology of Maududi's Jamaat-e-Islami in the UK—the Islamic Foundation—was keen to deny any such role. The foundation's spokesperson said that it 'does not have links with the Jamaat-e-Islami', even though its rector and chair of trustees, Professor Khurshid Ahmad, was also a vice president of the Jamaat-e-Islami in Pakistan.

Further highly publicised exposés and attacks on the alleged admirers of Maududi followed. In July 2006, Policy Exchange, an influential centre-right think tank close to David Cameron, published a paper by Martin Bright in which he attacked the Labour government for becoming too close to the Jamaat-e-Islami and its ilk, groups which he regarded as illiberal and reactionary and therefore inappropriate partners for a progressive political party.[21] The fact that Bright was by then the political editor of the leading centre-left weekly magazine the *New Statesman*, made his attack on the Labour government all the more powerful.

Another important component of the Maududist network, the UK Islamic Mission (UKIM), was investigated in Channel 4's 'Undercover Mosque' documentary in January 2007.[22] The UKIM had been praised by Tony Blair for its multi-faith and multicultural activities. Yet on 'Undercover Mosque' a UKIM imam in Birmingham was recorded calling on God at Friday prayers to 'help us win the fight against the kuffaar [unbelievers], in every field, in every department of life. We beg you to help us fight against the enemies of our religion. Help us fight the kuffaar.' An undercover journalist posing as someone interested in learning about Islam was given leaflets based on Maududi's writings and told by the man running the centre that the UKIM, although independent, was ideologically affiliated to the Jamaat-e-Islami. A Saudi-trained preacher, regularly booked to speak at UKIM events, told the reporter that Muslims had to live as a state within a state until ready to take over: 'Everywhere, King, Queen, House of Commons ... if you accept it then you are part of it. You don't accept it ... but you have to dismantle it ... So, you being a Muslim you have to fix a target. There will be no House of Commons. From that White House to this Black House, we know that we have to dismantle it.'[23] He was shown being booked by the Sparkbrook UKIM committee to give a talk after telling them 'You cannot accept the rule of the *kafir* [unbelievers]. We have to rule ourselves and we have to rule the others.'

In a statement the Sparkbrook Islamic centre told the programme that it had 'no organic links' with the Jamaat-e-Islami in Pakistan or any other Islamic party.

Perhaps the most significant blow to the Jamaat-e-Islami's UK offshoots came in May 2007 with the publication of *The Islamist*, the memoir of a British Muslim who had spent time in various Islamist groups. The author, Ed Husain, recounted his experiences in the Young Muslims Organisation and the Islamic Society of Britain, as well as the more radical Islamist group Hizb ut Tahrir. He blamed Islamist ideology for Muslim radicalisation in Britain and he described from the inside the Maududists' operations in the UK and what he felt was his own redemptive journey to Sufism and secularism. The book became a best-seller and the more controversial aspects of the Islamists' ideology became common knowledge.[24]

What made these works of journalism particularly shocking was the fact that the portrayal of these groups was so starkly at odds with their public image. Unlike many of the more traditional Islamic organisations in Britain, the MCB, the Islamic Foundation and the UKIM were, because of their eagerness to engage with British institutions, assumed to be at ease with British society. On the whole they presented a modern, professional image: the MCB with its spokesmen in suits; the Islamic Foundation praised by the Prince of Wales for 'its promotion of first-rate scholarship and learning'; the UKIM with its involvement in the interfaith network.

These revelations prompted a rethink by the government about the MCB's role. Furthermore, other Muslim groups—most notably the Sufis—were putting themselves forward as more moderate and representative of Muslims in Britain. In July 2006 the government minister then in charge of community affairs, Ruth Kelly MP, announced that in future the government would be working with a broader range of Muslim groups. She attended the launch of one of those groups, the newly formed Sufi Muslim Council, at which she praised its condemnation of 'terrorism in all its forms',[25] a comment perhaps intended as a subtle rebuke of the MCB for its refusal to disown Hamas.

The MCB suffered a further blow in the spring of 2009 when Daud Abdullah, its then deputy director general, was one of ninety Muslim leaders from around the world to sign a declaration which called for attacks on military vessels in 'Muslim waters' that were attempting to prevent the smuggling of arms into Gaza.[26] Given that the then Prime Minister Gordon Brown had offered Israel the support of the Royal Navy to block arms shipments to Gaza, this was taken as a call to attack British troops should such an operation take place. The government, already perturbed by the MCB's refusal to take part in the annual

Holocaust Memorial Day, announced that it was suspending links with the MCB over its refusal to eject Abdullah from its leadership.[27]

Since then the MCB's political influence has fluctuated with changes in ministerial personnel. However, it is unlikely to ever re-establish the position of privilege which it enjoyed before 2005.

How Maududist are the 'Maududists'?

The exposure of the Jamaat-e-Islami's hidden influence in Britain led many to adopt a fairly simplistic characterisation of all those groups in the JI network as Maududist. But the reality was that the extent to which the British offshoots of the Jamaat-e-Islami promoted a hard line Islamist ideology varied.

By 2009 the Islamic Foundation had undergone something of a makeover. At its Leicestershire campus, the halls once named after Islamist ideologues such as Maududi had been blandly renamed the Conference Hall, the IF Seminar Room and so on.

The foundation's website promoted its facilitation of interfaith gatherings; its expertise on the topic of Islamic economics; its New Muslim Project running courses and offering support to converts; the Policy Research Centre available to undertake research and run courses on the subject of Islam and Muslims in Britain; and Kube Publishing, a commercial spin-off of the Islamic Foundation. Included in the 2011/12 Kube catalogue were Maududi's commentary on the Quran plus six of his other titles.[28] However, under its commissioning editor, Yahya Birt, Kube also published titles intended for the mainstream commercial market such as a biography of the Victorian Muslim convert Abdullah Quilliam. Under Birt, children's books such as *Muslim Nursery Rhymes* became the big sellers as did simple religious books such as *Daily Wisdom* ('a hadith a day') which would be acceptable to almost any English-speaking Muslim. The fact that Birt, who is not one of Maududi's devotees, had been given this responsibility says a lot about the IF's direction of travel. For many years the largesse of Saudi benefactors meant that the IF had considerable funds at its disposal.[29] This source of IF funding influenced its work: publications talking of a desire to convert the non-Muslim population to Islam and to establish an Islamic state were perhaps intended to please their Saudi donors. There was also little need in that period for the organisation to manage its funds tightly. Pet projects could be funded, and books for which there would be little demand could be published. However, after 9/11, tighter controls in the Middle East on charitable donations meant the IF's funding was squeezed.

The foundation had for many years raised some of its income from Islamic awareness courses run for public sector workers, especially the police. After 9/11, even more of its work had to be run along similarly commercial lines. That meant attracting the right talent and giving power to those with the appropriate academic credentials and business acumen, even if they did not happen to be followers of Maudidi. The transition created tensions over how willing the organisation should be to ditch its Islamist roots. The foundation's decision to publish the eighteen-volume translation of a commentary on the Quran written by Islamist radical Sayyid Qutb, for example, was only taken after a heated internal debate. The argument was about ideas rather than money: the foundation was offered funding to publish the works and, according to its online book-shop, the £180 set of books was one of its best-sellers in 2011. However, those who opposed the publication still felt they had won an important concession: the IF adopted a policy of no longer publishing Maudidi's or Qutb's political writings, although it would consider publishing their work on other issues. To publish those writers' more radical texts would be incompatible, it was argued, with the foundation's heavy involvement in interfaith work.

There have also been changes within Young Muslims UK. In the 1990s the YMUK had clearly promoted the idea of creating an Islamic state in Muslim-majority countries. In 2001, its website even carried an article stating that any Muslim who died 'without ever participating in or yearning for Jihad (fighting), dies with a share of hypocrisy'.[30] But by 2009 it appeared to be a considerably weaker and less politicised organisation.

A YMUK branch disco serves as an illustration of the strange mixture of conservatism and liberalism that the organisation had become by the late 2000s. One outsider who was at the disco recalls girls arriving in headscarves and jilbabs. Yet once in the privacy of the all-female gathering they removed their modest outer clothing to uncover revealing evening dresses. The night was apparently spent 'gyrating to Justin Timberlake and the like' with a break half way through to cover up and pray.

Its parent organisation, the Islamic Society of Britain, is still run by those who were inspired by the Islamist ideas of YMUK in the 1990s.

However, those ideas seemed barely relevant to the ISB in 2009. The leading members of the ISB are mainly middle-class professionals, integrated in their worklives to mainstream British society and wary of being associated with Islamic militancy. Leading ISB member Dilwar Hussain recalls that in the 1990s he read Sayyid Qutb's *Milestones*—a book respected by many radical Islamists—and found it inspirational. When he re-read it after 9/11 he says he thought it was dangerous. He and his colleagues had never shared bin Laden's vision of a clash of civilisations, but by 2009 he worried that the organisations which had inspired the ISB had their roots in the anti-colonial movement and with that had come some anti-Western baggage.[31]

When attention was drawn to the fact that Anwar al-Awlaki, a Yemen-based preacher who by 2009 openly supported the agenda of al-Qaeda, had lectured six years earlier at one of the ISB's courses, the organisation lost no time in disowning him and making the (completely fair) point that al-Awlaki's views had become more extreme since the time of his visit to the UK.

Several leading ISB and former YMUK activists have attempted to pursue careers in politics. These include:

- Ajmal Masroor: an imam who frequently appears on television and who stood unsuccessfully as a Liberal Democrat parliamentary candidate in Bethnal Green and Bow at the 2010 general election.
- Salma Yacoob: a former YMUK member who narrowly missed winning a parliamentary seat when she stood as a candidate for the Respect Party in Birmingham in 2005 and 2010.
- Osama Saeed: a former Glasgow YMUK member and previous spokesperson for the Muslim Association of Britain in Scotland, who stood unsuccessfully as the SNP candidate in Glasgow Central at the 2010 Westminster elections.

In addition, at least two former members of the ISB governing committee attempted to get on to the Conservative parliamentary candidates list.

As for the UKIM, the first Jamaat-e-Islami organisation in Britain, the picture is mixed. While the revelations of 'Undercover Mosque' demonstrated that for some UKIM activists the link with the Jamaat-e-Islami and the ideology of Maududi are still important, anecdotal evidence suggests that their attempts to spread those ideas through the

UKIM's centres has been met with only limited success. One non-JI imam told me that when invited to preach at a UKIM mosque he was able to get away with imparting anti-Islamist ideas without the congregation noticing this subtle act of subversion. Another non-Islamist Muslim who has visited many UKIM centres observes that they are usually 'just middle-of-the-road mosques/community-centres', although the management committees usually include 'a rump of middle aged Maududists' who typically arrived in the 1970s or earlier with professional qualifications. The attractions of the UKIM centres for most who attend might be simply location, a middle-class management capable of communicating with those who do not come from South Asian backgrounds, and a lack of emphasis on traditional scholarship.

At the UKIM's largest centre, based in Oldham, the extent and the limits of the modernising trend can be seen. Abdul Hamid Qureshim, a member of the mosque committee, explains with pride the group's decision to opt for a modern-looking building without domes or minarets. The former office building was bought by the UKIM for £4 million with a plan to use the centre as the organisation's national headquarters as well as a mosque and community centre. Qureshim described himself to me as part of the 'new school' of UKIM. He explained that by this he meant that he thought promoting the idea of establishing an Islamic state is not appropriate in the Western context and that Muslims in Britain should play a full part in British society while retaining their Islamic values. He talked proudly of his daughter who was studying medicine away from home. However, he defended limiting women to a subordinate role in the mosque: although women were invited to the meetings of the executive council, they did not hold office on any of the mosque's committees. Qureshim said that family responsibilities and the difficulty of travelling made holding office impractical for women. I asked him what his attitude would be in the case of a woman who did not have family responsibilities and wanted to serve on the mosque committee. He did not see any point in considering this hypothetical question as he could not imagine a situation where a woman would be without responsibilities as a carer. 'The indigenous population might think differently,' he told me, 'but the indigenous population has family breakdown.'[32]

The organisation which seems to retain the strongest attachment to Islamist ideas is the Bangladeshi organisation the Islamic Forum Europe (IFE) and its youth wing YMO. An undercover reporter posing as a new

IFE recruit at the East London Mosque was told by an IFE official that although the group supported democracy, nobody would support a policy that had been arrived at democratically but which went against the sharia.[33]

The documentary also quoted from a lecture in which an IFE lecturer told new recruits: 'Our goal is not simply to invite people and give dawa [call to the faith]. Our goal is to create the true believer, to then mobilise those believers into an organised force for change who will carry out dawa, hisbah [enforcement of Islamic law] and jihad [struggle]. This will lead to social change and iqamatud-deen.' The filmmakers took iqamatud-deen to mean an Islamic social, economic and political order but they were told by the IFE that it meant simply 'establishing religious values'.

Dawatul Islam, the Bangladeshi JI group which the IFE was set up to usurp, has survived despite losing control of the East London Mosque. It owns a large former school in Tower Hamlets which it uses as its headquarters and community centre. Its main activity is running an independent secondary school for boys in which the emphasis is on secular qualifications rather than traditional Islamic scholarship.

The future for the Jamaat-e-Islami in Britain

By 2014, the Islamic Forum Europe appeared to be the only Jamaat-e-Islami organisation which was prospering. The role of the East London Mosque had been instrumental. Renamed the East London Mosque and London Muslim Centre, the building gained a huge extension which was opened by Prince Charles in 2004. Among its relatively narrow base of Bangladeshi Londoners, its position seems to have grown stronger. The hostility among Bangladeshis towards the Jamaat-e-Islami, caused by its role in the 1971 struggle for independence from Pakistan, is less of an issue for those in the younger generation who are more likely to be concerned about the 'war on terror' or the Palestinian issue. (Although in May 2013 a former trustee of East London Mosque, Chowdhury Mueen Uddin, was charged in Bangladesh with abduction, confinement, torture and murder in relation to the 1971 civil war in Bangladesh. Mueen Uddin, who said the accusations were wholly untrue, refused to return to Bangladesh as he did not believe he would receive a fair trial.)[34]

Yet, outside East London, the Jamaat-e-Islami seems to have failed to attract new adherents. Why? Perhaps because the overwhelming majority of Muslims who came to the UK from the subcontinent already had ties to other movements, most notably the Deobandi or the Barelwi Sufi movement. The mosques built by those other groups far outnumbered those which the Jamaat-e-Islami could sustain. This has allowed the Deobandis and the Barelwis to nurture a second and third generation of adherents. Furthermore, a general increase in religiosity among Muslims in Britain has meant enhanced authority for traditional Islamic scholars. But the Jamaat-e-Islami is a movement led by laypeople. Its main educational institution, the Markfield Institute, does not offer courses leading to qualification as a traditional Islamic scholar. The movement still brings in some imams from the subcontinent. But the JI's mosques now often rely on British scholars aligned to the Deobandi movement and traditional Islam to work as their imams and teachers—even if those scholars explicitly reject Maududist ideology.[35]

The Jamaat-e-Islami's focus on politics allowed it to punch above its weight in British society for over a decade. But it was also this emphasis on political activity above spirituality and religious knowledge which means it has remained, on the ground, a minority trend.

5

THE MUSLIM BROTHERHOOD

THE ARAB ISLAMIST EXILES

As many of the secular dictators in the Arab world fell during the 2011 Arab Spring, Islamist opponents who had spent years in exile returned home to take their place in the new democracies. Among them was a man from Hemel Hempstead: Sheikh Rachid Ganouchi, the leader of Tunisia's largest political party and one of the world's leading Islamist thinkers. Such was his influence that when he flew into Tunis airport at the end of his twenty-two years in exile he was greeted by around 10,000 jubilant supporters.

Ganouchi's political party, Ennahda, is the Tunisian equivalent of Egypt's Muslim Brotherhood (*ikwhan*). The Brotherhood network— which includes the Palestinian party Hamas—has followers from every Arab nation.

In the decades before the Arab Spring, many Brotherhood activists used the UK as a base from which to promote Islamist alternatives to the autocratic governments of their home countries. Some also became deeply involved in Britain's own Islamic scene, founding the Federation of Student Islamic Societies (FOSIS) and the Muslim Association of Britain (MAB).

The Brotherhood exiles have never made up more than a small proportion of Britain's Muslim population. Yet at times they have exerted huge influence. Their story is similar to that of the Jamaat-e-Islami: they achieved power out of all proportion to their size but, having raised their profile, they subsequently attracted greater scrutiny and suspicion.

History of the Muslim Brotherhood

From the outset, the Muslim Brotherhood was an organisation led by laypeople rather than religious scholars. Its founder in Egypt in 1928, Hasan al-Banna, was a schoolteacher, and many of those attracted to the organisation were from the literate, urban, lower middle classes.

Alongside its charitable work, the Brotherhood encouraged personal piety and promoted a vision of society living under Islamic law: 'Allah is our objective. The Quran is our Constitution. The Prophet is our leader. Jihad is our way. Death for the sake of Allah is our greatest wish', became the oath taken by members. Its branch network quickly spread across Egypt, and in the following decades similar organisations were formed in other Arab states too.

By the 1940s, the Brotherhood had a paramilitary wing, the Secret Apparatus. In 1947 it sent thousands of guerrillas to fight against Zionist forces in the emerging state of Israel. When a series of events in 1948 led the Egyptian government to realise that the Brotherhood was prepared to use violence to further its political aims at home too, it outlawed the organisation. The charges of violence made against the Brotherhood included the assassination of an Egyptian judge. The murder of the Egyptian prime minister in December 1948 was blamed on Brotherhood supporters. In February 1949, the Muslim Brotherhood's founder, Hassan al-Banna, was assassinated in what was thought to be a revenge killing by the Egyptian authorities.

In the decades that followed, the Brotherhood was at times brutally suppressed by the Egyptian authorities and at other times rehabilitated.

During one of the periods of persecution, the movement's ideology was developed in a radical direction by Sayyid Qutb, one of its leading thinkers.

Qutb was tortured by the Egyptian authorities and spent most of the 1950s and 1960s in prison. During his incarceration he took some of the concepts popularised by Sayyid Abul A'la Maududi, the founder and leader of the Jamaat-e-Islami in Pakistan, and developed them in a revolutionary direction.

Maududi had written that a true Muslim society was one in which the people worshipped God and were subject to his sovereignty. Societies which conferred power on parties or men who did not rule according to God's law were described by Maududi as having fallen into a state of pre-Islamic ignorance or *jahiliyya*. Qutb claimed that all societies on earth—including Muslim-majority countries—were living in *jahiliyya*. His radical work *Milestones* was an attempt to inspire a vanguard movement which would withdraw from the *jahiliyya* society around them and prepare to overthrow its rulers. He implied that violence would be necessary to achieve power. Some militants reasoned that ordinary members of a *jahiliyya* society could be legitimate targets, and not just the rulers and their apparatchiks, though Qutb himself did not make this clear.[1]

The Brotherhood's early history in Britain

While the Brotherhood was being suppressed in Egypt, many of those who supported its ideology were beginning to organise themselves in the more liberal atmosphere of British universities. In the UK, Brotherhood-supporting students from across the Arab world were able to network with each other and to link up with like-minded Islamists from Pakistan, Nigeria, Malaysia, Turkey and elsewhere.

This led to the founding of the Brotherhood's first British organisations: in 1961 the Arabic-speakers launched the Muslim Students Society; and in 1962 a joint effort by the Arab Muslim Brothers, the South Asian Jamaat-e-Islami activists and Malaysian Islamists led to the launch of the Federation of Student Islamic Societies (FOSIS).[2]

Within a few years of its foundation FOSIS was at the head of a network of student Islamic societies with branches at universities across the United Kingdom and Ireland. As well as providing fellowship for Muslim students, they promoted their Islamist vision through talks, publications and conferences. In 1966 the president of FOSIS, Adil Salahi, translated Sayyid Qutb's *Milestones* into English and published it in serialised chunks in the society's magazine.

Many of the early FOSIS and MSS activists remained in Britain after graduation. One such activist was Ashur Shamis, an engineering graduate, originally from Libya. In the early 1970s he helped to set up the Muslim Welfare House which served as a support service for Arab students and was the Brotherhood's London base. Shamis was its director until 1980 when he was advised by British intelligence that he was on a Libyan government hit list and that he should adopt a lower profile for his own safety.[3]

Shamis, like many of the Brothers, used Britain as a place to network with comrades from other Arab states. But he also explored the possibility of alliances with non-Brotherhood exiles: Libyan monarchists, socialists and more radical Islamists. In 1981 he and others founded a broad-based group called the National Front for the Salvation of Libya (NFSL). Shamis's involvement shocked many of the UK-based Brothers—not just because the NFSL was a rival to the Libyan Muslim Brotherhood Organisation—but because it was suspected of enjoying British and US government support. The NFSL's aim was to seize power from Colonel Gaddafi and, given the fact that Libya was a dictatorship, talk of doing this by democratic means seemed irrelevant. 'Our organisation did lots of work aimed at killing him,' says Shamis.[4] He believed that this was Islamically permissible, not because he had been told so by an Islamic scholar, but because he and his colleagues had read the relevant religious texts and come to their own conclusions. The Libyans' DIY scholarship was typical of the Brotherhood. According to one senior Brother, a Muslim who has been trained by the Brotherhood does not have to go to a scholar to learn what is permitted or forbidden. Nor do they have to follow one of the four main schools of Sunni jurisprudence. A trained follower can simply go to the Quran and hadiths to work things out for him or herself.[5]

UK-based Brothers from other Arab countries became involved in similar discussions about the permissibility and feasibility of removing their leaders by force. Usama Altikriti, for example—an Iraqi Islamist exile and former FOSIS president—was approached in the 1980s by dissident Baathist generals who wanted him to support a plan to overthrow Saddam Hussein's regime from the inside. Following the assassination of Egyptian President Anwar Sadat in 1981 there was some discussion among Altikriti's Muslim Brotherhood friends about whether they would ever carry out a similar attack on Saddam. While they were glad Sadat was out of the way, they concluded that this was not something they would ever do.[6]

1990s: democracy versus jihad

In the early 1990s, the Brothers found themselves having to compete with more radical Islamists for followers. So-called Arab-Afghans, veterans of the jihad against the Soviet Union, were seeking asylum in Britain.

Many regarded the rulers of their countries of origin as apostates who should be killed, so, unsurprisingly, they were no longer welcome at home.

Ashur Shamis recalls that it was a depressing time for recruitment for the Brothers: 'The jihadis came in and took over. They swept the landscape, even amongst the students and graduates.'[7]

Ashur had shared the jihadists' belief that dictators needed to be overthrown by force if necessary, but he did not agree with their justifications for attacking civilians and he found their ideas about an Islamic state too rigid and simplistic.[8]

Many of the Brothers during this period were becoming more attracted to the idea of democracy. Among the UK-based Brothers, one of the most influential promoters of the idea of Islamic democracy was Sheikh Rachid Ganouchi, the exiled leader of Tunisia's Ennahda party.

In 1994 he was joined by another leading Brotherhood activist and enthusiast for democracy, Dr Kamal Helbawy. In Brotherhood terms Helbawy had an outstanding pedigree. After joining the Muslim Brotherhood as a schoolboy in Egypt in 1951, he subsequently dedicated his life to the cause. He had spent the 1970s in exile in Saudi Arabia where he had worked as executive director of the World Assembly of Muslim Youth (WAMY). At that time, the Saudi government was happy to give shelter to Islamists from around the world, enabling Helbawy to network with other leading figures.

After leaving Saudi Arabia in 1988, Helbawy went on to become the Muslim Brotherhood's 'ambassador' to the leaders of various Afghan mujahideen groups fighting the Soviets. Among the Afghan leaders he had dealings with were Burhanuddin Rabbani, Abdul Rasul Sayyaf, Gulbuddin Hekmatyar and Ahmed Shah Masood. Helbawy was based in Pakistan where the Brotherhood helped to manage the Institute of Policy Studies, a centre run jointly with the Jamaat-e-Islami. Islamist volunteers from around the world would pass through the institute en route to do relief work or to fight on the front line. The centre had been established in 1979 by Professor Khurshid Ahmad, who by then was splitting his time between Pakistan and the Islamic Foundation in Leicester. Among Helbawy's other acquaintances were Abdullah Azzam and Osama bin Laden. Although Azzam is sometimes said to have provided the ideological inspiration for al-Qaeda, Helbawy insists that Azzam was always a member of the Muslim Brotherhood and was never attracted to more extreme ideologies. He says bin Laden was originally a moderate Islamist who was later radicalised by Egyptian jihadists.[9]

Helbawy's credentials meant he was regarded by many adherents as the 'grand sheikh' of the Islamic Movement in the UK.

The original purpose of his relocation to London had been to open a media centre aimed at increasing awareness among mainstream journalists of the Egyptian Muslim Brotherhood's cause. He became the Muslim Brotherhood's official spokesperson in the West, a job he did for three years. He also ran his own business, a care home for the elderly in Wembley.

In his spare time Helbawy argued the case for democracy with some of the jihadi leaders at a series of debates held in cities across Britain. A year before the Arab Spring, Helbawy told me that although the Muslim Brotherhood did not believe in seizing power by revolution or coup d'état, he did not rule out an Iranian-style revolution in certain contexts.[10] He believed that a successful Islamic state could only be created after a process of grassroots Islamisation resulting in popular support. He claims that democracy has roots in Islamic tradition: 'What is called in the West democracy, we call it shura, [which means] consultation.'[11] His vision of democracy is neither a crudely majoritarian nor a Western liberal one. Public opinion would only need to be consulted on issues about which the core Islamic texts are silent: democracy to him means 'to rule according to representatives in whatever issues that you have no text in the Quran and the Sunna [i.e. the Prophet Muhammad's example]'.[12] Few of his jihadi opponents were won over even to this Islamist version of democracy.

Relationship with the Jamaat-e-Islami

The relationship, which began in the 1960s, between the Brothers and the Jamaat-e-Islami in Britain was still strong when Helbawy came to Britain in the 1990s. The ethnic composition of the two groups was different but they regarded each other as being part of the same ideological network which they called the Islamic Movement. 'When we talk about the Islamic Movement attitude,' explains Kamal Helbawy, 'we mean those who are following mostly Hasan al-Banna or al-Maududi.'[13]

Helbawy was an old friend of one of the leading Jamaat-e-Islami figures in Britain: Professor Kurshid Ahmad of the Islamic Foundation in Leicestershire. Not only had the two men worked together in Pakistan, but from the 1980s they had run a coordination committee which brought together the Islamic Movement's leading politicians including the Malaysian former Deputy Prime Minister, Anwar Ibrahim, and the Turkish Islamist leader, Necmettin Erbakan.[14]

Links were made between the Brothers and those associated with the Jamaat-e-Islami at a more junior level too. In the 1990s, those who had come up through the Jamaat-e-Islami's youth organisation, Young Muslims UK, developed strong ties with the Arab Brothers. Many had met and admired the Tunisian Islamist leader Sheikh Rachid Ganouchi. Another source of inspiration was the Sudanese Islamist Hasan Turabi. At that time, Turabi was the ideological power behind Omar Bashir, the president who came to power in Sudan following the 1989 coup. Turabi's party was not part of the official Muslim Brotherhood but was a break-away group which put more emphasis on bringing about social transformation through politics than through grassroots community work.[15] Turabi met YMUK members on some of his frequent visits to London. He also hosted a delegation of them at his home in Sudan.[16]

Both Ganouchi and Turabi were seen by the YMUK members as liberals by Islamist standards in that both encouraged the participation of women in political life.

Most of the leadership of YMUK and its spin-off, the Islamic Society of Britain, were students and young professionals. In that sense they had a great deal in common with the Brotherhood exiles living in Britain and were willing to be nurtured by them. The Brothers ran study circles for these young people and had a syllabus written by Hasan al-Banna translated into English. Some YMUK members spent time at a Muslim Brotherhood-run college in France.

The Brothers set up a British organisation

While some of the UK Brothers remained focused on a desire for change in the Arab world, others were becoming more involved in the wider politics of the Muslim community in Britain. In 1997 the more UK-focused Brothers consequently set up a new organisation: the Muslim Association of Britain (MAB). The ambition was to reach out beyond the student and exile communities and to lead Britain's increasingly diverse Muslim population. MAB's founders attempted to recruit from the British-born youth who had come up through YMUK and the ISB, but in doing so they caused a split within the ISB and were met with only limited success. The reality was that the organisation served mainly the Arab Islamist exiles and their families.

MAB became an influential affiliate of the newly formed Muslim Council of Britain, controlled by the Brothers' friends in the Jamaat-e-Islami. Because the MCB umbrella organisation was accepted immediately by the government as the main representative body of Muslims in Britain, its leaders had direct access to ministers and a high media profile. When it came to campaigning for changes in policy, the strategy of the Jamaat-e-Islami activists on the MCB was to lobby ministers behind closed doors rather than to organise mass demonstrations. This might have been a reasonable tactic on some issues such as the demand for an expansion of the law on blasphemy to cover Islam as well as Christianity. However, in the post-9/11 years it failed to satisfy the expectations of many ordinary Muslims—the war in Afghanistan, anti-terrorist legislation which some feared would unfairly target Muslims and the prospect of an invasion of Iraq were all causes of growing anger among many British Muslims.

The Brothers, through MAB, capitalised on the growing politicisation of Britain's Muslim community in the run-up to the Iraq war. By becoming a partner in the Stop the War Coalition—an alliance that included trade unions, the far left and anti-nuclear activists—MAB found itself at the forefront of a rapidly growing movement. In February 2003 the Stop the War Coalition organised one of the largest political demonstrations in British history, with 750,000 people marching in London in protest against an invasion of Iraq. Muslims from a diverse range of backgrounds mobilised people at a local level to join the march. By providing the placards, MAB managed to create the impression that the masses belonged to their organisation.

MAB's enhanced profile led to a commensurate increase in influence. Senior members formed close relations with the then Labour mayor of London, Ken Livingstone, who was also an opponent of the Iraq war. Livingstone eventually became an ally of the movement despite his reputation as a supporter of socialism and progressive left-wing causes, and even hosted the Muslim Brotherhood's spiritual guide, Sheikh Yusuf Qaradawi, at a high-profile event in London's City Hall in 2004.

The Stop the War Coalition later evolved into the Respect Party. The Socialist Workers' Party gave Respect its backing. Although MAB did not formally join the Respect Party, some of its leading activists, such as

Anas Altikriti, did. He says that the Islamists he subsequently spoke to in the Middle East were appalled that he was prepared to collaborate on a long-term basis with socialists, atheists and homosexuals.[17] Altikriti, however, saw the alliance as a great success. Not only did it serve to raise MAB's own profile; with the success of former Labour MP George Galloway in winning a seat for the party at the 2005 general election, the Respect Party, and hence a number of MAB activists, also gained in political significance as well.

In the run-up to the anti-war demonstration, senior MAB members had regular and cordial contact with the police to discuss security at the protest. This in turn led to an introduction to the Metropolitan Police's Muslim Contact Unit, a division of Special Branch. The Muslim Contact Unit came to view MAB so favourably that in early 2005 it offered to help MAB take over the management of Finsbury Park Mosque in North London, displacing followers of the jihadi preacher Abu Hamza. After some internal debate, MAB decided to accept the police offer and took over the mosque.[18]

Further influence for the Brothers came with the growth of specialist television networks which meant that a wider audience would now be directly exposed to the Brotherhood's ideas. The Islam Channel, which was launched in 2004, was run by Mohamed Ali Harrath, a Tunisian Islamist exile. Harrath was not a member of Tunisia's main Islamist opposition party, Ennahda, but was the founder of a separate party, the Tunisian Islamic Front (FIT).[19] The Islam Channel gave leading Brotherhood activists a platform—Anas Altikriti, for example, had a weekly show—but it also gave airtime to presenters from a wider range of backgrounds. Kamal Helbawy was a frequent guest in the London studios of the Iranian state-sponsored English-language channel Press TV (though one other leading activist, Said Ferjani, told me he was sceptical about the benefits of engaging with an organisation controlled by the Iranian authorities). Al Jazeera TV in the era of the emir of Qatar Hamad bin Khalifa Al Thani gave a programme to Sheikh Yusuf Qaradawi, a scholar much admired by many Brotherhood activists, and the network regularly booked members of the Brotherhood to take part as guests on both its Arabic and English channels.

Buoyed by their newfound influence, MAB even made a bid in 2004 for the leadership of the Muslim umbrella organisation, the MCB. The Maududist groups which ran the MCB managed to keep control. The

Brotherhood, despite the audacity of its takeover challenge, retained enough influence to guarantee a senior role for one of their candidates on the governing committee.

Decline and fallout

While MAB had never advertised its Brotherhood sympathies to non-Muslim outsiders, these ideological links, like those of the Muslim Council of Britain, were to come under greater scrutiny from politicians and the mainstream media after the July 2005 London bombings.

The most controversial issue for MAB was its support for Hamas, the Muslim Brotherhood's Palestinian spin-off. One of MAB's most prominent members, Azzam Tamimi, defended the suicide attacks carried out by his fellow Palestinians against Israeli citizens.[20] So too did one of the Brotherhood's most popular clerics, Sheikh Yusuf Qaradawi.

There were also internal problems within MAB. Those, like Anas Altikriti and Azzam Tamimi, who had formed an alliance with the far left and led MAB to such prominence during the run up to the Iraq war were blamed by others in the organisation for trading MAB's relationship with the government for a brief moment in the sun. Altikriti, Tamimi and a small group of supporters decided to found their own organisation, the British Muslim Initiative (BMI).[21]

A leading member of the group which took control of MAB, Said Ferjani, felt that Altikriti and his colleagues were overly focused on international issues, and particularly the Palestinian cause. Ferjani says that while he cares about the Palestinians, he fears that firing up the emotions of young people over international issues risks 'disturbing them and creating a generation that only knows how to shout'.[22]

Under Ferjani, MAB managed to repair its relationship with the Labour government, gaining access to civil servants and occasionally to government ministers.[23] In 2006 MAB helped to establish the government-backed Mosques and Imams National Advisory Board (MINAB), a body that sought to encourage the professional governance of mosques and the provision of better training for imams.

The Brotherhood breakaway faction represented in the BMI found itself frozen out by the Labour government. Anas Altikriti, despite his extensive connections to Islamist politicians around the world (his father Usama, for example, became head of the Iraqi Islamic Party), says that his advice was never openly sought by the Foreign Office after the anti-war protests.[24] When the BMI directors organised the 2008 Islam Expo, a huge exhibition and conference held over several days in London, Labour politicians either refused to attend or pulled out under pressure from the government.[25]

It was perhaps not just the BMI's opposition to the Iraq war but also its links to Hamas which was the cause of the British government's aloof attitude towards it. Apart from Azzam Tamimi, the BMI had another prominent Hamas supporter on its team. Mohammed Sawalha, the BMI's president, is said to have been a Hamas commander and allegedly used London as a base to raise funds for the group's missionary and military activities.[26]

In the opinion of Kamal Helbawy, the founder president of MAB, the association was more effective and had more integrity when it was under the influence of Anas Altikriti and Mohammed Sawalha.[27]

After the Arab Spring

For many of the Brotherhood exiles, the collapse of the autocratic governments of Egypt, Tunisia and Libya in 2011 provided the first opportunity for them to put their political ideas into practice. Kamal Helbawy returned to Egypt, initially playing a leadership role in the Brotherhood but resigning after it broke its promise to refrain from fielding a candidate in the first presidential elections. In his final years in Britain, he had presented himself as an ally in the government's fight against violent extremism. He had condemned al-Qaeda and had explained in Islamic terms why he believed it was impermissible for British citizens to fight against British troops in Iraq. He also launched a think tank called the Centre for the Study of Terrorism and Security. However, in May 2012, he gave an interview to a pro-Brotherhood website in which he asked that God treat Osama bin Laden generously, 'enlighten his grave, and to make him join the prophets, the martyrs, and the good people'.[28] When I met Helbawy in London in 2013 he sought to justify his remarks on the basis that he would make such supplications on behalf of any Muslim. An Islamist friend of his who was sitting nearby rolled his eyes at Helbawy's explanation and suggested that he might be better leaving God to decide these things without the need for such pleadings.

Helbawy was part of a relatively liberal group which broke away from the Brotherhood soon after the Arab Spring. He said he would be content to see a woman or a non-Muslim rule Egypt and accused the Brotherhood-backed President Morsi of behaving in an autocratic manner.[29]

Sheikh Rachid Ganouchi returned to Tunisia, but declared that while he wished to help his Ennahda party, he had no desire to stand for election. Ennahda became the single largest party in the Tunisian parliament following the country's first elections in 2011. Ganouchi promised to work for a liberal Islamic regime similar in character to Turkey under the AKP, the reformed Islamist party. One of the Ennahda party's successful parliamentary candidates was an unveiled woman who described herself as a liberal—a sign perhaps of how broad-minded the party was prepared to be.

Other Brotherhood sympathisers from Britain decided to split their lives between the UK and their countries of origin. This included Ashur Shamis—the Libyan who had relinquished his formal affiliation to the Brotherhood to join a broader-based opposition group in 1981. He returned home to work as a media adviser to the prime minister who led the post-Gaddafi transitional government. Shamis saw his return as a temporary measure—like many of the UK Brothers, the decades he had spent in exile meant he had family that had never experienced life outside of Britain and were reluctant to move.[30]

The Brotherhood legacy

The Brothers' institutional legacy in Britain reflects the fact that the movement never really managed to win the loyalty of those beyond its core constituency of overseas students, graduate professionals and exiles.

Despite MAB's leadership role in the period immediately prior to the Iraq war, its membership ultimately remained a narrow one. While many in the wider Muslim community might have respected its leaders' abilities as activists, there were few ideological conversions.

As the Brotherhood's activities are concentrated in London and the red brick university cities, they are largely absent from the former mill towns in which many of Britain's South Asian Muslims live. There is a total of eight Muslim Welfare Houses located in London and the major cities. They provide prayer facilities, a meeting place and sometimes accommodation for students. The local office of the Muslim Association of Britain is often based in the same premises. According to the MAB website it has just nine branches in the UK. In a country with 1,700 mosques, this makes it a relatively small organisation at grassroots level.

In rural South Wales, a residential higher education college linked to the Brotherhood offers courses in Arabic and Islamic studies. The European Institute of Human Sciences is not a traditional seminary but a college offering courses in an Islamic environment, mainly to overseas students. The college struggled to receive accreditation for its higher courses after the University of Wales decided that, for academic reasons, it would no longer validate courses taken at the institute. The college has sub-branches in Birmingham and at the Muslim Welfare House in London.

The Brotherhood institution which has prospered the most is the Federation of Student Islamic Societies (FOSIS). The Brothers' activism and ideas appealed to students more than any other group, thus enabling FOSIS to benefit from the dramatic expansion of higher education in the UK. When FOSIS was founded in 1962 there were 129,000 full-time places in higher education. By 2008 the number had increased to 1.5 million. The Muslim student population changed significantly in its character as well as its size during that period: British-born Muslims of mainly South Asian origin now outnumber the overseas students in many university Islamic societies (ISocs). This has posed a challenge to the Brothers in terms of retaining control of the organisation when the intake is increasingly made-up of Muslims raised in Deobandi and Sufi communities. Further compounding these difficulties is the fact that the rival Islamist group, Hizb-ut-Tahrir, and the Salafis, have been aggressively competing for Muslim loyalty on campus since the 1990s.

In the past FOSIS had used its resources to promote Brotherhood ideas by distributing material such as 'Freshers' Packs' containing Hasan al-Banna's 'Letter to a Muslim Student in the West' to every student Islamic Society. By 2009, however, the organisation gave at least the impression of greater pluralism, with speakers at the annual conference coming from Salafi, Sufi and Deobandi backgrounds as well as the Brotherhood. Yet Sufi Muslim students from three different institutions complained to the author that this appearance was misleading. They felt that FOSIS was biased in favour of a coalition of Brotherhood and Salafi students, attempting to influence the branches by offering to arrange for Brotherhood-inspired speakers, such as Azzam Tamimi, or Salafis, such as Sheikh Haitham Haddad,[31] to visit their campuses. Some Sufis claimed that their attempts to organise alternative speakers were vehemently opposed (or even sabotaged) by the Islamists on campus and by FOSIS officials.

FOSIS is a genuine federation of university branches that is open to all and is run along democratic lines. So how could the Brothers maintain any degree of control over it? The answer to this perhaps lies in a combination of money and political skill. The FOSIS headquarters building in Kilburn is owned by a charity called the Muslim Student Charity. This latter charity in turn receives a substantial income from renting out a property which is registered to the Muslim Welfare House Trust. As a result, money that had initially been raised by the first generation of Brothers in the 1960s and invested in property is helping to provide an income for student activists fifty years later.[32] Although this does not guarantee that the Brothers will keep control of FOSIS, it does give them influence.

Possibly more significant than any institutional legacy, however, is the network of connections that the Brothers have built between Britain and the Arab Islamist world over the half century since they began to organise. The Brotherhood exiles who returned to their countries of origin after the Arab Spring of 2011 did so after forming friendships and political contacts, as well as raising families, in Britain. While many of the British Brothers will remain in the UK, they retain extensive connections to those with political power in the new democracies of the Middle East.

For these reasons the Brothers are important as a source of information and access to Islamist politicians abroad—but they do not represent the British Muslim masses. They are a modern Islamist, Arab organisation dominated by graduates. By contrast, the Muslim population of Britain remains mainly working class, South Asian and traditional in its religious practice. And to date, such boundaries of class, ethnicity and sectarian loyalty have proved to be more enduring than even the secular dictators of the Arab world.

6

THE BARELWIS

SUFIS AND TRADITIONALISTS

'We're the good guys. The antidote to extremism,' claimed Haras Rafiq as he showed me round the headquarters of the Sufi Muslim Council.

He gave me the same pitch that had worked so well with government ministers when his organisation first launched in 2006—Sufism, he said, promotes an aspect of Islam that is more moderate and has been more proactive in the fight against extremism than the Muslim Council of Britain with its links to the Pakistani Islamist party the Jamaat-e-Islami. Furthermore, according to Rafiq, the Sufi movements of Britain comprise a far larger proportion of Britain's Muslims than the combined affiliates of the MCB.

According to data from the MuslimsinBritain.org website, the Sufi-orientated groups control nearly 39 per cent of Britain's mosque capacity.[1] This estimate excludes Britain's Deobandi mosques, even though some Deobandis share elements of Sufi practice.

For the purposes of this chapter, when I talk of Sufi mosques and Muslims, I am not including the Deobandi Sufis.

Sufi mosques tend to have the inscription 'Oh God, Oh God's Messenger'[2] over the altar (*minbar*), reflecting their intense love of the Prophet Muhammad. All Muslims of course revere the Prophet Muhammad; however, the Sufis' emphasis on praising God's messenger as well as God is interpreted by their Salafi critics as a departure from strict monotheism.

The Sufis also venerate their deceased spiritual leaders, elevating them to the status of saints and making their graves into places of pilgrimage. The Salafis regard this as contravening the monotheistic principles of Islam too.

The Barelwis

Those Sufi mosques and organisations with origins in the Indian subcontinent tend to regard themselves as part of the Barelwi tradition—a movement established in the north Indian town of Bareilly in the nineteenth century. Its founder Maulana Ahmed Riza Khan used his knowledge as an Islamic scholar to defend Sufi practices against the ideological attack of the Deobandis. The type of Sufi practices that the Deobandis disapprove of include: celebrating the birthday of the Prophet Muhammad as a festival (known as *mawlid* or *milad al-nabi*); the more exuberant forms of religious meditation (*zikr*) such as those involving ecstatic jumping and dancing; and the use of musical instruments other than a single drum.

In Britain, around 90 per cent of Sufi mosques are managed by Barelwi groups; a reflection of the fact that South Asian Muslims make up a well-established majority of Britain's Muslims.[3]

Barelwi Sufism is the main tradition in the rural Mirpur district of Pakistan, the ancestral homeland of most of Britain's Pakistani Muslims. Mass migration from Mirpur was triggered in the 1960s by the construction of a huge dam which caused thousands of farmers to lose their livelihoods. Many of these displaced farmers came to Britain at a time when labour shortages meant they could easily find work in manufacturing industry.

The early Mirpuri migrants were male labourers who saw their presence in Britain as a temporary way of providing for their families in Pakistan. But by the 1970s many had been joined in Britain by their wives and children. As settlement began to look more permanent, these largely Barelwi immigrants began to establish their own mosques and institutions. The Barelwi settlers' spiritual sheikhs—known in South Asia as *pirs*—also began to pay annual visits to their followers in Britain. Oaths could thus be taken from anyone wishing to become a follower and the pir's tariqa could continue to develop in Britain.

Some of the Pakistani pirs established permanent mosques and centres in Britain. The Ghamkol Sharif Mosque in Birmingham, for example, was founded by an emissary of the late Sheikh Zindapir of Pakistan's North West Frontier Province. It serves as the headquarters of the Zindapir network in Britain and claims, as does another mosque in the city, to be the largest in Birmingham.[4] Another Pakistani tariqa, the Hazrat Sultan Bahu Trust, is also headquartered in Birmingham. Some of the pirs themselves, such as Pir Maroof in Bradford and Sheikh Faiz ul Aqtab Siddiqi in Warwickshire, are based permanently in the UK.

Some pirs have inherited their position as blood descendants of a Sufi master, whereas others are appointed by the sheikh to spread his spiritual teachings during his lifetime and to succeed him as head of the tariqa after his death.

Those, like Pir Maroof in Bradford, who have inherited their position by virtue of blood ties are known as *sajjada nashin*. The sajjada nashin are treated with deference—at the conclusion of a religious service, the congregation will often line up to kiss the hands of any sajjada nashin present.[5] However, they are not regarded as having the same authority as those appointed by another living sheikh to initiate and instruct new followers.[6]

One important Barelwi organisation which operates without the traditional tariqa structure is Minhaj ul Quran (MuQ), a network of mosques and religious education centres which was founded in Pakistan in 1980 by Sheikh Muhammed Tahir al Qadri. MuQ claims to operate in over ninety countries. In the UK it runs mosques and Islamic centres in Glasgow, Bradford, Nelson, Oldham, Manchester, Birmingham, Walsall and Forest Gate in East London. Some of MuQ's scholars work as teachers and imams in other Barelwi mosques and institutions.[7] MuQ has 'friends' and 'members' rather than mureeds; the organisation's leader, Sheikh Tahir al Qadri, sees himself as the head of a revivalist movement which has political and social ambitions as well as a desire to promote religious knowledge and spirituality.[8] The organisation has strong Sufi characteristics in that it promotes 'ardent love for the Holy Prophet' and the celebration of the Prophet Muhammad's birthday, and it is happy for its adherents to become mureeds of traditional sheikhs.[9]

The Barelwi equivalent to the Tablighi Jamaat (the Deobandis' proselytising wing), is the missionary organisation known as Dawat-e-Islami, the international headquarters of which are in Karachi, Pakistan. In the UK, its headquarters are in Dewsbury, the same West Yorkshire town in which the Tablighi Jamaat's headquarters are based. Dawat-e-Islami is also particularly active in Birmingham, Bradford and Accrington.[10] Unlike the TJ, Dawat-e-Islami makes use of modern technology to supplement traditional methods of spreading its message: preachers can be heard in Urdu and English via a website, mobile phone apps and a dedicated television channel called Madani TV. According to Dawat-e-Islami UK's accounts, the group's income—which mainly comes from donations—was over £800,000 in 2010/11.[11]

While attachment to the Pakistani tariqas is still strong among the immigrant generation, British-born Sufis have begun looking beyond South Asia for spiritual guidance. Haras Rafiq of the Sufi Muslim Council, for example, is from a Pakistani Barelwi background but became a follower of Sheikh Hisham Kabbani—a Lebanese Sufi based in the United States and a deputy of the Cyprus-based Sufi master Sheikh Nazim. Both Sheikh Nazim and Sheikh Hisham Kabbani have visited the UK regularly to meet with their followers and to take oaths of allegiance (*bayat*) from recruits who wish to join their tariqa. They even have their own permanent centres at Tottenham in North London and Feltham in West London.

Being a Sufi in Britain

At a church hall in Maida Vale, West London, a group of Sheikh Nazim's followers gather for a weekly meeting where they will practise zikr, the Sufi meditation designed to encourage remembrance of God and to purify the soul.

With the room in darkness, a group of around ten men sit cross-legged in a circle. The chanting is led by a young accountant, deemed by the others to have the best voice. He sings verses from the Quran which the others then repeat in unison. As the hour goes on the zikr becomes more intense, with the men repeating single words or phrases in Arabic over and over again, growing louder and louder and faster and faster. Then suddenly the leader reverts to singing quietly and melodiously and the mood becomes less intense. The session ends as the men, speaking in English, take it in turn to ask God for his blessings and they begin to pray for others including Queen Elizabeth. Then the lights go on and a meal is served.[12]

The zikr is even more exuberant at the Zawiya in the Small Heath district of Birmingham. The small, single-storey building is run by followers of Sidi Hamza, a Sufi sheikh based in Morocco. The male followers gather there on Saturday nights. A group of men will sit round the edge of the room on the floor as the session begins in a similar way to the Maida Vale group. As the atmosphere intensifies and people enter a trance-like state, one of the men gets to his feet and begins to jump up and down to the rhythm of the singing, raising and lowering his arms in front of him as he does so. Gradually, the other men get to their feet and start to do the same. 'When the soul dances, the body moves,' explains Sajad Ali, a follower of Sidi Hamza and a regular at these Saturday night gatherings. 'Our hearts get enthusiastic because of the singing and we get so illuminated that we jump into the air. When we do that we're in a form of rapture. Sometimes people are crying and shaking. Your soul just takes over and you connect with your sheikh spiritually and you are present in front of your Lord. It's called hadhra.'[13]

The women followers sometimes come to these gatherings, but only to observe. They have their own gatherings on another night where their zikr will take the same form. Sajad Ali explains that the men will not be present as the women's voices might be sexually arousing, especially if they reach a state of ecstasy.

This more exuberant expression of Sufism is not what Sajad Ali grew up with as the British-born child of Pakistani Barelwi parents. His family celebrated the birth of the Prophet Muhammad and observed other Sufi practices such as *khatum*—by which he means, after the death of a loved one, reciting the Quran, praying and giving money to charity in the hope of raising the deceased in the eyes of God or, when a new house or extension was built, having the whole Quran read in two hours as a form of blessing. At the time he was not even conscious that these were distinctly Sufi practices: 'there were no badges then. It was just Islam.'[14]

Abu Khadeejah, who is now a Salafi but was brought up with a traditional Pakistani form of Islam, recalls other rituals from childhood: 'Thursday night was an important night for us, as it would be in many Sufi homes. We believed that dead spirits were released on that night and would roam the earth. We would cook some food, blow over it, eat it, offer some to the neighbours and then present some of this food to the dead.' He says such practices made no sense to him at the time, and as a Salafi he now rejects them completely.[15]

The sheikhs who head the tariqas are experts in Sufi spirituality known as *tasawwuf*. They are not necessarily experts in Islamic law, although most are. They believe in the importance of adherence to the sharia and referring to the traditional ulema for guidance. Haras Rafiq of the Sufi Muslim Council quotes the founder of the Maliki school of Islam: 'He who practices tasawwuf without learning sharia can become a heretic and he who follows sharia without practising tasawwuf is cheating himself.'[16] It is possible to find practising Sufis in Britain who do not attach such importance to the sharia—but they are the exception.

In Sufi circles, a sheikh in tasawwuf is the latest link in a chain (silsila) of living saints that goes back more than thirty generations to Prophet Muhammad's closest companion, Abu Bakr, or to the Prophet's son-in-law, Ali.[17]

These sheikhs are often believed by their followers to have knowledge of the unseen, or even to have had conversations with God or the Prophet Muhammad. Some of their claims to esoteric knowledge sound wildly superstitious to outsiders. In the 1980s, for example, Sheikh Nazim forecast that Jesus would return before the turn of the century and that the year 2000 'will not be completed'. He has also stated that Prince Charles is a descendant of the Prophet Muhammad and will one day rule Britain and North America as a monarchy.[18]

Many of the Sufi orders present in Britain are branches of the Chishti, Naqshbandi and Qadri tariqas. However, these labels are much less important than the influence of individual living sheikhs in defining the practices of followers.

Tariqa also means 'method', an allusion to the fact that each sheikh will prescribe for his followers the spiritual exercises that they should follow.

Sajad Ali, the Sufi who attends the exuberant Saturday night gatherings in Birmingham, explains his tariqa's methods: 'The first is excessive meditation. For example we might say the words "La illaha ill Allah" (there is no god but God) 15,000 times.' Others, he says, think nothing of spending two hours per week watching TV soap operas. He would rather commit that time to God. 'The Sufi is the one who says I will do the things I must do and then I will do more. I am going to do the extra.' Another principle of his tariqa is love and companionship: 'We have love for each other. I don't just mean smiling and saying "Hi how are you?" I mean a burning love.'[19]

The goal is to fight against one's ego, surrender oneself to God and become a better human being.

Many Muslims say that the word 'Islam' means peace. Sajad disagrees: 'It means surrender. So once you have surrendered you are a slave. I have surrendered myself to my Lord. Western ideology is such that a lot of people find that hard to accept.'

As a Sufi, Sajad aims to develop a tolerant and forgiving disposition: 'When someone says something bad to you, reply with something better. Find seventy excuses for your brother or sister when they do something wrong. Have mercy on them and they will have mercy on you. Allah is *rahman wa rahim*—merciful and most forgiving.'[20]

Although Sajad Ali's reaction to his mildly Sufi upbringing was to explore Sufism in more depth, many British Muslims from similar backgrounds took the opposite course, dismissing the Sufism of their parents as a departure from Islam in its true form.

Sufis versus Salafis

In the 1990s, the Sufi mosques on the whole did little to stop the younger generation drifting away. Sermons continued to be delivered in Urdu by imams who were often unable to speak English. Efforts to cater for the younger generation were usually limited to classes aimed at teaching children to memorise the Quran without necessarily understanding its meaning or pronouncing the Arabic correctly. Then, as now, women were often banned from the mosques.

Those who were competing with the Sufis for Muslim loyalty made a more direct and effective appeal to the youth. The Salafis, the radical Islamist group Hizb ut Tahrir and the groups affiliated to the Jamaat-e-Islami and the Muslim Brotherhood addressed the political issues of the day such as Bosnia; they empowered their followers with the idea that they could help bring about political change rather than just relying on God's will; and they appeared to offer textual justification for each and every view they held.

Furthermore, the Sufis' rivals publicised and preached their messages in English, thereby offering followers the chance to join with British Muslims of other ethnic backgrounds and to develop a sense of identity based on a universal faith rather than a foreign culture.

Women might not have been offered the chance to lead these new Islamist and Salafi movements or to mix freely with the men, but they were at least given the chance to become activists and to put their intellectual and organisational abilities to use.

What must have made these alternative forms of Islam even more appealing for many teenagers was the opportunity it afforded for a form of adolescent rebellion that their parents would find difficult to counter—having spent years emphasising the importance of Islam to their children, the older generation now found itself criticised by the youth for not being Islamic enough.

Such teenage rebellions can put severe pressure on family relationships. Haras Rafiq of the Sufi Muslim Council recounts the story of a family which was delighted when the son, a university student, decided to take his religious obligations seriously. However, when the son returned home for the vacation it was clear that he had turned against his parents' Sufi practices. At mealtimes the son took to dividing the food on his plate in two and eating only half. His mother asked him what he was doing. He told her that his imam had advised him that he should eat half because that portion had been provided by God. He had been told to leave the other half because that portion was provided by a heretic (i.e. his Sufi-following father) and he was forbidden from eating it. 'That story blew my mind,' says Rafiq, for whom this was an early indication of what the Sufis were up against.

The consequences of the Barelwis' failure to compete for the loyalty of the youth were evident to Sufi-follower Mas'ud Ahmed Khan even in the early 1990s. Khan had grown up in a Pakistani family in the Buckinghamshire town of Aylesbury, where he found the local Barelwi mosque uninspiring: the main activity that it provided for Muslim youth was the usual after-school Quranic instruction classes where the discipline was harsh and the emphasis was on rote-learning rather than understanding. Yet he subsequently felt the pull of Sufism when, as a student, he stumbled upon the works of the celebrated eleventh-century Sufi scholar and mystic, Imam Ghazali. Due to his upbringing in a Barelwi family, Khan felt comfortable with the rituals and the mysticism. As he began to amass his own collection of Sufi scholarship, he felt he was beginning to understand its appeal more fully.

Khan could see that Sufis were losing the youth, particularly converts, to Salafi preachers who attracted large crowds to the lectures they gave in hired halls. Khan's local Barelwi mosque was not particularly receptive to his ideas about how to avert decline, so he turned instead to the Internet as a way of spreading the Sufi message to a younger audience. With a degree in computer studies and a job in IT, Khan was part of the vanguard of Internet users. In the early 1990s he began to transcribe his collection of Sufi literature before sharing it via Internet 'newsgroups'—a text-based forerunner to web pages. His intention was simply to make these works available to friends and family, but the collection was soon noticed by other Internet users and it became clear to Khan that there was a sizeable audience for this type of material.

Among those whose writings Mas'ud Ahmed Khan made available to a wider readership were Sheikh Abdal Hakim Murad (an English Sufi and convert to Islam, also known as Tim Winter, who lectures in Islamic studies at Cambridge University) and Sheikh Nuh Ha Mim Keller, an American convert, scholar and Sufi. They formed part of a group of Sufi scholars who were prepared to address the claims of the Salafis directly, and in English. In 1995, Khan arranged for Sheikh Nuh to come to the UK for a series of speaking engagements in Bradford, the Midlands and London. The tour was not restricted to Sufi venues, taking in as it did the Jamaat-e-Islami-controlled Islamic Foundation in Leicestershire and some university campuses.

'He gave a series of lectures in which he addressed some of the differences between the traditional Muslims and the Wahhabis. For example, he gave a talk on the tradition of Sufism in Islam and another entitled "Where is God?"'[21] Sheikh Nuh characterises the Salafis as too literal in their interpretation of the early Islamic scholars' position that God is above his throne above the heavens. God, according to Sheikh Nuh, cannot literally be above the heavens as this would contradict the Quranic verses which state that God is unlike anything in this world and is absolutely free of need for anything created. To believe that God is literally above the heavens would, argues Sheikh Nuh, erroneously imply that God needed a time and space to inhabit.[22] The Salafis argue that the Sufi position promotes what they regard as the false belief that God is omnipresent.[23]

Sheikh Nuh was offering a vision of Sufi Islam that urban, Western-educated Muslims could respect—one that was firmly rooted in Islamic scholarship and tradition rather than appearing to be mixed up with the folk rituals of a foreign, rural culture.[24]

Khan feels that the speaking tour was something of a turning point for his generation of British Muslims: 'It helped to galvanise support for traditional Islam, enabled like minded people to establish networks of co-operation and set the ball rolling with regards to combating Wahhabism on campuses and in towns.'[25]

The effects of Sheikh Nuh's visit were reinforced a couple of years later when Khan organised a similar tour by Sheikh Hamza Yusuf, an American convert and scholar.

Other Sufi scholars who made an impact through their writings and lectures in the effort to counter the growing Salafi influence were Sheikh Nazim's US-based deputy, Sheikh Hisham Kabbani, and the British convert Sheikh Abdal Hakim Murad, both of whom used a mixture of traditional Islamic scholarship with English-language preaching and modern methods of communication. Popular Sufi scholars from the Arab world also played their part, such as Habib Ali Jifri from Yemen and Muhammad al-Yaqoubi from Syria. One prominent expert and admirer of their methods calls them 'neo-traditionalists'.[26]

These Sufi scholars disputed the Wahhabi–Salafis' claim to orthodoxy. The importance of following one of the four major madhabs, Sunni schools of Islamic law, with over 1,000 years of tradition was explained.[27] The modern Islamist and Salafi groups which had rejected this were portrayed as 'innovators'—a charge usually levelled at the Sufis.

The neo-traditionalist scholars were given a further boost in 2005 when the UK government decided to fund tours of Islamic scholars preaching an anti-terrorist creed under the banner of 'The Radical Middle Way'. The programme, which also included non-Sufis, helped bring the neo-traditionalist message to a wider audience and re-enforce the more intellectual image that it brought to Sufism.

In Sufi circles a scholar is usually only recognised as competent to give guidance on an area of Islamic law or theology when he has been given permission (*ijaza*) by another recognised scholar. Thus each scholar has an academic lineage going back to the early days of Islam in much the same way as the sheikhs in tasawwuf have a spiritual lineage. For these reasons, many Sufi Muslims prefer to call themselves 'traditional Muslims' to distinguish themselves from some of the Salafi and modern Islamist groups which might recognise the traditional madhabs but do not strictly adhere to the rulings of any single school, and do not necessarily have the same formal systems of scholarly authority.

The Sufis' ability to produce British-born qualified Islamic scholars is severely hampered by their lack of UK seminaries. While the Deobandis have over twenty darul ulooms in the UK, aspiring traditional scholars from a non-Deobandi background have often travelled abroad to Syria and Egypt to study.[28] A 2003 survey of Islamic seminaries in Britain listed just five small Barelwi institutions among a list dominated by larger Deobandi darul ulooms.[29] By 2013 there was still no Barelwi equivalent to the Deobandi darul uloom network. Jamia al Karam, a Barelwi-run Islamic boarding school in Retford, Nottinghamshire, was offering a mix of secular and Islamic education. Students who wished to qualify as a scholar could complete their studies at Al Azhar University, Cairo's ancient seat of Islamic learning. Hijaz College, a Barelwi institution in Nuneaton, offered a full-time darul uloom course for adults as well as boarding facilities for boys to study an Islamic syllabus in the evenings after attending a local state school during the day. In 2013, several Barelwi institutions in Britain offered part-time courses for aspiring Islamic scholars. These included the Hazrat Sultan Bahu Trust darul uloom in Birmingham, which ran part-time courses for male and female students. In East London, a branch of Al Azhar University was running part-time advanced courses for those who could already demonstrate fluency in Arabic. Other initiatives to spread traditional scholarship and provide an alternative to the Deobandi school included iSyllabus, an Islamic studies programme led by British scholars who have been classically trained abroad. Courses were held in Glasgow, Edinburgh, Bradford and Birmingham. The educational director of iSyllabus, Sheikh Ruzwan Mohammed, graduated from Glasgow University before spending twelve years studying in Turkey, Yemen, Egypt, Morocco and Syria. He illustrates a trend among some British Muslims who are drawn towards classical Islamic scholarship but not necessarily Barelwi tradition. He says he respects Sufism but is wary of the 'cultish' aspects that are sometimes associated with it.[30]

The British Muslim Forum and the Sufi Muslim Council

The Sufis of Britain initially concentrated on establishing mosques and keeping their spiritual networks alive. However, by 2003 they were feeling the need for political recognition too. The Muslim Council of Britain had become accepted as the representative body of British Muslims, yet as it was dominated by the Jamaat-e-Islami many of the Barelwi mosques wanted nothing to do with it.

One of the driving forces behind the effort to establish a Sufi Muslim umbrella organisation was Sheikh Muhammad Imdad Husain Pirzada, a Barelwi pir and the principal of Jamia al Karam Islamic boarding school in Retford, Nottinghamshire. In 2003 he instigated the formation of the British Muslim Forum. All of the main Barelwi tariqas agreed to be represented. When the organisation launched in 2005, it was able to list 200 mosques and Islamic organisations as affiliates on its website. The idea was to engage in grassroots work while also representing Muslims to the Labour government and opposition parties. Within a short time its leaders managed to establish good relations with several influential politicians, including the then Race Equality Minister Fiona MacTaggart MP and the Conservative opposition's homeland security spokesman, Patrick Mercer MP. The BMF got the impression that the politicians who attended their events were taken aback by the size of the gatherings and were slowly beginning to accept the BMF as a viable group. Following the 7/7 London Underground bombings a few months after the group's launch, the politicians seemed even more receptive. When the government invited Muslim community representatives to sit on its Preventing Extremism Together (PET) task force it thus came as a blow that representation was weighted in favour of the Jamaat-e-Islami groups.[31]

Another umbrella organisation, the Sufi Muslim Council, was launched by Haras Rafiq in the following year. He too was concerned about the fact that the Muslim Council of Britain was perceived as the representative body of Muslims and he felt that the Sufis could gain influence by offering to play a role in countering extremism. Rafiq, a former corporate manager, built the necessary political connections to get ministerial backing. Yet his big breakthrough came when a Labour MP from a Sufi background, Mohammed Sarwar, agreed to sponsor the official launch of the Sufi Muslim Council in the House of Commons. The then secretary of state for communities and local government, Ruth Kelly MP, and the then shadow attorney general, Dominic Grieve MP, gave the SMC their tacit support by attending the event.

Haras Rafiq was prepared to adopt a far more confrontational approach than the BMF when it came to the non-Sufi groups. He felt no inhibitions about publicly criticising what he regarded as the extremism of the other Muslim movements in Britain: he repeats an accusation frequently made of the Tablighi Jamaat that it is the ante chamber of radical Islam; Wahhabi ideology, he says, is unable to exist without having an enemy; and the ideas of the founder of the Jamaat-e-Islami, Abul A'la Maududi, he describes as 'negative and violent'.[32]

These are sentiments the British Muslim Forum would not express, according to Hafiz Gul, the BMF's first general secretary: 'Our relationship with the Sufi Muslim Council is very, very close but we feel we couldn't be that vocal.'[33]

The other difference between the remit of the Sufi Muslim Council and the BMF was that the latter intended to concentrate more on work at community level, such as training imams in child protection laws or establishing local groups for Muslim women. This was a reflection of the fact that BMF had a large number of affiliated mosques, whereas the SMC had none.

Despite the BMF's solid base of community support and its early success in gaining political recognition, it was in decline within three years of its launch. By 2012 the accounts filed with the Charity Commission showed no income or expenditure.

As for the Sufi Muslim Council (SMC), its detractors cast doubt on the extent to which it had a broad base of Sufi support in Britain, given that the organisation's website heavily promoted Sheikh Nazim and Sheikh Hisham Kabbani, respectively the leader and deputy of one tariqa. The SMC's original executive director, Haras Rafiq, is one of the sheikhs' followers and was ordered directly by Sheikh Hisham Kabbani to set up the organisation as a counter to extremist influences.[34] In 1999 Kabbani told a US State Department forum that 80 per cent of mosques in the United States were run by extremists and that there was an imminent danger of a terrorist attack.[35] At the time he was condemned for his remarks by over 100 US Muslim organisations and Islamic centres but, after 9/11, he was also seen as an ally with the gift of foresight by senior members of the Bush administration. Some of Kabbani's political activities remain controversial: in 2001, for example, he was a guest of President Islam Karimov, the head of Uzbekistan's highly oppressive government.[36]

Did the SMC ever really have much of a claim to represent Sufis beyond the followers of Sheikh Nazim and Sheikh Hisham Kabbani? According to one study, it certainly did.[37] It is true that the SMC did not have universal support among Sufi and Barelwi leaders—the followers of at least one pir were privately disdainful about some of Sheikh Nazim's forms of religious worship, which included a UK tour with the 2005 *X Factor* contestant Chico. But the researcher who investigated the SMC's support base found that its campaign to counter 'extremist trends' had struck a chord with Sufis beyond Sheikh Nazim's tariqa, enabling it to mobilise support from some of the most important Sufi sheikhs.[38]

But much like the BMF, the Sufi Muslim Council foundered within a few years of its launch. Its original chief executive, Haras Rafiq, resigned for health reasons in 2009. Its website, as of the summer of 2013, did not appear to have been updated for three years.

Sufis, jihad and foreign policy

The modern jihadi movements, such as those inspired by al-Qaeda, have tended to be less attractive to those who identify themselves as Sufis. In the UK, none of those convicted of involvement in terrorist activities appear to have been practising Sufis at the time they committed their crimes.[39]

However, that does not mean that the Sufis are the Islamic equivalent of the Quakers.

Sufi scholar and BMF official, Hafiz Gul, believes that defensive wars against foreign occupation are justified and that at the stage at which the state of Israel was being created, the Palestinians were entitled to fight against those trying to establish the Jewish state 'because we are told to defend our lands as Muslims'.[40]

Yet he is keen to distinguish between this type of situation and attacks on civilians carried out by modern day jihadi groups: 'The indiscriminate killing of innocent victims is not acceptable or lawful within Islam wherever it may be.' Hafiz Gul does not regard the tactics of jihadi groups in such places as Kashmir, Palestine, Iraq or Afghanistan as religiously justified: 'Calling jihad is not something that any Muslim can do. It has to be called by the leader of a Muslim nation.'[41] Osama bin Laden, the leaders of the Kashmiri jihadi groups and the Iraqi insurgent groups were not leaders of Muslim nations and therefore lacked the requisite authority to call a jihad, according to Hafiz Gul's understanding.[42]

Some Muslims argue that, in the case of a defensive jihad, no national leader is required to lead military action and that it is an absolute duty for all Muslims to help eject infidel occupiers from Muslim land. Hafiz Gul does not accept this interpretation: while spontaneous acts of self-defence in the face of an immediate threat to an innocent person's safety or a country's sovereignty are legitimate, he does not believe it is permissible within Islam to take part in a defensive jihad without the authority of a Muslim leader: 'If anyone could call jihad then Muslims all over the world would have responded to the call. The reason why they haven't responded to such calls is because that is not the way most Muslims view it.'[43]

He would also oppose attacks carried out on Israeli targets even if done so with the blessing of the elected Palestinian Authority: 'In my opinion, military action is not achieving anything for either side in Palestine at this moment and, when you're not achieving something, then you are better to leave military means and start working together.'[44] This is not just a pragmatic stance. He believes that Islamic law obliges Muslims to abandon military attacks if they are failing to achieve positive results.

Hafiz Gul felt that the British invasion of Iraq in 2003, which the UK government had sought to justify on the grounds that the Iraqi regime possessed weapons of mass destruction, was not warranted. However, he did not see the subsequent attacks by insurgent groups on US and British troops operating in Iraq as legitimate either: 'If America was trying to occupy Iraq then Iraqis would be required to defend their country. But it wasn't about trying to occupy Iraq.'[45]

In the 1990s, Sufi opposition to British foreign policy was articulated more loudly. The author Philip Lewis describes how, following the Iraqi invasion of Kuwait in 1990, a conference of British Muslims, led by a Barelwi, issued a statement that shocked non-Muslims with its one-sidedness: it condemned 'the US-led aggression against Iraq' and criticised the government of Saudi Arabia for allowing non-Muslim troops access to the Islamic heartlands, even though they were there to defend Saudi Arabia and Kuwait against Iraqi invasion. An earlier statement spoke of British involvement in the First Gulf War as part of a conspiracy to 'eliminate the threat of a Third World Muslim power developing economic and technological capability'.[46]

But Sufi opposition to Western foreign policy during the run up to the First Gulf War was perhaps in part motivated by the fact that Western governments were in alliance with the Sufis' arch enemies: the Wahhabi-backed state of Saudi Arabia.

An alternative to Islamism?

The Sufis are often contrasted with the politicised Muslims of the Islamist groups who advocate the establishment of an Islamic state that will enforce sharia law in Muslim lands.

Birmingham-based Sufi Sajad Ali echoes the views of many ordinary Sufi followers on the issue. He believes that the sharia and an Islamic state will only be re-established after the appearance on earth of a messianic figure known as Imam Mehdi and the return of Jesus. He describes in great detail a time, foretold by the Prophet Muhammad, when the world is at its darkest point for Muslims. Only after a period of tribulation will peace under Islamic rule be established. 'So to all these people,' he says, referring to the Islamists, 'who go on about the khilafah [Islamic state] we say "Why don't you just read what the books of the end of time say?"'[47]

Muslims believe that the Prophet Muhammad gave advice regarding the signs which believers should look out for as an indication that the 'end times' are coming. Sajad Ali sees many of these signs around him today: 'The end of time will come when your shoe will talk to you. Well now you can get a Nike talking shoe that tells you how many miles you have walked. There will be a spider's web—the Internet is known as the world wide web! You will be clothed yet you will be naked: we now have see-through clothes! The nomads will have tall buildings to the sky—well look at Dubai! Alcohol and homosexual behaviour will be rampant. Men will dress as women; women will dress as men. Divorce will be common. Well look at this country!'[48]

Sheikh Nazim believes that Imam Mehdi is already on earth, living in the desert area between Saudi Arabia and Yemen known as the Empty Quarter, and that the anti-Christ is on the earth, with thirty deputies performing his work around the world.[49]

Not all Sufi leaders oppose political activism as a means to establish an Islamic state. The leader of the Sufi group Minhaj-ul-Quran (MuQ), Sheikh Mohammed Tahir al Qadri, was the founder of an Islamic political party in Pakistan. In 2013 he led a mass march as part of an unsuccessful attempt to prompt the dissolution of the government of Pakistan's President Asif Ali Zardari.

Sheikh Tahir al Qadri reinforced the image of Sufi opposition to militancy when he held a highly publicised launch in London for his fatwa against suicide bombing in March 2010.[50] However, it would be wrong to assume that he also opposed the Islamist ideology of groups like the Jamaat-e-Islami and its founder Maulana Maududi.

According to an analysis of Sheikh Tahir al Qadri's pronouncements by the leading academic expert on Sufism in Britain, Ron Geaves, there are signs that the sheikh takes a position similar to Maududi in that he argues the case for a state which receives its authority from God rather than the people.[51] A thesis on the Sheikh's ideology written by one of his followers (and tacitly endorsed by MuQ via its British website) identifies some subtle differences between al Qadri and Maududi but, more strikingly, describes the Sheikh as one of the 'three eminent contemporary Muslim revivalists' alongside Maududi and the Muslim Brotherhood's founder, Hassan al-Banna. The author of the thesis writes that all three of these revivalists share a belief that 'political activity and attainment of enforcement power and authority' are 'vital for successfully materialising the struggle for Islamic Revival'.[52] One of al Qadri's close political allies—a Shia Muslim and journalist called Murtaza Pooya—described himself to the author as influenced by Maududi and an advocate for the 1979 Islamic Revolution in Iran.[53]

A slightly different emphasis is given to the concept of an Islamic state by Sheikh Faiz ul Aqtab Siddiqi, a British-educated Barelwi pir and scholar based in Nuneaton: 'We're a traditional spiritual centre of guidance and the circles of politics are not for us.'[54] However, the sheikh says that 'an Islamic state of mind' among the majority would ultimately result in an Islamic state, 'because a political state is a manifestation of the state of the mind of the people essentially'.[55]

Sheikh Faiz inherited the leadership of his tariqa from his late father Pir Muhammad Abdul Wahab Siddiqi, who was an influential figure among Muslims in Britain from the early 1970s onwards.

However, his father was highly active in Islamic political circles. Pir Wahab Siddiqi was elected in the 1970s as the overseas president of the Jamiatul Ulema e Pakistan, a Barelwi political party.

In the early 1990s Pir Wahab Siddiqi was at the centre of a radical British Islamist experiment—the Muslim Parliament. The parliament was set up following the failure of Muslim protestors to persuade the British government to ban the publication of Salman Rushdie's novel *The Satanic Verses*. It was established in response to Muslim disillusion with British society and its aim was to allow Muslims to become more independent of the non-Muslim population. The vision was for Muslims to set up their own schools, trade with each other and to become an enclave within society.

A four-page eulogy to the late Pir Wahab Siddiqi, published on the Internet, describes how he was a close friend of, and adviser to, the Muslim Parliament's founder leader, Dr Kalim Siddiqui.[56]

In his inaugural address to the Muslim Parliament, Dr Kalim Siddiqui told members that the Prophet Muhammad had shown Muslims 'how to generate the political power of Islam in a minority situation and how to nurse ... it until the creation of an Islamic state and the victory of Islam over all its opponents'.[57]

Despite being a mainly Sunni organisation, the Muslim Parliament was supported by the Shi'ite Islamic Republic of Iran. Its leaders were treated as VIPs on visits to Iran and Pir Wahab Siddiqi apparently visited the Republic many times, meeting with, among others, Ayatollah Khomeini and the then President Rafsanjani to 'draw on the experiences of the Islamic revolution'.[58]

Sheikh Faiz shows no signs of wanting to become involved in the sort of political activities that engaged his father in his final years. But he is involved in what some might see as an Islamist development: working towards the establishment of the UK's first sharia courts.

Sufis and sharia law in Britain

The Sufis, like the Salafis, Deobandis and Shia Muslims, operate sharia councils—tribunals to which Muslims can refer for advice or rulings on civil and family law disputes. The authority that these councils enjoy comes not from having any formal legal status but from the willingness of community members to submit voluntarily to their decisions.

Mohammed Shahid Raza, a Sufi scholar who runs the Muslim Law (Shariah) Council based in Ealing, would like to see Islamic family law made available to Muslims through the mainstream legal system: 'When Britain was ruling India, there was a separate legal code for Muslims, organised and regulated by British experts of law.'[59] But such a change would require parliamentary legislation and would almost certainly be too controversial to receive the necessary political support.

Sheikh Faiz al Aqtab Siddiqi of Hijaz College has a vision for the establishment of an Islamic court in the UK which would avoid the need for any change in the law. As he qualified as a barrister in the English legal system, he knew that under existing legislation it would be possible to set up an Islamic court of arbitration, the decisions of which would be enforceable in English law under the terms of the Arbitration Act. To that end he formed the Mahkamah Council of Jurists. He says he has arbitrated in a number of disagreements between Muslim businessmen and in mosque disputes. The decision of such a religious arbitration board on civil disputes (other than family law cases) will be enforced by the High Court so long as: (i) the ruling is not 'inherently unreasonable';

(ii) the parties to the dispute agreed in advance to abide by the council's ruling; and (iii) enforcement would not be against the public interest. Through these activities Sheikh Faiz says that he envisages a sharia court being established in Britain without the need for legislation. Such a system already exists in the orthodox Jewish community in Britain, where a religious court of arbitration (Beth Din) adjudicates in civil disputes and family law cases.

Sufism and militancy

Since 9/11, Britain's Sufi leaders have emphasised their spirituality and lack of militancy. Yet this has not always been the tone set by Sufis in Britain.

The Sufis' intense veneration of the Prophet Muhammad meant that they were at least as offended as other Muslim groups by the publication of Salman Rushdie's *The Satanic Verses* (1988). The man who bought a copy of the book to be publicly burnt in a notorious protest in Bradford was a leading Barelwi in the city.[60]

The sense of anger and hurt that Sufis feel as a result of any insult directed at the Prophet Muhammad has been seen more recently. Following the publication of provocative cartoons of the Prophet in a Danish newspaper Jyllands-Posten in 2005, British Sufis organised a protest march which was far better attended than the more highly publicised protest of the extremist group Islam4UK.

In 2011, when the governor of the Punjab, Salman Taseer, was assassinated for opposing Pakistan's blasphemy laws, the Jamat-e-Ahle Sunnat, a Barelwi political party, issued a statement declaring that no Muslim should express 'any kind of regret or sympathy over the incident'.[61] Taseer had caused anger by appealing for the pardon of a Christian woman who had been sentenced to death for allegedly insulting the Prophet Muhammad. The man who admitted killing Taseer was a policeman in Punjab and a follower of the Barelwi missionary group Dawat-e-Islami.[62] A Muslim from a different Barelwi organisation in the West Midlands was among those who paid their respects at the family home of the assassin.[63] By contrast, another Barelwi organisation with links to the UK, Sheikh Tahir ul Qadri's Minhaj-ul-Quran, defended Governor Taseer on the basis that the accusations of blasphemy were unjustified.[64]

Conclusion

It would be a mistake for the British government to see the Sufi Muslims as a monolithic group, straightforwardly supportive of any policy passed in the name of fighting religious extremism and threats to security. There is certainly much less of an atmosphere of militancy among Sufi Muslims than there is in some other groups, and many follow a theology that is highly compatible with secularism. But the Sufis' relative moderation in some areas does not make them liberal on every issue. Support for freedom of speech, for example, does not extend to those who criticise or insult their religion.

Links to the Sufi pirs who lead the tariqas of the Indian subcontinent appear to be weakening. But in their place a new generation of English-speaking sheikhs, often based in the United States, is providing a new source of inspiration and loyalty for Sufi followers in Britain.

Yet the Sufis lack a network of UK Islamic seminaries to match that of the Deobandis. This means that the next generation of Sufi religious leaders is small by comparison: Sheikh Faiz ul Aqtab Siddiqi estimates that he is one of only 150 native English-speaking Sufi scholars in Britain. The Deobandis' British seminaries probably produce more than that number every year.[65]

The Sufis may have won the fight to counter the influence of the Salafis. But when it comes to the bigger battle for Muslim hearts and minds—that against the Deobandis—the Sufis still have a long way to go.

7

THE SHIA 'TWELVERS'

NAJAF IN BRENT

In the aftermath of the Iraq war, Jordan's King Abdullah famously used the phrase 'Shia crescent' to describe an arc of Shi'ite-backed movements and governments stretching from Iran, into Iraq, Syria and Lebanon.[1] Britain's equivalent is a triangle rather than a crescent. Fanning out from a point among the Arab cafes of central London's Edgware Road, the Shi'ite centres of population and influence are to be found to the north and west in the boroughs of Westminster, Brent and Harrow.

For a tour of the Shia Triangle, Willesden High Road is a good place to start. The area looks like a typical inner London suburb with its multicultural mix of grocery stores and cafes, side streets of Victorian terraces and plush villas up the hill. But on a walk along the main street with a local Shi'i to show me around, the area's importance as a political and religious hub becomes clear. Every few minutes we pass a person or a place with impressive Shia connections: 'That guy across the street is the cousin of Nouri al-Maliki, the Iraqi Prime Minister ... That shop belongs to a nephew of a famous religious leader in the Iraqi government.'[2]

The Sunni—Shia divide

The Shia trace their split from the main Sunni branch of Islam back to the death of the Prophet Muhammad in the seventh century. Most of the early Muslim community accepted Abu Bakr, a close companion of the Prophet Muhammad, as their new spiritual and political leader or 'caliph'—that majority became known as the Sunni branch of Islam. The dissenting minority, which became the Shia, thought that the Prophet Muhammad's son-in-law and cousin, Ali, should have been the successor instead. The term Shia is an elided form of the phrase Shiat Ali, meaning the Partisans of Ali. The Shia give extra reverence to those they refer to as the Ahlul Bayt—a term which literally means 'the people of the house', but in the Shi'ite context means the Prophet Muhammad's family.

The Shia share certain core beliefs and rituals with the Sunnis: observant followers offer five daily prayers towards Mecca; they fast during the holy month of Ramadan; and religiously observant women tend to wear the hijab. But centuries of parallel development have also resulted in some differences in belief and practice.

Dr Rebecca Masterton, an English convert to Sunni and then Shia Islam, has researched both interpretations of the religion. In her Sunni days she says she heard 'the classic bits of misinformation': that the Shia curse the first three caliphs; that they worship Ali rather than God alone; and that Shi'ism was made up by a converted Jew who was trying to break up the Muslim community. She revised her views when, while still a Sunni, she got a job translating Shi'ite religious texts and decided that the scriptural evidence was on the Shia side. She was shocked to read, for example, sources indicating that Umar, the second caliph, had made changes to the practice of Islam. She cites as an example the practice of saying additional prayers during Ramadan: 'There is actually a hadith in Bukhari which says that the Prophet got angry because people started to treat the additional prayers like it was an obligation ... Then Umar came along later and formalised the extra prayers.'[3] Bukhari is a collection of hadiths (sayings and doings of the Prophet Muhammad) which the Sunnis regard as well sourced.

In 2010 Masterton was presenter of an advice programme on the Shi'ite satellite channel Ahl ul Bayt TV, taking calls from viewers throughout the English-speaking world. She was often asked about relationship issues, including the controversial Shia practice of temporary marriage whereby a couple can enter into a marital relationship on a pre-agreed, time-limited basis with the option of renewing the agreement at a later date. 'I had a man call in, and I could tell from his tone that he was trying to be a little bit provocative,' recalled Masterton, 'and he was saying "I really like temporary marriage and I want to have lots of wives. Can I do that?" And my answer to that was what most women want out of a relationship is love and care and support. So if you're going to be doing lots of temporary marriages, ask yourself what love and care and support are you giving them. In addition to that ... it's got to be based on the whole ethics of the religion which is about how you treat people. Deceiving or taking advantage of people or manipulation is obviously prohibited.'[4]

That answer might make Masterton sound as if she is sidestepping the issue, however she is a candid supporter of the principle of temporary marriage and wonders on what authority Umar (the second caliph who is followed by Sunnis but is regarded with suspicion by the Shia) thought fit to ban it. But is it practised in Britain? 'Yes, it's quite common!' she says, laughing, 'But it's kept under wraps because of the social taboo. It often suits divorced women who don't want to introduce a man into their children's lives ... It can be used for an engagement or if someone goes on a journey for a long period of time.'[5]

Although Shia Muslims make up a majority of the population in Iran, Azerbaijan, Bahrain and Iraq,[6] in the Muslim world as a whole they are vastly outnumbered by Sunnis. This is also the case in Britain: in a country with nearly 1,700 mosques, the Shia run around 100 places of worship.[7] In most areas of significant Muslim population in Britain, there is usually at least one Shia mosque or centre among the more numerous Sunni ones. North West London is the exception to that pattern, with Shia institutions holding their own—or perhaps even dominating—the Islamic scene.

'Up the hill is the European office of the most important *ayatollah* in the world today,' says my guide in Willesden, referring to Grand Ayatollah al-Sistani of Iraq. 'Along the High Road is a college set up with money from Iran. Towards Cricklewood there is a very old foundation which is more for the Urdu speakers. Behind that is a place with very strong ties to the Iraqi Dawa Party ...' My guide continues to run through an extensive list of Shia organisations which are all within a fifteen-minute drive.

The leading figures of the various Shia communities in the area often work together cooperatively. 'The atmosphere is very polite,' according to my companion. But beneath the surface, ethnic divisions and sub-divisions, ideological differences and personal rivalries are at least part of the reason this community has spawned so many separate institutions.

Marjas, Ayatollahs and Grand Ayatollahs

One major factor in the organisation of the community is the role played by the *marjas*—the leading religious scholars deemed worthy of emulation whose advice is followed on matters of religious practice. Those marjas who are recognised as the most outstanding are referred to by the title ayatollah and the most esteemed of those as grand ayatollah. In the UK, and around the world, the marja with the largest number of adherents is Grand Ayatollah al-Sistani, an Iranian-born cleric who lives in the holy city of Najaf in Iraq.

'The relationship between the follower and the marja is that of lay person to a specialist,' explains Dr Saeed Bahmanpour, who served as the principal of the Islamic College for Advanced Studies, a Shia-run institution in Willesden, until December 2011.[8] In accordance with a principle known as *taqleed*—which literally means emulation—most practising Shia believe that it is a religious obligation to follow a marja. The marja, an expert in philosophical reasoning as well as Islamic law and theology, will advise followers on technical matters of religious practice. Opinions on issues often differ from marja to marja, so following just one of these scholars is recommended in order to prevent followers from choosing between different rulings on different topics.

Deciding who to follow is a matter of personal choice and not all the members of a single mosque or centre will necessarily follow the same marja. Asking who someone follows is akin to asking a British person who they voted for: not everyone is comfortable discussing their affiliations.

Pious followers are obliged to pay a tax, known as *khums*, to the marja. The amount paid should be equivalent to one-fifth of the follower's annual surplus. The money is paid to a trusted representative of the marja who can either spend it locally on a number of projects including charitable activities like helping the poor, producing educational publications or running a madrassa. Alternatively he can pass it on to the marja for religious projects, investment or other charitable purposes.

The living marja who is most familiar to non-Muslims in the West is Grand Ayatollah Sayyid Ali Khamenei, the supreme leader of the Islamic Republic of Iran. However, in some quarters Khamenei is not considered a scholar of the highest rank, although he is certainly respected.

Grand Ayatollah al-Sistani in Najaf not only outranks Khamenei but represents a Shi'ite school of thought which rejects the legitimacy of the constitutional model upon which the Islamic Republic of Iran is based.

After the 1979 revolution in Iran, Khamenei's predecessor, the late Grand Ayatollah Khomeini, instituted a system of Islamic governance known as Guardianship of the Jurist (*wilayat al-faqih*) with an ayatollah sitting above the elected parliament as an expert on Islamic law. Some Shia believe that this was an innovation that went against traditional Shi'ite notions of how an Islamic state might arise. Mainstream Shia are known as 'Twelvers' (or *ithna'ashari*) because they recognise Ali as the first of twelve leaders of the Muslim community, known as Imams. According to the ithna'ashari, the twelfth Imam, Muhammad al-Mahdi, went into 'occultation'—that is, he became hidden from human sight—at the end of the ninth century. The Twelvers believe that the Hidden Imam will one day return to usher in an age of justice and peace where the world will be governed according to God's law.

While Grand Ayatollah Khomeini did not discard the traditional expectation of the Twelfth Imam's return, he proposed that Muslims should strive to create a society in the intervening period that was governed by God's law. Given that the marjas were experts on the sharia, Khomeini consequently argued that a learned ayatollah should govern over society.

At the time of the Iranian Revolution the most formidable critic of Khomeini's theory was Grand Ayatollah al-Khoei. Then the Shia world's most respected cleric, he denounced the guardianship concept as a deviation from Shi'ism and is said to have done more than anyone else to create a barrier to Khomeini's influence in the wider Shia world.[9]

While Khomeini took action against some dissident clerics based in Iran, Grand Ayatollah al-Khoei remained in the Iraqi city of Najaf, beyond Khomeini's jurisdiction and determined to hold fast to the more traditional school of Shi'ite thought.

The 'Najaf School' in London

In 1989 Grand Ayatollah al-Khoei despatched a team of former students, family members and close aides to London. The needs of the growing population of Shia Muslims in the West, he had learnt, were not being catered to. One of his sons had persuaded him to establish a charity, the Al-Khoei Benevolent Foundation, with branch offices in London and New York.[10]

The foundation existed to carry out the traditional charitable functions of education and help for the poor. But it also developed an important networking role: the trusted representatives of al-Khoei now based abroad were able to make links with influential political and religious figures in the Islamic world and the West.

The diplomatic role of the overseas branches of the Al-Khoei Foundation became even more important as Grand Ayatollah al-Khoei's ability to operate in Saddam Hussein's Iraq became increasingly difficult. In 1991, following the Shia uprising in southern Iraq, Saddam attempted to pressurise al-Khoei into issuing a fatwa in his support. When al-Khoei refused, Saddam had him placed under house arrest and the funds his organisation held in an Iraqi bank were confiscated. It was at this point that the headquarters of the foundation were moved to London,[11] where al-Khoei's representatives had bought a former synagogue, offices and a school in the North London suburb of Queen's Park.

Grand Ayatollah al-Khoei died in 1992 while still under house arrest. After an interregnum caused in part by the death in the following year of al-Khoei's successor, most of the faithful transferred their allegiance to Grand Ayatollah al-Sistani, who had been one of al-Khoei's most gifted students. The management of many of al-Khoei's charities was also transferred to Sistani. In London, however, the Al-Khoei Benevolent Foundation continued to operate as a separate entity, with members of the al-Khoei family among the trustees. The foundation's income rapidly declined as it no longer had access to the marja's funds, but it did hold on to its substantial property assets in Queen's Park, including the former synagogue it had converted to a prayer hall, as well as the adjoining offices and the private day schools for girls and boys.

The Al-Khoei Foundation's London offices have continued to act as a kind of embassy for the Najaf school of Shi'ism. 'Every British Prime Minister and Leader of the Opposition has visited the Foundation since it was established,' says Yousif al-Khoei, the foundation's public affairs director and a grandson of the grand ayatollah.[12] The walls of the foundation's entrance hall are covered in framed photographs of the many politicians, religious leaders and royalty who have met with its representatives, including King Hussein of Jordan, Benazir Bhutto, the mufti of Egypt and the Duke of Edinburgh. A photograph taken at the funeral of Pope John Paul II in 2005 shows two representatives of the Al-Khoei Foundation sitting on the front row beside Italian Prime Minister Silvio Berlusconi. 'We were only meant to have one seat but the Al-Azhar guy didn't turn up so we were offered his seat too,' explains Yousif al-Khoei.[13]

When a UK government-backed body, the Mosques and Imams National Advisory Board (MINAB), was established in 2006, the Al-Khoei Foundation took a leading role. The aim of the state-funded body is to improve the governance of Britain's Sunni and Shia mosques through voluntary affiliation. The Al-Khoei Foundation was one of four organisations which founded MINAB, and Yousif al-Khoei became its treasurer.[14] MINAB's constitution grants the Shia 20 per cent of the seats on the fifty-member executive board.

Since the death of Grand Ayatollah al-Khoei in 1992, the Al-Khoei Foundation has continued to be the main bridge between the Shia in Britain and the wider society. It has also maintained its role as a link with the most followed marja: in 1994 Grand Ayatollah al-Sistani accepted an invitation to become the foundation's patron. Although the relationship has been mutually beneficial, it has not always been cordial. Tensions arose when a representative of al-Sistani sought to take control of the foundation and, having failed so to do, resigned as a trustee. In an attempt at reconciliation, a trustee and member of the al-Khoei family offered al-Sistani the keys to the foundation's offices. The marja declined the offer but renewed his blessing of the organisation.[15] Although Grand Ayatollah al-Sistani remains the organisation's patron, the foundation is not his official representative body in the way it once was for Grand Ayatollah al-Khoei. So which organisation does represent Grand Ayatollah al-Sistani? The answer can be found just a short walk away.

Around the corner from the Al-Khoei Foundation is the UK head-quarters of one of Grand Ayatollah al-Sistani's charities, the Imam Ali Foundation (IAF).[16] The IAF, which is run by Sistani's son-in-law Sayyid Kashmiri, did not attempt to emulate the Al-Khoei Foundation's work as a provider of education, nor did it attempt to engage with UK institutions to any great extent. Yousif al-Khoei attributes this to a wish not to duplicate work that is already being done. Relations are positive, he says, and the Al-Khoei Foundation works with the IAF by, for example, helping to run a family mediation service.[17] Yet my anonymous local guide says that the IAF's lack of local activity has attracted some private criticism from al-Sistani followers in London: 'Many feel that it simply exists as a liaison office to collect money, to distribute some books and maybe gather some of the Iraqi exiles for a little chat with some food.'

Perhaps because of this lack of emphasis on engagement with the wider community, a second al-Sistani British charity was founded in

2000. The Alulbayt Foundation, which operates from a large detached house on the same street as the Imam Ali Foundation, was set up with the assistance of Seyed Jawad Shahrestani, another son-in-law of al-Sistani, and his official representative in Iran.[18] In contrast to the Imam Ali Foundation, the Alulbayt Foundation made more effort to reach out to the wider community and to operate at least partly in English. In 2010 it was trying to find premises for a full-time school and was already running an English-language Saturday school for children, a creche and a library. It also organised special programmes of talks during religious festivals. Charitable obligations to the wider world were also met through, for example, providing help to orphans in Iraq.[19]

The Alulbayt Foundation was involved with the Islam and Citizenship Education Project, a British government-sponsored programme to teach citizenship values from an Islamic perspective.[20] But apart from this, it did not appear to be as well connected with the British political system as the Al-Khoei Foundation.

Shi'ite seminaries in Britain

Among the significant figures sent to the UK by Grand Ayatollah al-Khoei in 1989 was one of his former students, Ayatollah Dr Sayyid Fadhil al-Milani. As well as acting as the senior religious scholar at the Al-Khoei Foundation in Queen's Park, Dr al-Milani helped to establish a seminary, the International Colleges of Islamic Science (ICIS), which operates from Dollis Hill, North West London. The college teaches the traditional Islamic seminary (*hawza*) curriculum of Najaf and students can study up to PhD level by correspondence or at the college itself.

Dr al-Milani is probably the most prominent Shia scholar to represent the apolitical view of al-Khoei. But Dr al-Milani is wary of articulating that view too loudly in public, perhaps for fear of causing disunity. When asked to explain his position on the Guardianship of the Jurist during a BBC Radio interview he was reluctant to answer and would say only: 'The majority of Shia *fuqaha* [jurists] do not believe and do not support the theory unconditionally.'[21] According to one of his former students, Dr al-Milani is always careful to say that this is the view of 'most jurists' rather than to state his own opinion or to repeat the more forthright condemnations of his former teacher Grand Ayatollah al-Khoei.[22]

Dr al-Milani also does some teaching at another institution, the Iranian-sponsored Islamic College of Advanced Studies (ICAS) in Willesden. Established in 1998, ICAS offers an alternative *hawza* programme.

The former principal, Dr Saeed Bahmanpour, describes the *hawza* course as demanding, with the minimum period of study usually taking around eight years. As the course was only launched in 2004, it had not been completed by any ICAS students by 2010. Some ICAS *hawza* students had transferred to Qom, the main seat of Islamic learning in Iran, in the hope of finishing their studies there. ICAS therefore plays a fairly minor role in seminary education in Britain. Its main business is the provision of A level courses for students who want to study in an Islamic environment and it also runs a degree course in Islamic studies which is validated by Middlesex University.

For those who do not wish to spend eight years gaining the basic scholarly qualifications, the Al Mahdi Institute, a Shi'ite seminary in Birmingham, provides a fast track alternative. Founded by Sheikh Arif Abdulhussain, a Shi'ite scholar brought up in the UK, it offers students from Britain and overseas the chance to complete the curriculum in four years. According to the former principal, Shazim Hussayn, few of the students have any intention of becoming full-time clerics: 'Most want to do the course for reasons of personal piety.'[23] A British former student of the institute said that he and several of his peers used the course as a prelude to postgraduate study elsewhere and to prepare them for performing clerical duties in the community. Part-time, less-advanced courses are also offered.

Shazim Hussayn says that the college is largely funded through regular donations from 'non Middle East sources', which allows it to offer bursaries to all its students. In 2012 the institute paid over £2 million for the lease of a former Christian college, allowing it to move from premises above a shop in Balsall Heath to an attractive campus in Selly Oak. Although the precise source of the college's funding is not made public, the former principal says that the college fiercely guards its independence.[24]

The influence of the Islamic Republic of Iran

The Islamic College of Advanced Studies in Willesden receives the greater part of its funding from Iran.[25] The man who was until 2011 its principal, Dr Bahmanpour, is very much an admirer of the Iranian constitutional model.[26] Of the Iranian Islamic Republic he says, 'For an

Iranian, patriotic about their country, you couldn't get a better thing than what we have now.'[27]

Brought up in Iran, Dr Saeed Bahmanpour came to the UK as a student in the late 1970s, initially to study engineering at Queen Mary College before switching to sociology at the London School of Economics. Soon after he had arrived in the UK he met some Iranian Marxists who told him that that there was no god. He was shocked rather than persuaded by their atheism. It provoked him to embark on a journey of religious exploration, during which he came across the writings of Ali Shariati—an Iranian intellectual who fused revolutionary Marxist and Shi'ite ideas.[28]

Bahmanpour was impressed by Shariati's modernistic approach: 'He gave the sociological context to everything. It connected to me.' Bahmanpour was also inspired by the ideas of Ayatollah Khomeini, who was then exiled in Paris and thus close enough for Bahmanpour and a group of friends to pay a personal visit. Bahmanpour says it is difficult for Westerners to understand the charismatic appeal of Khomeini that he and many other young Iranians felt so powerfully: 'The first time I even just saw his picture it had that sort of pull.'[29]

In the UK, few Shi'ite institutions are strongly identified with the Islamic Republic of Iran. This is perhaps, as Dr Bahmanpour says, because many of the Iranians living in the UK are not particularly religious, due to the fact that some are dissidents while others have chosen to live in Britain precisely because it is free of the restrictions of an Islamic theocracy. Yet Dr Bahmanpour cautions against reading too much into the fact that most Shia in the UK, and even in Iran, are the followers of Grand Ayatollah al-Sistani—it is merely an indicator of their devotional practice, he says, and not necessarily their political affiliations.[30]

The British institution with the clearest ties to Grand Ayatollah Khomeini is the Islamic Centre of England, just south of Willesden in Maida Vale. The imam, Ayatollah Abdolhossein Moezi, is the representative in Britain of Iran's supreme leader, Ayatollah Ali Khamenei.[31]

The Islamic Republic of Iran's most significant attempt to spread its influence in Britain came via Press TV, a twenty-four hour English-language channel that was launched in 2007. An offshoot of the Iranian state broadcaster, it was a bold attempt at cultural diplomacy. Programmes were broadcast from studios in Tehran and London. With the emphasis on news and current affairs as opposed to religious programming, Press TV was a vehicle for Iranian influence rather than a Shi'ite channel as such. London-based presenters included Sunni Muslims such as the famous convert Yvonne Ridley and the left-wing MP George Galloway. Much airtime was given to championing the cause of the Palestinians. While this might have helped Press TV find a niche audience which was not exclusively Shi'ite, it alienated some within the Shia community: 'The more aware Shia recall that Hamas supported Saddam,' says one young Iraqi-born Shi'ite scholar. He describes those younger Shia of South Asian origin who admired the channel as being part of a 'naive trend' unlikely to be followed by Iraqis: 'If Saddam was the guy who killed your grandfather or your uncle you're not going to be all that keen about supporting Hamas. Where was the Muslim unity in the Saddam years?'[32]

Press TV's most serious setback came in January 2012 when the channel lost its UK broadcasting licence. The ban came after Ofcom, the regulator, carried out an investigation into the transmission of an interview with a *Newsweek* journalist imprisoned in Iran. The journalist complained that Press TV had broken the broadcasting code because the interview was recorded under duress: he said his captors had threatened him with execution unless he cooperated. Ofcom upheld the journalist's complaint. Furthermore, Ofcom's investigation revealed that the channel was under direct editorial control from Iran. It was Press TV's refusal to move editorial control to London that resulted in the ban.[33]

The Indian and Pakistani Shia—the hidden majority

'All these people are from different cities in India and Pakistan,' explains one of the congregation at the Idara-e-Jaaferiya, a Shia centre in Tooting, South London.[34]

In a Deobandi or Barelwi mosque in Britain one might expect to find a concentration of people from a particular district of India or from the same village in Pakistan or Bangladesh. But worshippers at the Tooting Idara can trace their origins back to a wide range of towns and cities. Some hale from Hyderabad and Lucknow in India, while others came to the UK from Karachi, Lahore and elsewhere in Pakistan. A shared language—Urdu—as well as a common religious identity has created this community.

'There is none of the biradari thing here,' says one of the Idara elders, referring to the Pakistani clan system which encourages marriages to close kin. Marriages here are often made across the Pakistan–India national divide.

The Khoja Shia Ithna'ashari—a mainly Gujarati-speaking Shia community—will not be found here in any great number. They have their own distinct identity and a separate network of mosques and centres.

Given the high profile of Iraqi and Iranian Shia institutions in Britain, it comes as something of a surprise to discover that away from the powerbase of North West London, it is Muslims of Indian and Pakistani origin who run over three-quarters of Britain's Shia mosques and Islamic centres.

'There are nine centres for the Iranians in this country, thirteen for the Arabs, nine for the Khojas and sixty-eight or sixty-nine for the Indian/Pakistani [Urdu-speaking] community,' according to Maulana Syed Ali Raza Rizvi, president of the Majlis E Ulama E Shia Europe, an organisation representing Shia scholars of mainly Pakistani origin.[35] He also knows of ten places in London and the Midlands where religious programmes are run for newly arrived Persian-speaking Hazara refugees from Afghanistan and Pakistan.

'The Pakistanis were the pioneers,' according to Maulana Rizvi, and South London was the first place they settled.

'It started in my basement,' explains Zainab, an elderly woman who worships at the Tooting Idara. From the early 1960s Shia Muslims were arriving in London from towns and cities scattered across India and Pakistan. The urge to gather as a community was particularly strong in the holy month of Muharram which the Shia dedicate to the remembrance of the martyrdom of the Prophet's grandson Hussain. Somehow word got round that the place to go was Zainab and her husband's basement.[36]

As numbers grew, the community hired halls in which to gather. A large house in Clapham was acquired but they outgrew that too. So in 1979 the trustees of the Idara-e-Jaaferiya bought their long term base, a former church in Tooting.[37] Further out into the South London suburbs, another group established the Muhammedi Trust in Kingston around the same time.[38] According to Shia scholar Syed Ali Raza Rizvi, there are seven South Asian Shia centres in South London, the latest of which is the Ahl ul Bayt Centre in Clapham which he agreed to take over after the original Iraqi management committee moved away.[39] Beyond this concentration in South London there are Indo-Pakistani Shia centres spread across the UK.

'They only know how to beat themselves and cry,' my anonymous guide to the Arab Shia districts of North West London told me dismissively. He was referring to the ritualised mourning and self-flagellation practised at gatherings to commemorate Shia martyrs. The suggestion that this practice is confined to the South Asian Shia is incorrect. So too is the implication that there is a lack of religious scholarship among the South Asian Shia. According to Maulana Rizvi, there are around seventy Pakistani and Indian Shia scholars in Europe, most of them based in the UK. Like their Middle Eastern equivalents, they have mainly been educated at seminaries in Najaf in Iraq, Qom in Iran and the Syrian capital Damascus. Maulana Rizvi himself studied under a scholar in Birmingham before obtaining a master's degree from one of the oldest seminaries in Qom. 'I always wanted to go to Najaf but I couldn't ... because of Saddam's time,' he says, 'Qom may be more advanced, stronger in many ways. But the spirituality is something different in Najaf.'[40]

A less textual, extremely emotional strand of South Asian Shi'ism can be found in Britain too but, according to Maulana Rizvi, it is a minority trend. The so-called *malang*—which in Urdu means 'crazies'—say they are crazy with love for their religion. But their ardour for the Shia martyrs is often accompanied by violently anti-Sunni rhetoric from populist Shia preachers. According to Maulana Rizvi, it is a trend which he regrets is spreading to the more educated and to non-South Asian Shia.

On the whole it is subtle cultural rather than major doctrinal differences which distinguish the Urdu speakers from the Arabs and Iranians.

At a gathering in the Tooting Idara to mark the death of one of the centre's founders, women visit a shrine dedicated to commemoration of the Prophet Muhammad's family, the Ahlul Bayt. A woman reads poetry melodically in Urdu. Mourners stand in prayer around a table upon which is placed a symbolic offering of food from the deceased's family.[41]

A survey of over 1,000 Muslim places of worship in the UK found that every Shia mosque or centre in the survey was open to women as well as men. Around a quarter of Sunni mosques in the survey had no prayer facilities for women.[42]

The walls of the shrine at the Tooting Idara are decorated with flags. Each flag (or *alam*) represents the battle standard of a Shi'ite martyr. The women gently touch the flags as a sign of respect. As is common in many South Asian Shia centres, along one side of the shrine are miniature replicas of holy buildings in places such as Najaf and Karbala, modelled in polished metal. Various other objects in the shrine are reminders of events in the Shia Muslim story: a water bag symbolises a time when the martyr Hussain and his family were deprived of drink for three days; a double-edged sword recalls Ali's weapon in battle; and each finger in a hand-shaped symbol represents a member of the Ahlul Bayt.

In common with other Shia prayer rooms, there are stacks of small clay discs. Worshippers place a disc (*turbah*) in front of them and touch with their foreheads as they bow in prayer. A member of the congregation explains that the disc she holds is made of clay from Karbala in Iraq, the place where Imam Hussain was martyred. 'It is better to pray on something natural,' she says.

The sermon is delivered in Urdu from the men's prayer hall and relayed via a television link to the women who sit in small groups on the floor in the adjoining hall. After some time, the tone of the preacher becomes more emotional. Many in the congregation then stand. The women raise one hand and start to tap their chests rhythmically and chant 'Ya Hussain!' [Oh Hussain!]. The action is a symbol of their empathy with Hussain and is known in Arabic as *matam*. As the preacher recites stories from the tragedy of Karbala, the chest-beating and chanting in the men's hall becomes louder. The men use alternate hands and more of a slap than a tap against the chest. A British Indian woman who is visiting from the Arab heartlands of North West London tells me that her sons prefer to worship here because 'they do the Pakistani *matam*'. The Iranians and Iraqis, she says, tap both hands simultaneously against their chests, while here the men use one hand after the other.

The most extreme form of *matam* involves men stripping to the waist and flaying their own backs until they bleed with a multi-bladed beater known as a *zanjeer*. The ritual takes place at the festival of Ashura, the tenth day of the month of Muharram when Shia Muslims commemorate the martyrdom of the Prophet Muhammad's grandson Hussain. Many of the scholars see the use of the *zanjeer* as a cultural practice for which there is no religious necessity.

Maulana Rizvi, the Pakistani scholar who runs the Ahl ul Bayt centre in Clapham, says that the *zanjeer* is not used on his premises.[43] But a quick search of YouTube shows videos of male worshippers flaying themselves in front of chanting crowds at Shia Islamic centres across the UK, including the Idara in Tooting. The videos show men performing this ritual either in car parks or in halls with plastic sheeting covering the floor—presumably because so much blood is spilt during the process.

One gets the impression that the Shia scholars would be happy if the use of the *zanjeer* was abandoned, but they know that those who practise the ritual are unlikely to be dissuaded.

Despite the linguistic and cultural differences, the Urdu-speaking Shia tend, like the majority of the Shia around the world, to view Grand Ayatollah al-Sistani in Najaf as the supreme living source of religious authority.

One British Asian worshipper at the Tooting Idara tells me that she thinks the Iranian Revolution had a profound effect on Shia Muslims in Britain in that it made them more aware of their religious identity and more conscious of their faith. She says that the revolution influenced her decision to start wearing the hijab and believes it is part of the reason that so many other South Asian Shia Muslims have done the same.

The Iranian-managed Islamic Centre of England in Maida Vale makes efforts to connect with Indo-Pakistani Shia by hosting events of particular relevance to them and running programmes in English rather than Farsi. But there is a long tradition among the Indo-Pakistanis of loyalty to the Najaf school of Iraq. The Idara in Tooting, for example, was set up in the 1960s by Indian and Pakistani followers of one of al-Sistani's predecessors.[44]

This affinity with Najaf was reinforced by Grand Ayatollah al-Khoei who, when he sent a team of emissaries to set up his foundation in London in the late 1980s, included on the first board of trustees clerics of Indian and Pakistani origin as well as a Khoja businessman, Mustafa Gokal.[45]

Despite the close ties and lack of doctrinal differences between the Al-Khoei Foundation and the Indo-Pakistani Shia, there is resentment among some of the South Asian leaders of the position that the Al-Khoei Foundation has assumed as the supposedly representative body of Shia Muslims in Britain. One Pakistani Shia elder told me that he felt that the leadership of the Al-Khoei Foundation had been imposed on his community by the government. 'Everything goes through Yousif al-Khoei,' he complained, '[but] they make us do all the work, organising the community.' In the foundation's defence, Yousif al-Khoei says he has done much to help the Urdu-speaking Shia leaders make connections outside their own community, promoting their participation, for example, in the Mosques and Imams National Advisory Board (MINAB).

MEDINA IN BIRMINGHAM, NAJAF IN BRENT

The Khoja Shia Ithna'ashari

Within the Shia community the Khojas are famed for their excellent administrative and leadership skills. 'They play a huge part in the community,' says my guide to Shia London, 'Very organised and "clean" with the money.'

The Khojas are a community of Shia Muslims who trace their roots back to Indian landowners known as Thakkers. In the fifteenth century, a group of Thakkers converted to a form of Ismaili Shi'ism. To distinguish themselves from the Hindu Thakkers they called themselves Khwaja or Khoja.

In the nineteenth century, the community split as some converted to the Twelver branch of Shi'ism. Around the same time, many Khojas began migrating from their main centres of population in Gujarat and Kutch to East Africa where they thrived as traders and administrators in the colonies of Britain and other European powers.

The British Empire connection meant that members of the Khoja Shia Ithna'ashari community often came to the UK as students or to work. The Khoja presence in Britain grew dramatically from 1972 when large numbers of Ugandan Asians began to arrive in the UK, after being expelled from the country by President Idi Amin. The families often came with nothing and had to stay in refugee centres set up in village halls. The British authorities helped the newcomers locate relatives already settled in Britain who might be able to look after them. The dispersal of the new arrivals meant that in towns and cities where there might have been just a small number of Khoja families, substantial new communities were established. There are now Khoja Ithna'ashari organisations—'jamaats'—in Chelmsford, Peterborough, Milton Keynes, Watford, Birmingham, Leicester, Fareham and London.

Even before Grand Ayatollah al-Khoei sent his emissaries to set up a foundation in the UK in the late 1980s, the Khojas had established a well-organised network of Shia mosques and centres in Britain.

They have umbrella organisations at European and international level: the Council of European Jamaats based in South London and the World Federation of Khoja Shia Ithna'ashari Muslim Communities, which is headquartered in a large property with extensive grounds in Stanmore on the outskirts of North West London.

At the Peterborough Jamaat, the coherence and organisational talents of the Khojas are clear to see. In 1978, just six years after being forced out of Uganda and having to start new lives in the UK, a group of Khojas here had built their own mosque. The success of the Peterborough community attracted more Khoja families, many of which arrived from Tanzania and elsewhere in East Africa. In 2001, the new imam, Mulla Mohammed Kassamali, arrived from Nairobi and decided that most of the sermons should be in English rather than Urdu. By 2008, there were around 250 Khoja families in the community and plans to spend over £2 million extending the mosque on to an adjoining site.[46]

The imam describes the congregation as 'neither affluent nor poor'. The early immigrants were mainly non-professionals. Some of the women were schoolteachers, while others found work in local factories. The next wave opted more for the professions. The new generation, both male and female, are branching out away from science and accountancy into a broader range of careers including journalism and academia.

Although the Khoja communities have a hierarchical structure, the elders are prepared to allow young people to assume positions of responsibility. In Peterborough the imam allows the youth wing to run itself: 'They can do anything within the boundaries of the religion.' One of its former members, Abbas Ismail, was acting as a spokesperson for the Khojas' World Federation at the age of thirty, a role in which he oversaw the mainly young staff and volunteers in one of the departments at its Stanmore headquarters.[47]

The total Khoja population worldwide is estimated to be just 120,000: 'No more than a medium sized town,' according to Abbas Ismail, 'this has necessitated good organisation, raising income and being bound together.' Khojas tend to marry other Khojas, often finding partners in Khoja communities in Canada, the United States or Africa. In Britain, some non-Khoja Shia have married into Khoja families. The children of such marriages are considered Khoja if brought up within the community. In some areas, such as Chelmsford, the local KSIMC affiliate is made up of Pakistanis, Afghanis and Iranians, as well as Khojas. The incorporation of these new ethnic groups has helped to ensure the longer-term viability of the local jamaat.[48]

The Khoja Ithna'ashari have their own seminary in Nairobi,[49] and Peterborough Imam Mulla Kassamali was once its director. But, the imam explains, 'Khoja isn't a theological distinction.' Like the Urdu speakers, the vast majority of Khoja Shia Ithna'asharis follow Grand Ayatollah al-Sistani in Iraq. Abbas Ismail of the World Federation, however, cautions against overemphasising adherence to al-Sistani: 'Grand Ayatollah al-Sistani does not dominate the consciousness of the ordinary Khoja in all aspects of life.' The Khojas have their own structures and decision-making processes as far as their own social affairs are concerned. Abbas Ismail says, 'We would definitely look to Sistani on matters of Islamic law and other relevant areas. But he is a leader not the leader for everything.' According to Ismail, the late Mulla Asghar—the Khojas' worldwide leader who moved to the UK from Kenya in 1973—is seen as a figurehead. Even after his death in 2000, Khojas often still ask themselves 'Would Mulla have done it this way?'[50]

The Shia Ithna'asharia Community of Middlesex—Khoja modernisers

The religious orthodoxy of the Khoja network and its cautious attitude towards incorporating other cultures is something which one small group of Khojas has decided to reject. At the Shia Ithna'asharia Community of Middlesex (SICM), also known as Mahfil-e-Ali, the leadership takes a more liberal approach to religion, at least by Islamic standards. At an evening talk held in their prayer hall in North Harrow, the organisers do not enforce the sort of gender segregation seen in the vast majority of mosques in Britain. Men and women sit in only vaguely distinct groupings on the floor and at the front of the hall a young couple sit together. Several of the women have not covered their hair. Only when they rise for the evening prayer at the end of the meeting is a curtain pulled between the sexes, and the women without hijab grab sheets from a box marked 'prayer garments' to cover their heads. Sunni women pray alongside the Shia, observing their own distinct ritual.[51] The Kuwaiti imam who comes most nights to lead the prayer thinks that they are too liberal. 'But I only lead the prayers,' he says.[52] The rules are made by the committee of young professionals which runs the centre, not him. Even the older generation of trustees who control the funds support the liberal approach.

The older generation here tended to recognise Ayatollah Fadlallah as their marja—a political and religious leader based in Lebanon until his death in 2010. Some in the younger generation do not follow anyone and even question the practice of *taqlid* (taking a single marja as a source of emulation): 'Islam is a very simple religion and most Muslims have a good basic knowledge of it. The sheikhs all have their own websites now so if there is something you don't know, you can always look it up on the internet or send an email asking for advice,' says a member of the youth-ful executive committee.[53]

That same young committee member is engaged to a convert from Scandinavia and says that marriages to non-Khoja Shia and even Sunnis are common in this liberal Khoja community.

The talks programme is eclectic and highly intellectual. One night the book group is discussing the writing of American liberal political philoso-pher Michael Sandel. The following evening a young academic is giving a short talk after the screening of an art house film.

An interest in philosophical ideas is considered essential by orthodox Shi'ite thinkers. However, the SICM has at times been regarded by the mainstream Shia leaders as too open-minded and too indiscreet in its willingness to air internal debates. In 2006, the SICM's youth group hosted a series of talks by Abdulaziz Sachedina, an Islamic scholar and academic who had been banned from lecturing on religion by the Khojas' worldwide body and by other Sistani-following congregations.

In the late 1990s, Sachedina fell out with the Khoja leadership in Canada, where he was based, after delivering a number of lectures in which he explained that his theological research had caused him to reject certain orthodox religious practices and doctrinal positions. He argued that Christianity, Judaism and Islam should be regarded as equally true and he challenged the idea that a woman's testimony should be worth half that of a man's in contractual disputes and other matters. He also made allegations, disputed by eminent Shia theologians, about the late Grand Ayatollah al-Khoei's views on slavery. Grand Ayatollah al-Sistani was asked to become involved in the dispute and issued a statement advising that Sachedina should not be invited to speak to the faithful nor should he be consulted on matters of belief.

According to Sachedina's account of a showdown between himself and al-Sistani in 1998, the censure was issued because al-Sistani concluded that some of Sachedina's views were incorrect; moreover, by publicly criticising one of the opinions of the late Grand Ayatollah al-Khoei, Sachedina was breaching a social convention among seminarians not to create confusion among the faithful by airing disagreements in public.[54]

The SICM youth have also hosted AbdolKarim Soroush, another controversial Shi'ite intellectual. Soroush, originally an enthusiast for the Islamic Revolution in his native Iran, fell out with the regime over his liberal Islamic theories.

Unlike the other Khoja Ithna'asharia jamaats, the SICM never became an affiliate of the Khojas' umbrella organisation, the World Federation. A founder member of the SICM says that they remained independent because their open membership policy went against the Khoja jammat system.[55]

The isolation of these liberal modernisers and freethinkers reveals as much about the strictures and authoritarianism of mainstream Shi'ism as it says about the SICM.

The Arab Shia and the Dawa Party

At the Dar Al Islam Foundation in the Shi'ite heartland of Cricklewood, everyone arriving for Friday prayers is speaking in Arabic.

The man in charge of the office inside the foundation says that the mostly Iraqi congregation are from Najaf, Basra and Baghdad.[56] The Shia from Karbala and the Lebanese, he explains, have their own places of worship nearby.

But the Dar Al Islam Foundation's significance has more to do with its political connections than its sub-ethnic loyalties. It is closely associated with the Islamic Dawa Party, the leading partner in the State of Law coalition led by the Iraqi Prime Minister Nouri al-Maliki. Many of the leading figures at the Dar Al Islam Foundation left to pursue political careers in Iraq after the fall of Saddam Hussein in 2003. Among the regular worshippers during the Saddam era were Dr Walid al-Hilli, a senior member of the Iraqi Dawa Party, and Abdel Falah al-Sudani, who went on to become a trade minister under Nouri al-Maliki. The links to the party remain even though some of its leading exiles have left the UK. Haider al-Abadi, a senior Dawa Party member in Iraq, was still an official trustee of the charity which runs the foundation in 2010.

Hanging on the wall inside the main office at the Dar Al Islam Foundation are framed photographs of the Dawa Party's spiritual guides, Grand Ayatollah Mohammed Baqir al-Sadr and Grand Ayatollah Mohammed Hussein Fadlallah.[57] Ayatollah al-Sadr was the party's living inspiration from its foundation in 1957 until his execution by Saddam in 1980. Aytollah Fadlallah took over as the movement's leading cleric until his death in 2010 (although whether or not he actually was a member of the party is a matter of dispute).

According to Saeed Shehabi, a former Dawa Party activist exiled in Britain since the 1970s, al-Sadr inspired Shi'ites with a vision of a modern and more just society governed by Islamic principles: 'The details of how that would work were not discussed—we thought that we would work that out later.'[58]

Shehabi admired al-Sadr's pioneering work on Islamic banking and economics and was also excited by his more abstract philosophical ideas: 'He used mathematics and probability theory to show that God's existence could be proved by statistical methods. He read Marx and Hegel and contemporary philosophers and produced Islamic doctrines in philosophy.'[59]

Al-Sadr's vision, according to Saeed Shehabi, particularly resonated with those who were governed by dictatorships; it appealed not just to Shia in Saddam's Iraq but also to Shia governed by unelected rulers in the Gulf states of Bahrain, Kuwait and Saudi Arabia. Activists from Afghanistan and Lebanon were recruited too.[60]

These individuals shared Grand Ayatollah Khomeini's anti-secularist, Islamist agenda.

While there were various schools of thought within the party, under Fadlallah's guidance the Dawa was steered towards an ideology that was subtly different from that of Khomeini: the ambition should be to create a state where elected laypeople governed using Islamic principles, rather than one in which sovereignty lay in the hands of a cleric appointed for life.

Fadlallah's refusal to endorse the concept of the Guardianship of the Jurist was also one cause of a rift between him and Hezbollah, the Lebanese political party and militia group which he had advised in its early years. Hezbollah adopted Grand Ayatollah Khomeini, and then his successor Grand Ayatollah Khamenei, as the supreme source of emulation. Fadlallah by contrast recognised the more orthodox Grand Ayatollah al-Sistani as the supreme source of emulation. In 1995 Fadlallah openly challenged the Guardianship of the Jurist concept and declared that he himself was a source of emulation.[61]

In Britain, the Dawa movement had its roots in the Muslim Youth Association (MYA), originally a club for Arab, South Asian and Iranian Shia students.

The Muslim Youth Association was founded as an apolitical organisation. But in the 1970s the membership was becoming increasingly politicised as it discovered the leading ideologues of Islamic governance. Apart from the writings of the Dawa Party's Ayatollah Mohammed Baqir al-

Sadr, there were radical ideas coming from Ayatollah Khomeini and the Iranian intellectual Ali Shariati. Through their friendships with the Sunni Islamists who controlled the Federation of Student Islamic Societies, MYA members also became aware of the ideas of the Muslim Brotherhood. The Dawa's spiritual guide, al-Sadr, encouraged followers to see the Muslim Brotherhood as a model to emulate and recommended the writings of its leading thinkers.[62] Saeed Shehabi felt that the Brothers were kindred spirits: 'Organisationally I did not become a Muslim Brotherhood man but I was with them and they liked me.'[63]

By 1977 the MYA was splitting along ethnic lines. Some of the Arab members found the Iranians wary and secretive. 'When some Iraqi brothers sensed that the Iranians had some political thing, they started to become edgy,' recalls Saeed Shehabi.[64]

The Iranians, with some help from the Khojas, set up their own centre, known as Kanoon Towhid, in Hammersmith. They also became affiliated to a revolutionary vanguard movement of Iranian students in Europe.[65]

The leading Khoja members of the MYA became the freethinkers behind the Shia Ithna'ashari Community of Middlesex (a fact which explains the tendency among the older members of that community to follow Ayatollah Fadlallah).

The MYA, which had originally operated in English, switched to Arabic to reflect the exclusively Arab composition of the membership.

Although the different ethnic groups were never reunited in one organisation, collaboration between them was later resumed. Most of the Iranian students who had split from MYA returned home after the revolution and were replaced with a younger generation with whom there was no animosity. Monthly meetings, conducted in English, brought the Arab, Iranian, Khoja and Pakistani students and graduates together. To smooth relations further, the Iranians were allowed to keep a library in the Arab students' centre.[66]

Saeed Shehabi became a member of the Dawa Party's leadership in Europe in 1978 and served until 1985. Originally from Bahrain, he was opposed to the rule of the Sunni royal family over the Shia majority state. He says his objection was not sectarian—he would accept a Sunni ruler who governed fairly and in the interests of the people. But there was no opportunity to remove the hereditary rulers democratically, so the Dawa's strategy, according to Shehabi, was 'to prepare the cadres, to try to organise so we were strong enough to make a move against the regime'.[67] The revolutionary threat that the party posed to those in power meant that the Dawa had to operate as a clandestine organisation. According to Shehabi, the government of Bahrain was not aware of the Dawa's activities until 1983: 'Then word came to me from Bahrain: "Don't come home because your name was mentioned in an interrogation. Your party links have been exposed."'[68]

During the same period the Dawa Party in Iraq was subject to brutal suppression, with many activists being executed or fleeing the country in the 1980s. Some Dawa activists took refuge in Iran where they formed a breakaway group—the Supreme Council for the Islamic Revolution in Iraq (SCIRI)—which recognised Grand Ayatollah Khomeini rather than Ayatollah Fadlallah as their spiritual guide. Many came to Britain, making it a base from which the Dawa and other anti-Saddam activists campaigned.

From London the Dawa published an Iraqi newsletter, *The Dawa Chronicle*, and a separate publication for the party's Bahraini supporters. Saeed Shehabi edited the Bahraini newsletter and co-edited its Iraqi equivalent.[69]

Another wave of refugees arrived following the failed Shia uprising in southern Iraq in 1991. Other significant figures that had spent the 1980s in exile in Iran relocated to London where they had easy access to English-language and Arab media. Among them was the future prime minister of Iraq, Ibrahim Jaaferi, who became the Dawa Party's spokesman in London.

Operating separately from London's Dawa movement—but with an overlap in personnel—is the Abrar Islamic Foundation, a community centre for Arab Shia. Religious advice is provided at the foundation by the same imam who leads the Friday prayers at the Dar Al Islam Foundation in Cricklewood.[70] The Abrar Islamic Foundation operates from the relatively luxurious Abrar House—a £3 million office block and meeting hall off Edgware Road in central London. According to Saeed Shehabi, the funds used to buy the building came from the sale of property originally bought for them decades earlier by a businessman from the Gulf.[71]

The Muslim Youth Association, which in the 1970s brought together Shia students for apolitical gatherings, became focused on Iraq and effectively turned into an arm of the Dawa Party.[72] Its obvious legacy is the contribution it has made to developing the political consciousness of those who went on to play a role in the government of post-Saddam Iraq. But in its more ethnically inclusive early days, the MYA also helped to nurture some non-Iraqis who went on to become influential activists in Britain and elsewhere. Among them were, most notably, the Iranian liberal Islamic intellectual AbdolKarim Soroush; the editor of the UK's first Muslim newspaper *The Muslim News*, Ahmed Versi (a Khoja member of the MYA who in the 1970s edited, with Saeed Shehabi's help, its monthly magazine *Islamic Echo*); and Mohamed Iqbal Asaria, a Khoja member of the Muslim Council of Britain's leadership team who, as an economist and accountant, advised the Bank of England on Islamic finance and was awarded a CBE in 2005.

Many of the friendships made in the 1970s have endured, helping to maintain links between activists across different Shia ethnic groups. Connections have also been maintained with some of the Sunni Islamists who ran the Federation of Student Islamic Societies and other Islamist youth organisations. On a visit to Abrar House in 2013, I find Saeed Shehabi talking politics with Dr Kamal Helbawy, the leading Muslim Brotherhood figure who once ran the World Assembly of Muslim Youth. It transpires that Shehabi and Helbawy go back a long way: another friendship forged through the youthful Islamic activism of the 1970s and one, intriguingly, which is still going strong in the more sectarian era of the Syrian civil war and the Arab Spring.

The British Shia and the Iraq War

Less than a month after the 9/11 attacks, Prime Minister Tony Blair convened a meeting of Britain's faith leaders at 10 Downing Street. The first retaliatory bombs were being dropped on Afghanistan and the phrase 'war on terror' was already common currency. But many Muslims in Britain and around the world felt that US and British military actions were tantamount to a war against Islam. The faith leaders' summit was an attempt to change perceptions, and it appeared to have been a success: a bearded, turbaned Muslim cleric and the chief rabbi flanked the then Archbishop of Canterbury George Carey as he declared after the meeting, 'we are quite clear this is not, and must not, be seen as a confrontation between religions or with a particular religion'.[73]

The Muslim leader at the archbishop's side was Abdul Majid al-Khoei, son of the late Grand Ayatollah al-Khoei and one of the trustees of the Al-Khoei Benevolent Foundation.

While a representative of the Muslim Council of Britain urged the government to attempt 'further diplomatic moves to resolve the situation', Abdul Majid al-Khoei not only endorsed action against the Taliban in Afghanistan but was sanguine about the prospect of an invasion of Iraq too.

Many Shi'ites in southern Iraq were disappointed that the defeat of Saddam Hussein after his invasion of Kuwait had not been followed by Western support for their uprising against the dictator.

But Blair was mistaken if he thought that most Shi'ites in Britain were as accepting of his plans as Majid al-Khoei was.

Although many Shia in Britain wanted to see the fall of Saddam, the issue of whether or not they should support a Western invasion was the subject of passionate debate within the community. Those of non-Iraqi origin were the least likely to support an invasion. The Khojas were mostly opposed. The Khoja governing bodies—the World Federation and the Council of European Jamaats—issued statements opposing invasion and many took part in demonstrations led by the Muslim Association of Britain (MAB).[74]

Not even all the Iraqis were supportive of Western plans to invade. In Britain, Dawa Party supporters took part in the anti-war demonstrations after their spiritual guide, Grand Ayatollah Muhammad Hussein Fadlallah, spoke against a Western military invasion. (Although some of the Dawa Party's natural supporters were pro-invasion and temporarily switched allegiance to Sistani.) Former Dawa Party activist Saeed Shehabi says he wanted to see Saddam removed but not under the pretext of his alleged possession of weapons of mass destruction: 'I would have preferred to see Saddam indicted for human rights abuses by the International Criminal Court, just as they did for Omar Bashir in Sudan.'[75]

Despite their opposition to President Bush's plans for a military attack, the exiled Islamists of the Dawa were involved in power-sharing negotiations, led by the United States and held in London, even before the first bomb had been dropped.[76] And as soon as Saddam was toppled, those exiles with ambitions to enter politics returned home to take up positions of influence in the new Iraq.

Apart from those members of the Dar Al Islam Foundation in Cricklewood who took up influential positions in the Dawa Party and in government, some from the foundation joined the more secularist alliance of Ayad Allawi and 'some were with others', according to one of the foundation's managers.[77]

Ayatollah Sayyid Muhammad Bahrul Uloom, the former imam of the Ahl ul Bayt centre in Clapham and a moderate cleric not aligned to any party, became a president of the Iraqi Governing Council. One of his sons also became the oil minister.

Hamid al-Bayati, a spokesman in London for the more pro-Iranian Supreme Council for the Islamic Revolution in Iraq (SCIRI), became deputy minister of foreign affairs and subsequently his country's permanent representative at the UN.

Majid al-Khoei, the cleric who was thought to have encouraged Blair in his plans for an invasion, was murdered just seven days after returning to his home city of Najaf.

The militant Shia faction, the Mahdi Army commanded by Moqtada al-Sadr, was suspected of al-Khoei's assassination. 'I think it was more a case of Moqtada refusing to save him rather than ordering his death,' says Omar Ali Grant, a British Muslim convert who claims to have fought in al-Sadr's militia against the Americans in 2004.[78]

Grant, who now regards his past support for al-Sadr as a mistake, says his actions were atypical of British Shia: 'In England there are no Sadrists. The Iraqi Shia in London are mainly pro the Iraqi government. They support the Dawa Party or they support SCIRI.'[79]

Relations with British Sunnis

At an institutional level there is dialogue but not unity between the Sunnis and the Shia.

The Khojas' umbrella bodies, the World Federation and the Council of European Jamaats, are affiliated to the Muslim Council of Britain (MCB), as is the Iranian-backed Islamic Centre of England. But the Shia do not play an influential role in the Muslim Council of Britain, and in 2010 the MCB angered Shia Muslim leaders by defending a controversial Indian preacher, Zakir Naik, who was known for his anti-Shia rhetoric and had been banned from the UK by the Home Office. The Al-Khoei Foundation, the World Federation, and the Council of European Jamaats issued a joint press release condemning the MCB's stance.[80]

Yet at other times the Al-Khoei Foundation and the MCB have come together for the sake of Muslim unity. When a Shia Muslim was physically attacked by jihadi Salafis in Edgware Road in May 2013, Yousif al-Khoei rang the MCB to ask for their support. Within a few hours the general secretary of the MCB, Farooq Murad, had arrived at the Al-Khoei Foundation's offices to embrace the victim. The MCB also issued a statement acknowledging the sectarian motivation for the attack and condemning it unequivocally. 'That defused the whole sectarian tension,' says Yousif al-Khoei.[81]

The Al-Khoei Foundation has also played a part in addressing Shi'ite sectarianism: when a controversial Shia cleric called Sheikh Yasser al-Habib was accused of broadcasting anti-Sunni rhetoric on his UK-based Fadav TV network, Yousif al-Khoei challenged him to sign up to a voluntary code of conduct requiring Islamic broadcasters to refrain from insulting other religious groups.[82]

On the Mosques and Imams National Advisory Board (MINAB) the Shia are on at least an equal footing with Sunni members, although the largest Sunni network in Britain—the Deobandis—has declined to participate.

The Islamic Human Rights Commission—founded by Massoud Shadjareh, a prominent Shi'ite of Iranian origin—brings together Sunni and Shia Muslims to raise awareness of issues such as the persecution of Muslims abroad, changes to UK law which they believe disproportionately affect Muslims and the situation of the Palestinians.

Sectarianism is an acute problem for Shia Muslims in Pakistan. Bomb attacks on Shia areas and places of worship are a frequent occurrence. Human Rights Watch (HRW) estimated that in 2012 at least 325 Shia Muslims were killed in targeted attacks in Pakistan. HRW blamed the Pakistani Taliban and other Sunni militant groups linked to the Pakistani military and intelligence agencies.[83]

According to the British Pakistani Shia scholar Maulana Syed Ali Raza Rizvi, there are few signs of this sort of violence being replicated in Britain. The only significant incident of which he is aware is the burning down of a hall attached to a Shia centre in Birmingham in 2004.[84] He suspected a sectarian motivation, as the centre had received anonymous warnings after some local Sunni Muslims converted to Shi'ism.[85]

As far as contact with the non-Shia groups in Britain is concerned, Maulana Rizvi says he is in touch with some of the Barelwi scholars and 'even the Deobandis sometimes'.[86] If he wants to talk to any of the Sunni scholars he will simply telephone them. They will contact each other on issues of common concern, such as the offence they felt at the publication of cartoons of the Prophet Muhammad in a Danish newspaper in 2005. Maulana Rizvi says that he also meets Muslims from other denominations through an interfaith group, the Christian Muslim Forum.

Relations between the Shia and the Barelwis are warmer than those between the Shia and the Deobandis. 'The Barelwi are closer to the Shia because they have regard for the mystics,' according to Dr Sayyid Ali Murtaza Zaidi, a Shia leader from Pakistan who was addressing Shia audiences across Britain to raise awareness of sectarian violence in 2012.[87] In Pakistan, almost all the militant attacks on Shia Muslims (and Barelwis) have been carried out by Deobandi groups.[88] However, Shia scholar Dr Zaidi was keen to emphasise that not all Deobandi Muslims should be assumed to be anti-Shia: 'There are tens of groups in the Taliban. Most are simple people working for Islam and they were befooled.'[89]

On university campuses, the Shia students often operate an alternative Islamic society—usually known as the Ahlul Bayt Society or 'ABSoc'. In 2011 there were twenty-three Ahlul Bayt Societies operating in UK universities.

Since 2009, the ABSocs have had an umbrella organisation—the Muslim Student Council (MSC)—to coordinate at a national level. Among the reasons given on the MSC's website for its existence were: the need to counter the influence of Wahhabi-influenced Islamic societies on campus; to 'raise the standards of political activism' among Muslims; and to prevent students being pulled into 'mainstream secular lifestyles based on "drinking, dancing and partying."'[90]

Conclusion

The most striking feature of Britain's Shia community is the lack of influence that the Islamic Republic of Iran exerts over it, despite all of its resources. To a certain extent this is due to the secular nature of most ordinary Iranians living in Britain. But the more important factor is that the religiously observant among the mainly South Asian and Arab Shia Muslims of the UK tend to regard Grand Ayatollah al-Sistani of Najaf as the leader of Shi'ites worldwide, rather than Grand Ayatollah Khamenei.

The fact that Najaf school secularism has triumphed over Tehran's Islamism will be something of a relief to a British government which is worried about Muslim radicalisation at home, and which views Iran as a diplomatic threat.

The Al-Khoei Foundation's position as the 'go to guys' of the Shia community has been justified by the fact that most observant Shia in Britain are in accord with its Najaf school loyalties. If anything threatens the Al-Khoei Foundation's position it is probably ethnic rather than doctrinal differences. Although the foundation has, from its inception, incorporated leading figures from the Khoja and Urdu-speaking Shia communities, it is perceived by many as Iraqi-controlled and therefore unrepresentative of the majority of practising Shia in Britain. But the Al-Khoei Foundation has managed to maintain its position as the most prominent Shia organisation in Britain, in large part because it is highly skilled at the sort of networking and public relations work needed to build relationships with the government, the media and other faith communities. Until the leadership of the Urdu-speaking community decides to raise its profile outside Shia circles it will remain, like the Twelfth Imam, potentially powerful but hidden from view.

THE ISMAILIS

THE DAWOODI BOHRAS AND THE FOLLOWERS
OF THE AGA KHAN

The Ismailis make up no more than 2 per cent of the UK's Muslim population. But their resources and influence within Britain are out of proportion to their numbers. Furthermore, they have an important place in Islamic history, and one Ismaili sect has as its leader the intriguing figure of the Aga Khan.

There are two branches of the Ismaili faith that have a significant presence in Britain, with that led by the Aga Khan (the Nizari Ismaili tradition) being the largest. Estimates of the Nizari population of Britain vary widely from 10,000 to 50,000.[1] The other Ismaili tradition with a significant presence in the UK is that of the Dawoodi Bohras, which is led by a spiritual leader based in Mumbai. They form a community which estimates having around 6,000 adherents in Britain.

The Nizaris and the Bohras express their Muslim identities in very different ways. The Bohras display more of the outward signs that have come to be associated with a Muslim identity: the men are mainly bearded and the women often wear a distinctive form of hijab, and through a network of mosques and seminaries the Bohras' leader propagates a textual version of Islam. The Nizaris, by contrast, have no seminaries; dress codes reflect the norms of the societies in which followers live; and in the Aga Khan the Nazaris have a spiritual leader who is a businessman and philanthropist rather than a full-time cleric. But the two groups also have a great deal in common: in Britain both are dominated by East African Asians and followers are predominantly middle class. Most strikingly, both groups show that it is possible to be loyal to the leader of a religious diaspora while simultaneously maintaining a strong sense of patriotism towards Britain.

Who are the Ismailis?

The Ismailis are Shia Muslims in that they believe that the rightful successor to the Prophet Muhammad was his son-in-law and cousin, Ali, and thereafter only direct descendants of the Prophet were entitled to become Imam—the leader of the Muslim community. The Shia split over the issue of succession in the eighth century, following the death of the fifth Imam. The Ismailis recognised Ismail as their sixth Imam, while the followers of what subsequently became the majority 'Twelver' branch of the Shi'ite faith followed a rival successor.

The Ismailis were at their most powerful in the tenth century when they established the Fatimid state. During the period of Fatimid rule, the Ismaili Imam became the head of an empire which ruled over North Africa and Egypt, the Hijaz, Sicily and parts of the Levant. The Fatimids became the custodians of the holy cities of Mecca and Medina. In their capital Cairo they founded Al Azhar, the most prestigious seat of Islamic scholarship. However, in 1094, after nearly 200 years in power, a dispute over who should succeed as Imam occurred and the Ismailis split into two factions: the Nizari Ismaili branch, whose Imam would later go by the title Aga Khan, and the Mustali branch, of which the Dawoodi Bohras are part. This split marked the beginning of the end of the Fatimid Caliphate. Under Mustali rule, the caliphate lost the city of Jerusalem and other territory to the Crusaders. In 1171 what remained of the Fatimid Empire finally fell to Sunni Muslim warriors led by Saladin.[2]

The Nizari branch of the Ismailis founded their own state based around a mountain fort at Alamut in Persia. The Nizaris' castles and their state were eventually destroyed by the Mongol invaders. Accounts of the Nizari state's 150-year existence tend to be based more on legend than history and portray the Nizaris as a militant group responsible for political assassinations. The questionable myth has it that young Nizari men were intoxicated with hashish and taken into a secret garden to give them a foretaste of the paradise which awaited them if they lost their lives carrying out the assassination of a Nizari enemy. The hashish-intoxicated killers were called 'hashishins' and this, so the disputed theory goes, is the origin of the term assassin.[3] Dr Farhad Daftary of the Institute of Ismaili studies traces the popularisation of assassin myths back to European Crusader propagandists, and points out that none of the variants of these myths can be found in Muslim accounts recorded around that time.[4]

The Nizari Ismailis today

The Nizari Ismailis are certainly unusual, not least because their Imam, the Aga Khan, does not fit the stereotypes of an Islamic leader.

His Highness Prince Karim Aga Khan IV is best known to the British public as a billionaire race horse-owner. But to the Nizari Ismaili Muslims around the world he is a spiritual successor to the Prophet Muhammad.

The Aga Khan is the most European of the Islamic figureheads: a British passport-holder, he lives in France and Switzerland and speaks fluent English and French. When his photograph appears in the British press he usually has the appearance of a debonair individual wearing a suit and tie. His grandmother was an Italian ballet dancer, his mother an English aristocrat and his stepmother was the Hollywood actress Rita Hayworth.

To understand the Aga Khan's claim to authority, we have to go back to the origins of the Shi'ite branch of Islam.

The majority branch of Shia Muslims (the so-called 'Twelvers') believe that the twelfth Imam to lead the Muslim community after the death of the Prophet Muhammad became hidden from human sight, since which time they have been awaiting his return. However, the Ismaili Nizaris believe that the line of living Imams has continued unbroken since the seventh century and that Aga Khan IV is their forty-ninth Imam. Only a very small proportion of Muslims recognise the Aga Khan's leadership: his followers throughout the world are thought to number 15 million, which would represent just under 1 per cent of the world's total Muslim population. In parts of the Islamic world there are enclaves where the Nizari Ismaili followers of the Aga Khan are in the majority: for example, in the Pamir Mountains of Tajikistan where, according to one report, virtually every home and business has a portrait of the Aga Khan on the wall,[5] or in the Hunza region of northern Pakistan.[6] But in no nation do followers of the Aga Khan make up more than a small percentage of the population.

The Aga Khan now recognises communities of Nizari Ismailis in Afghanistan, Tajikistan, East Africa, Pakistan, India, China, Malaysia, Portugal, France, the UK, Canada, Bangladesh, Australia, New Zealand, Papua New Guinea, Iran, Syria and the United States.

The Aga Khan regards himself as responsible for the Nizaris' material welfare as well as their spiritual leadership. 'An imam is not expected to withdraw from everyday life. On the contrary, he's expected to protect his community and contribute to their quality of life,' he told *Vanity Fair* magazine in a rare interview.[7] The Imam will make contingency plans for communities in parts of the world where their safety might be threatened. He will provide financial assistance to those, like the Ismailis ejected from East Africa in the 1970s, who find themselves needing help to start new lives in a foreign country.

Much of the Aga Khan's time is spent travelling the world to visit his followers. These visits are often combined with a meeting with the local head of state, government ministers or royalty: between January 2010 and December 2011, for example, the Aga Khan met with the emir of Qatar, the Prince of Wales, the wife of President Mubarak of Egypt, the prime minister of Canada and the presidents of Tajikistan, Afghanistan, the Kyrgyz Republic, Kenya and Mozambique.

The Aga Khan has no state—yet he is treated like a king. The title Aga Khan was originally bestowed on Prince Karim's great-great-grandfather by the shah of Persia in 1834. When the first Aga Khan fell out with the shah and fled to colonial India, the British honoured him with the prefix 'His Highness'. It is a title which the British have granted to all his successors.

In India, the first Aga Khan assumed the leadership of the Shia Ismaili Muslim community there, dealing on its behalf with the British. Within that community were a large group known as Khojas—ethnic Indians whose ancestors had been converted centuries earlier by Ismailis who had abandoned the Middle East following the fall of the Fatimid Empire. After a legal dispute over tithes, many of the Khojas converted to Twelver Shi'ism, but a large number remained loyal.

It was during the Imamate of the third Aga Khan that the relationship between the British and the Nizari Ismailis developed significantly. Aga

Khan III was born in British India in 1877. He inherited his title as a boy following the death of his father in 1885. After that he was sent to England where he became a friend of Queen Victoria and the Prince of Wales. In India the Aga Khan used his speeches and writing to promote support for the British Empire and its monarchy.

The Aga Khan's support proved to be particularly useful during the First World War. The British government feared a rebellion by Muslims living under their authority in India, after the Ottoman caliph sided with Germany. The caliph was regarded by many Sunni Muslims as the most important Islamic leader in the world and one who had the authority under religious law to authorise a jihad. While some of the Deobandi Muslim leaders of India were making contact with the caliph's officials and secretly seeking authorisation to launch a jihad against the British in India, the Aga Khan was urging his own followers and the wider Muslim community of India that it was in their best interests to remain loyal to Britain. Although the Ismaili leader at times felt it necessary to berate British ministers for ignoring Muslim sensibilities, he expressed a deep patriotism towards the empire, speaking shortly after the outbreak of war of 'India's desire to share the responsibilities, no less than the privileges, of membership of this great Empire.'[8]

Aga Khan III was also a modernising Imam. He declared that women need not wear the veil and that his followers should, while giving due regard to modesty, adopt the dress of the society in which they lived. He also put great emphasis on the need for both men and women to be educated.

It was during the reign of Aga Khan III that the position of Imam became linked in the public's mind with fabulous wealth. In 1936, to mark his fiftieth year as Imam, the Aga Khan was presented with his weight in gold at a ceremony carried out in Bombay in front of 30,000 followers. Dr Shams Vellani of the Institute of Ismaili Studies points out that such ceremonies had no religious symbolism but were rooted in India's feudal traditions of social welfare and were used as a means of raising money for charitable purposes, such as providing hospitals and schools.[9]

His Highness Prince Karim Aga Khan IV succeeded to the title at the age of twenty following the death of his grandfather in 1957. The title skipped a generation, passing over the fourth Aga Khan's father Prince Aly Khan. Once a well-known socialite, Prince Aly had, even according to a historian from the Institute of Ismaili Studies, 'led a controversial private life'.[10] The succession was revealed in the will of the last Aga Khan who had privately decided that his grandson Karim, then a student at Harvard University, should be heir to the title rather than his son Prince Aly.

Through the Aga Khan, the Nizari Ismaili community is well connected to the top level of the British establishment. During a seven-day visit to Britain in 2008, the Aga Khan was honoured by the queen with a private banquet to celebrate his fiftieth year as Imam. On the same trip the Aga Khan had private meetings with Prime Minister Gordon Brown, the foreign secretary, the lord chancellor, the international development secretary, the then leader of the opposition David Cameron and the Mayor of London Boris Johnson. The Aga Khan has hosted the Prince of Wales and Duchess of Cornwall on a trip to an Ismaili enclave in Pakistan and on a visit to Al Azhar Park in Cairo, a heritage and leisure project funded through one of the Aga Khan's charities.

Who are the Aga Khan's followers in Britain?

In the nineteenth century many of the Indian Ismailis known as Khojas migrated to Zanzibar. They had been encouraged to do so by the sultan of Oman and Zanzibar who was keen to increase trade with the subcontinent. From Zanzibar many Khojas migrated to the mainland of East Africa, establishing communities in Mombasa, Dar es Salaam, Nairobi, Kampala and Tanga, where they prospered as business people.[11]

The Nizari Ismaili community in Britain today is largely made up of the descendants of those migrants to East Africa. Small numbers initially came to the UK as students in the 1950s, often staying at the Nizaris' hostel/community centre in Kensington. From the 1970s there was a more significant influx following the expulsion of Asians from Uganda by the dictator Idi Amin in the 1970s and Africanisation policies in neighbouring countries. A smaller wave of economic migrants from India and Pakistan has added to the community more recently.

The structure of the Nizaris' community organisation in Britain conforms to that set out in a written constitution which applies to Nizari Ismailis around the world. At the top is a National Council and below that are regional and local groups. The president of the National Council is appointed by the Aga Khan himself and serves for a term of three years.

Although such roles are unpaid, they carry a high-level of prestige within the Nizari Ismaili community and are usually undertaken by wealthy business people and professionals.

Each member of the National Council takes responsibility for one of the dozen or so 'portfolios' which cater to the social needs of the community. 'The economics portfolio for example is about how to be successful in business,' explains Shams Vellani, a prominent Ismaili in the UK, 'They will invite outsiders to give talks to members.'[12] There are also portfolios to promote education, healthy living, to organise sporting and youth activities and to cater to the specific needs of women. Almost every Ismaili family in the UK has graduates in it, according to Vellani, so finding appropriate volunteers to take on roles requiring professional expertise is not difficult.

The Ismailis operate their equivalent of a sharia council, known as the National Arbitration and Conciliation Board. In the UK, the Board handles between 200 and 300 cases per year, adjudicating on divorce and separation issues and business disputes between Ismailis. The arbitrators may have legal or other relevant expertise and will always be respected members of the Ismaili community. The guiding principles are 'fairness and natural justice'.[13]

The Nizaris have no Islamic seminaries, although they do have religious teachers (*mu'allimun*) and preachers (*waezeen*) who instruct members about their faith and heritage.

The education of ordinary Nizaris in the principles and history of their tradition is handled by the Ismaili Tariqah and Religious Education Board (ITREB). Voluntary teachers deliver a six-year curriculum developed by the London-based Institute of Ismaili Studies to children attending weekend classes run at over sixty locations in the UK. The curriculum was devised in English before being translated into French, Portuguese, Urdu, Gujarati, Arabic and Persian for the benefit of Nizari communities worldwide.

The Aga Khan's own instruction in the tenets of his faith and Ismaili tradition was overseen by a young Ismaili religious teacher.[14] The Aga Khan also has a degree in Islamic studies from Harvard University. The Nizari Ismailis' equivalent of fatwas are called firmans—religious orders handed down by the Aga Khan which followers are expected to obey.

The Nizaris call their meeting halls jamatkhanas, a term sometimes used by other Muslim groups to describe their own places of congregation. Observant followers try to meet several evenings a week for the purposes of worship and community organisation, with Friday evening gatherings being the most important of the week. The British Nizaris' most significant meeting place is the Ismaili Centre in South Kensington, a purpose-built prayer hall and social centre which was opened by Prime Minister Margaret Thatcher in 1985. The centre has done much to raise the profile of the Ismailis in London: it is a striking building which mixes modern architecture with traditional Islamic designs and is situated on a prominent site on the Cromwell Road. The Nizari Ismailis have other purpose-built jamatkhanas in Leicester, Croydon and East Finchley, as well as some permanent centres in converted buildings elsewhere in London and one in Birmingham. But most of the fifty jamatkhanas in Britain are located in smaller towns and cities such as Milton Keynes, Guildford, Haverhill and Bolton, where jamatkhanas are held in rented premises such as school halls.[15]

The rituals of the Nizaris' worship are not disclosed to outsiders. 'They are very sensitive when it comes to their religious practices because they are not very orthodox,' explains a former employee of an Ismaili institution, 'If you go to the Ismaili Centre [in Kensington] you can be shown round and see into the main prayer room but you will not ever be allowed in during the religious service.'[16] Their most important festivals are the two Eids which are celebrated by Muslims generally, as well as the birthday of the Prophet Muhammad; the day of the appointment of Imam Ali; the commemoration of the martyrdom of Imam Ali; and 'Imamate Day'—a commemoration of the day on which the Aga Khan succeeded to his position.

Shams Vellani of the Institute of Ismaili Studies says that the Aga Khan's followers are free to go to any mosque of their choice for common prayers with other Muslims, but that they 'prefer mosques where the ethos is guided by the Quranic values of a shared humanity, pluralism, the role of intellect in matters of faith and life, respect for human dignity and the like'.[17]

Although the European wives of the Aga Khans have converted to Islam, there is apparently no pressure on those who marry an Ismaili in Britain to adopt the faith. According to Shams Vellani, in earlier times 'marrying out' was regarded as crossing over into the enemy camp. For women it would have necessitated the surrender of their faith on the basis that only Muslim men were permitted to marry a Christian or a

Jew. But now, says Vellani, marriage is regarded as a matter of personal choice rather than as a concern for the community.[18]

The newspaper columnist Yasmin Alibhai-Brown personifies the more liberal approach to Islam that is possible for Nizari Ismailis in Britain. She identifies herself as a practising Muslim, yet she is married to a non-Muslim (something still regarded as forbidden for Muslim women in most branches of Islam) and is not only unveiled herself but is a vocal critic of the mullahs who say all Muslim women have a duty to wear the hijab.

The consumption of alcohol is discouraged rather than regarded as a major sin by the Nizaris. A framework of ethical ideals published by the Aga Khan Development Network states that: 'Any substance abuse which interferes with the normal functioning of the mind is a greater violation of the ethical code for it amounts to self-inflicted loss of personal dignity and of the ability to fulfill one's responsibility to oneself, to one's family and to society.'[19] According to a former insider, 'The basic philosophy is all things in moderation. His Highness [the Aga Khan] serves wine when he gives lunch but does not drink himself. And no Ismaili would consume alcohol in his presence.'[20]

While most practising Muslims in Britain follow one of the groups which believe that music for the purpose of entertainment should at least be discouraged, the Nizaris have a group of amateur orchestral musicians—the Ismaili Community Ensemble—which holds an annual concert at the Cadogan Hall in London.

The Aga Khan Development Network

The National Council and the jamatkhanas serve the needs of the Ismaili community in Britain. But much of the Aga Khan's work is focused on philanthropic activities aimed at serving not just his own followers but others in need.

The Aga Khan's most important organisation is the Aga Khan Development Network (AKDN). Run from an office block on the estate of the Aga Khan's chateau just north of Paris, it has been described as his own UN. The AKDN focuses mainly on development activities in Africa and Asia, where most of its 80,000 employees are based. Profits generated by the Aga Khan from a portfolio of businesses—in sectors which include aviation, energy, pharmaceuticals, telecoms, hotels, banking and a tannery—are invested in development work.[21]

The Aga Khan Development Network has eleven 'agencies' engaged mainly in educational, cultural and humanitarian work. They include an emergency relief agency known as FOCUS; a micro-finance provider; a not-for-profit healthcare provider running health centres and hospitals in Asia and Africa; the Aga Khan University; the University of Central Asia, which was founded in 2000 as a joint venture with the governments of Kazakhstan, the Kyrgyz Republic and Tajikistan; the Aga Khan Trust for Culture, the work of which includes restoring buildings of historic importance in the Muslim world; and a development aid organisation, AKFED, which employs over 30,000 people in businesses set up to provide economic activity in parts of the world where there is a lack of foreign direct investment. In 2010, AKFED had an income of US$2.3 billion, equivalent to around one-fifth of the UK government's development aid budget.[22]

The UK government is one of the AKDN's sources of income. Between 2006 and 2008, the UK's Department for International Development paid the AKDN £1.3 million for work in unspecified countries in the field of 'democratic participation and civil society'.

Some young, professionally qualified Nizari Ismailis will take time out of their careers in the West to work in development projects in the poorest parts of Africa and Asia. But those employed to run AKDN's various offshoots are selected on merit and are often non-Ismailis.

Assistance is delivered in countries where poorer Ismailis live, but the beneficiaries are not necessarily Ismailis. For example, in 2002 the AKDN agreed to develop a five-star hotel in Kabul after the new Afghan government said it thought that increasing hotel capacity would aid the country's general economic development.[23] The rebuilt and extended building, which opened as the Serena Hotel in 2006, subsequently came under attack from the Taliban.[24]

The Aga Khan University's main campus is in Karachi, Pakistan, where the emphasis is on courses in medicine, nursing and teacher training. It is a non-denominational institution and Ismailis are not given preference in the allocation of university places: Nizaris make up just 2–3 per cent of the student population. The AKU also has a campus in London: the AKU Institute for the Study of Muslim Civilisations offers short courses and a two-year full-time MA in the study of Muslim cultures. In 2011 the AKU's London base was housed in rented accommodation in an office block on Euston Road. The Institute of Ismaili Studies was based on another floor in the same building but operated as a separate institution. Both institutions plan to move to a purpose-built campus near King's Cross station in 2015.

The Dawoodi Bohras

Among the luxury mansions on a back street in Notting Hill is a small 1970s block of flats called Bonham House. I used to pass this building every day—it was a source of curiosity for me as I would often see men and women dressed in what looked like a distinctive national costume coming in and out of it. The men were all bearded and wore white pill box caps embroidered with gold thread. The women were dressed in outfits which were unfamiliar yet recognisably Islamic: full-length dresses made of patterned or embroidered cotton and a matching cape with a bonnet-like hood attached to cover the hair. I concluded that it must be accommodation for the staff of a national embassy, but I was too shy to ask any of these supposed diplomats which country they represented.

The mystery was solved a few years later as I drove through the entrance to the Mohammedi Park Masjid Complex in Northolt, West London. I had come to meet a member of the Dawoodi Bohra congregation at his home in this small gated community. The mini-housing estate was full of men and women dressed in the same mysterious costumes I had seen in Notting Hill, and their attire, I discovered, is unique to this offshoot of the Ismaili Shia tradition.

The Dawoodi Bohras are mainly of Gujarati Indian origin and can trace their ancestral journey to Britain back through the South Asian trader communities of East Africa. Today the Dawoodi Bohra population is still concentrated in the subcontinent: around 700,000 of the estimated 1 million Bohras worldwide are thought to live in India.[25] Most of the 6,000 Dawoodi Bohras living in Britain are descended from those Gujarati traders who settled in East Africa. The UK community grew rapidly in the early 1970s with the mass emigration of ethnic South Asians from East Africa. According to the community's own estimates, there are now around 3,000 Dawoodi Bohras living in London and another 3,000 elsewhere in the UK, with organised communities— known as jamaats—in Leicester, Manchester, Bradford and Birmingham.

'We are very much a nation without a state,' Shabbir Abidali, then a senior member of the Bohra community in London, told me on my visit to Mohammedi Park in 2010.[26] He has close relatives in Sri Lanka,

Egypt, the United States, India, Kenya and Canada. Their communal identity is reinforced by maintaining their traditions, keeping in touch and through encouraging marriage within the faith. Abidali estimates that 99 per cent of those brought up in their tradition marry another Dawoodi Bohra. It is through marriage that Dawoodi Bohras from places as far afield as Canada, Sweden and India have joined the East African immigrants and their children in Britain.

As the Bohras neither proselytise nor exclude, conversion from other faiths or branches of Islam is possible but not common. Would-be converts have to go through a process of education before filling out an application to be accepted into the community. If their application is approved by the Bohras' spiritual leader in India, they will swear an oath of allegiance to him before acceptance is complete. Senior Bohra Shabbir Abidali knows of a Filipino Catholic, a Hindu and 'someone from Kyrgyzstan' who have converted.

In common with most observant Muslims, Dawoodi Bohras fast during Ramadan, celebrate the Eid festivals, and are commanded to offer five daily prayers. They also share with the Shia Twelvers the tradition of commemorating the martyrdom of the Prophet Muhammad's grandson Imam Hussain at the festival of Ashura, when emotional sermons are accompanied by the ritual chest-beating (*matam*) in congregation. Like the Twelvers, the Dawoodi Bohras also regard Najaf and Karbala in Iraq as important places of pilgrimage. In 2005, three members of the Bohras' Northolt mosque were killed in Iraq having travelled to the Shia shrines during the insurgency.

The Dawoodi Bohras' leader until his death in January 2014 was Syedna Mohammed Burhanuddin, the 52nd Dai. Unlike the Aga Khan, he was not regarded by followers as a successor to the Prophet Muhammad—in other words, he was not seen as a 'living Imam'. The Bohras believe that the last known Imam went into seclusion in the twelfth century and that since that time the line of succession has continued in secret. According to Ismaili historians, the twentieth Imam recognised by the Bohras' branch of the faith was murdered a few months after his son al-Tayyib was born. Al-Tayyib, the designated heir to the Imamate, then disappeared. The Bohras believe that Al-Tayyib survived and that the Imamate has continued in secret through his heirs.[27] In January 2014, Syedna Mufaddal Saifuddin succeeded his late father to become the 53rd Dai-al Mutlaq. According to an official Bohra publication, the twentieth Imam made preparations for the coming period of withdrawal from human sight by leaving instructions that the Dai al-Mutlaq should govern in the Imam's absence.[28] The Dai's role is to act as the Imam's deputy, leading the community, guiding the faithful and appointing a successor until the Imam returns. The Dai and his family, based in Mumbai, are referred to by followers as the royal family (or Qasr-e Ali, meaning noble house). The Dai's children and grandchildren have the title prince or princess and live in (not necessarily luxurious) properties owned by the Dai.[29]

Despite the ethnic dominance of Indians in this branch of the Ismaili faith today, the sect has its roots in the Fatimid Empire and for the first 400 years of its existence it was led by a Dai based in Yemen. After that time, the seat of the Dai moved to India, which was the other main area where followers were concentrated at the time. The leadership has remained in India ever since. Ties between the Yemeni Ismailis and the leadership in India grew weak but were revived in the 1960s by the 52nd Dai. Today in Yemen there are still Muslims who, like the Dawoodi Bohras, recognise the authority of the India-based Dai pending the return of a new Imam. But the Yemeni community of 'Tayyibis', having dwindled to around just 5,000 people, is now smaller than that of the Dai's followers in the UK.[30]

A Bohra publication on the life of the 52nd Dai describes him as leading with 'the authority of the Imam' and states that his pronouncements were 'to be regarded by his believers as being the same as the Imam's'.[31]

The 52nd Dai tried to be present in the lives of his followers as much as is possible. He used to travel until he suffered a stroke during a trip to London in 2011, the year of his 100th birthday. The mysterious 1970s block in Notting Hill was his London residence where he would stay on regular two- to three-week visits. (The organisation's British headquarters are nearby in Notting Hill Gate.) Personal visits were supplemented then replaced by taped sermons and regular live satellite broadcasts to followers around the globe. Such was his embrace of new technology as a means of keeping in touch with his followers that the author of an authoritative study of the Dawoodi Bohras was inspired to call it *Mullahs on the Mainframe*.

The Bohras, unlike the Nizaris, have their own Islamic seminaries: the Aljamea tus Saifiya in Surat, India; Jamia Saifiya in Karachi, Pakistan; and, since 2011, an academy in Nairobi, Kenya. Most study there for reasons of personal piety rather than with the intention of becoming full-time clerics.

It comes as a surprise to discover that the obligation upon Bohras to wear the 'traditional' dress is the result of a twentieth-century revival in outward religiosity. The Bohra community in India and elsewhere went through a period of being relatively relaxed about such issues as the wearing of the hijab and the free mixing of men and women. However, in the late 1970s the 52nd Dai decided to order his followers to adhere to more recognisably Islamic habits. In 1979 he decreed that male followers should wear a beard and that women should dress in the Bohra version of the burqa, known as a *rida*. This was followed up in 1981 with a further directive that men should wear the white embroidered cap known as a *topi*, a long white shirt and an optional long jacket.[32]

'Every cap is different,' explains Bohra elder Shabbir Abidali. The Bohra women embroider the white cloth hats with different designs in gold embroidery to make each one unique. Many of the Bohra men will wear these caps whenever they are in public, even if they work for non-Bohra employers. The women's uniform is so distinctive that it takes more nerve to wear it outside the community. At the Mohammedi Complex in London, one Bohra woman who wears the costume to visit the mosque says she would never dream of dressing that way for work: 'I'm a teacher and if the people I work with ever saw me dressed like this I'd be a laughing stock.'[33] Yet a Bohra man assures me that 'there are innumerable independent and professional women in our community who wear the *rida* with pride'.[34]

Another aspect of revived orthopraxy under the 52nd Dai was a ban in 1979 on the payment or charging of interest on loans. Although a ban on interest is widely observed by Muslims from most Islamic traditions, as traders and businessmen the Bohras had come to rely on such loans for investment. At the 52nd Dai's instigation, Bohra communities, including the Bohras of Britain, established trusts offering interest-free loans mainly to their own followers.[35] Shabbir Abidali of the Bohra community in Northolt has no hesitation in backing the 52nd Dai's ruling on this issue: Abidali says that the Islamic scriptures are quite clear on the subject and he is sceptical about financial innovations designed to make the payment of interest appear Islamically compliant.[36]

Since the 1970s, each Bohra community leader—known as an *amil*—has had to issue certificates indicating the level of an individual follower's adherence to Islamic orthodoxy, as defined by the Dai. Followers are asked about their behaviour on a number of issues such as how often they pray, how consistently they adhere to the dress code and whether they drink alcohol or smoke. Green cards are awarded to the most adherent, amber cards to those who err on some minor issues and red cards to those who err on at least one major issue, such as the avoidance of alcohol or the payment of taxes due to the Bohra headquarters. A card of some colour is needed to have access to community services such as marriage and funeral rites. But even a mere red card-holder is still within the fold on the basis that he or she accepts the 52nd Dai's authority.[37]

The fact that the 52nd Dai managed to change the practices of the worldwide Dawoodi Bohra community in less than a decade is perhaps a sign of the strength of his authority among followers who referred to him as 'His Holiness'.

But the 52nd Dai's willingness to wield such authority gave rise to a dissident, reformist Bohra movement which called for the democratisation of the community.

In Britain, relations between the Bohras and other Muslim groups are cordial but not strong. Neither the Bohras nor the Nizaris are affiliated to the Muslim Council of Britain; nor are they represented on the Mosques and Imams National Advisory Body (MINAB).

Invitations to important events are extended by the Bohras to leading figures in Britain's Shia 'Twelver' organisations. Their contacts beyond the Muslim communities included a visit to their main mosque in London by the then Archbishop of Canterbury Dr Rowan Williams.[38]

The Mohammedi Park Complex

The Mohammedi Park Complex in Northolt, West London, is the result of the Bohras' most ambitious project in Britain. Consisting of twenty-two modern town houses built around a central square and mosque, it was completed in 1996 after years of struggle to obtain planning permission. The minaret of the purpose-built mosque is visible from the main A40 route heading west out of London. A slip road leads down to this tranquil enclave in the incongruous setting of an industrial estate.

On Saturday mornings the mosque and central square are busy as members of the community from across London and the south-east of England bring their children to classes. The mosque at its centre is capable of accommodating 1,000 worshippers. It combines modern design with elements of Fatimid architecture in recognition of the Ismailis' tenth-century glory days.

Walking along cloistered corridors on the mosque's first floor on a Saturday morning, one can see small classrooms of children and mothers talking casually outside. The basement of the mosque serves as a dining room where groups of eight sit on the floor to share a meal around a large circular tray known as a *thaal*. The huge main hall is where the men perform their communal prayers. It is also the venue for wedding celebrations at which men and women will socialise separately, divided by a screen. In a room off the main hall, men, women and children queue to pay their respects at the grave of the wife of the 52nd Dai. She died on a visit to London in 1994 and, as followers reach the plinth on which her casket sits, they pray, bow and kiss her grave.

The sitting room inside Shabbir Abidali's town house on the complex is furnished in the style of a typical English executive home. He explains that covenants attaching to the houses prevent residents from selling to non-Bohras. But despite the physical separation of this neighbourhood, those who live here perhaps lead more integrated lives than some of those Muslims concentrated in the regular housing of Midlands cities or former mill towns in the north of England. The children brought up in this complex, for example, all go to non-Muslim state and private schools (although some may study at the Bohra seminary in India for a few years). And many residents of Mohammedi Park are successful business people and professionals whose careers take them outside their own immediate community on a daily basis.

The community's tradition of entrepreneurship and self-employment has been incorporated into the religious identity of followers in Britain (Bohra literally means trader). 'We believe that God is the only provider,' explains one member of the community.[39] Many of the younger Bohras have qualified in professions such as law, medicine and accountancy, where a comfortable life is easily achievable as a salaried employee. But the true Bohra will still aspire to run his own business, according to senior Bohra Shabbir Abidali: 'If he is a doctor, he will be thinking about opening his own practice.'[40]

The Bohra's most prominent entrepreneur in Britain is Lord Noon who, as Gulam Noon, made a fortune supplying microwaveable curries to supermarkets. It was perhaps Lord Noon's connections which helped to ensure that the 52nd Dai was received at 10 Downing Street by Prime Minister Gordon Brown during a visit in 2008.

Despite their strong, distinctive identity and international links, the Dawoodi Bohras resident in the UK feel themselves to be British and exhibit strong feelings of patriotism. According to Shabbir Abidali, most members of his community have only British citizenship. He believes that England stands for fair play and he regards loyalty to one's country of residence as important. He was sceptical about the 2003 invasion of Iraq but sees no reason why a Bohra should not join the British armed forces (a member of their small community is in the RAF).[41] The Bohras also regard the British royal family with respect and affection. The Prince of Wales has visited the Bohra's Mohammedi Park Complex twice, and his Foundation for the Built Environment was consulted over some of the architectural details of its design.[42]

The Dawoodi Bohra Reformists

On the edge of Birmingham's Jewellery Quarter, the construction of a Bohra mosque was approaching completion in 2013. Visible from one of the city's busiest roads, this striking example of Islamic architecture looked set to become a local landmark, much like the Ismaili Centre in South Kensington.[43]

The new mosque will be open to both men and women, but the Dawoodi Bohra woman who points it out to me does not expect to be allowed inside. Haki Kapasi is a former president of the Dawoodi Bohra Welfare Society of Great Britain, a branch of the Bohra reformist movement which regarded the 52nd Dai's leadership style as unacceptably autocratic. Twelvers, Sunnis and non-Muslims may be welcome to visit the new Bohra mosque when it opens, but not the likes of Haki Kapasi. 'It's easier for a Hindu to go into the mosque than a reformist!' she tells me.[44]

Haki Kapasi's reformist Bohra community in Birmingham has new premises too: a converted factory less than ten minutes drive away from the new orthodox mosque. The reformists will gather there for all the major religious festivals: Ashura, Ramadan, Eid and the commemoration of saints. Although orthodox Bohras will be welcome, it is unlikely that any will dare attend.

Openly questioning the Dai's authority can lead to excommunication (*baraat*) and orthodox Bohras are forbidden to have even casual contact with the excommunicated, including members of their own family.

'There are mainstream guys who come to my house but they don't tell anyone they have been,' says Haki Kapasi's reformist father, Fazlehusein Hassanbhai Kapasi. 'Likewise, I go to their house but I won't tell other people I have been there.' They might spot each other at a wedding celebration hosted by a neutral third party like a Shia Twelver, but the orthodox and the reformist will probably not talk 'in case somebody spies'. Fazlehusein Kapasi becomes almost tearful at times as he recounts stories of exclusions from funerals and families torn apart as a result of someone going over to the other camp.[45]

Mr Kapasi and many of the orthodox Bohras with whom he has a clandestine friendship go back a long way. They grew up in Uganda in the 1940s and 1950s and were part of a community of around 100 Dawoodi Bohra families based in the capital Kampala, where the local jamaat owned a mosque, a boarding house, religious schools, accommodation for the poor and properties for rent. However, when the 52nd Dai took over in 1965, he brought in a new constitution which included a requirement to transfer ownership of community assets to the Dai himself. While most of the Dawoodi Bohras acceded to the Dai's request, in Kampala a majority decided to disobey. The Dai's attempt to acquire the community's property was thwarted after a Ugandan court ruled that it belonged to the dissidents instead.

When ethnic South Asians were expelled from Uganda by President Idi Amin in the 1970s, Bohras from both the reformist and orthodox sides settled in England where they continued to live as separate religious communities.

The Dawoodi Bohra Welfare Society of Great Britain estimates that there are around 800 reformists in the UK. The largest community is in Leicester where the society has around 250 members. The other organised communities are in Peterborough and London as well as Birmingham.

The reformists do not wear the orthodox Bohra garb. Haki Kapasi wears jeans and, like other reformist women, only covers her hair at religious gatherings. Her father regards the topi hat as authentic, traditional Bohra dress, but he does not wear it when he goes to work at his motor parts business in Birmingham. He feels no obligation to wear the white robes or even grow a beard.

Some members of the first generation of reformist Bohras brought up in Britain have married outside the community. Interfaith marriages have taken place with Sunni Muslims, Nizari Ismailis, Hindus, Sikhs and English Christians. These non-Muslim partners are welcomed into the community, according to the Kapasis. Two of Mr Kapasi's own children are married to non-Bohras: 'It's a wonderful mix.' He would prefer it if his new relatives by marriage converted to the Bohra tradition. But if they do not do so, he says that he reassures them: 'You are part of the family even if you are not part of the faith.' It is a mark of how liberal the reformists are that they should have previously elected a woman, Haki Kapasi, as the president of their British organisation.

Despite the relaxed attitude towards marrying out, the community is growing rather than integrating itself into extinction. Some of the children of those mixed marriages have been brought up as reformist Dawoodi Bohras. Furthermore, among the second generation, marriage within the community is on the rise, according to the Kapasis.

Some reformists in India have complained that the Dawoodi Bohras there practise female genital mutilation ('female circumcision'). Mr Kapasi says it certainly went on among his community in Uganda and he has arguments with orthodox Bohra acquaintances in India who still support the practice even now. But he concedes that the orthodox Bohras he knew regarded it as a traditional rather than a religious practice and it was not carried out as the result of any order of the Dai or accompanied by any religious ceremony. Haki Kapasi co-chaired an international gathering of Bohra reformist women in the 1990s when they agreed that the practice should end: 'It was culture and tradition. When we came here, we realised it wasn't right.'[46]

Without access to any of the Dawoodi Bohra seminaries, how have the reformists managed to produce their own religious leaders? 'Ah, this is the crux for us,' says Mr Kapasi, 'We have to train our own people into leading our rituals.' Responsibility for researching different aspects of the faith and traditions is delegated to lay members. 'We're like the Quakers,' says Haki Kapasi. Sometimes a Sunni or a Shia Twelver imam from Birmingham will preach to them or preside at a funeral. At other times a leading Dawoodi Bohra reformist from Leicester will carry out their religious ceremonies: 'He doesn't have the title of a priest but he is as good as,' according to Mr Kapasi.

Despite the official shunning by the orthodox of the reformists, Fazlehusein Hassanbhai Kapasi reported signs of pragmatism when we met in 2013. It had become possible for reformists to attend funerals presided over by an orthodox priest, particularly if it was the wish of the deceased's family. What was the cause of this apparent rapprochement? Mr Kapasi suspected it was all about money and influence. The local *amil* might be more inclined to abide by the wishes of a deceased person's family if the family in question happens to be wealthy and willing to give a large donation, he said. Furthermore, the orthodox community cares about its image in Britain. 'They still want the invitation to Downing Street,' said a sceptical Mr Kapasi.

Conclusion

The Bohras and the Nizaris confound much of the received wisdom about Islam and Muslims in Britain. Islamism—a belief in a pan-Islamic state governed by a caliph—is often identified as the ideology responsible for Muslim radicalisation and antipathy towards secular government. Islamist ideologies, think tanks such as The Quilliam Foundation have argued, encourage Muslims to feel that their first loyalty is towards a yet to be realised Muslim state rather than Britain.

However, the Bohras and the Nizaris are the most patriotic of Muslim groups in Britain—yet they could still be called Islamists: they look back with pride to the days when they ran an empire led by an Ismaili caliph and, in the run-up to Indian independence, Aga Khan III attempted to negotiate with the British, at the urging of his Indian followers, for the creation of a separate Ismaili state.[47]

Both the Aga Khan and the Dai al-Mutlaq lack the sovereign territory or the mass following needed to realise the dream of an Islamic state. But modern communications allow them to be present in the lives of their followers more than ever and to exert increasing authority over the diaspora.

The use some Muslims in Britain make of sharia law to settle disputes between themselves has been the source of anxiety about the erosion of secularism and the idea of 'one law for all'. But even the Nizaris, who appear at ease with secularism, make use of Britain's arbitration law to give effect to their own parallel legal system in which the Aga Khan himself is the ultimate arbiter.

The Deobandis and the modern Islamist groups might point to the Nizaris and argue that Ismaili integration has been achieved only by sacrificing scripturalism and the outward signs of the Muslim faith. But the Bohras are living proof that this need not be the case: they put at least as much emphasis as the Deobandis and Islamists on complying with the sharia and adopting an outwardly Islamic identity.

The Bohras of the Mohammedi Park Complex even demonstrate that it is possible to be integrated into British society while living in a religiously exclusive neighbourhood.

The willingness of the Ismailis to embrace British society might have something to do with the fact that their followers are probably the most economically and educationally successful Muslims in Britain. But this is clearly an insufficient explanation because, in socio-economic terms, Britain's Ismailis are very similar to many of the Gujaratis who play a prominent role in the Deobandi movement in Britain, coming as they do from the relatively well-educated and affluent Indian diaspora communities ejected from East Africa in the 1970s and '80s.

So how do the Ismailis manage to display such loyalty to queen and country without feeling some sense of contradiction? Perhaps it is because of the attitudes of their leaders. Both the Aga Khan and the Bohras' 52nd Dai emphasised the duty of their followers not just to obey the law of the land in which they live but to be loyal to that country. More importantly, the leaders have displayed affection towards Britain, its institutions and its rulers. By refraining from campaigning on pan-Islamic political causes, the Aga Khan and the late Dai are no doubt regarded by many non-Ismaili Muslims as 'sell outs' who have cared too much about keeping cordial relations with the British establishment. Whatever the fairness of that criticism, the attitude of the Ismailis' leaders has allowed their British followers to feel that their religious identity reinforces rather than contradicts their feelings of belonging to Britain.

The Ismailis have shown that integration into Britain need not mean losing one's Islamic identity and that it can mean more than just claiming citizenship and obeying the law. As the 52nd Dai reminded followers at the celebrations of his 102nd birthday in 2013: 'Prophet Mohammed (peace be upon him) has taught us that to love one's country is part of one's faith.'

If true faith and true integration for British Muslims are about feeling a love for Britain and its people, then the Ismailis have led the way.

NOTES

INTRODUCTION

1. Tahir Abbas (ed.), *Muslim Britain: Communities Under Pressure*, New York: Zed Books, 2005; Waqar Ahmad and Ziauddin Sardar (eds), *Muslims in Britain: Making Social and Political Space*, London: Routledge, 2012; Peter Hopkins and Richard Gale (eds), *Muslims in Britain: Race, Place and Identities*, Edinburgh: Edinburgh University Press, 2009.
2. The programme was *Panorama*, 'A Question of Leadership', broadcast on BBC1, 21 Aug. 2005. Transcript available at: http://news.bbc.co.uk/1/hi/programmes/panorama/4171950.stm (last accessed 3 Feb. 2014).
3. Based on Apr. 2013 data collected and analysed by Mehmood Naqshbandi, webmaster of www.muslimsinbritain.org
4. A survey of over 1,000 mosques conducted by Mehmood Naqshbandi suggests that around 84 per cent of Barelwi mosques provide prayer facilities for women compared to 57 per cent of Deobandi mosques.
5. Confidential cable written by Richard LeBaron, deputy chief of the US embassy in London. Passed by WikiLeaks to *The Daily Telegraph* and published on *The Telegraph* website on 3 Feb. 2011. Available at: http://www.telegraph.co.uk/news/wikileaks-files/uk-terrorism-wikileaks/8302239/EUR-SENIOR-ADVISOR-PANDITH-AND-SP-ADVISOR-COHENS-VISIT-TO-THE-UK-OCTOBER-9-14-2007.html (last accessed 5 Feb. 2014).
6. MuslimsInBritain.org, www.muslimsinbritain.org/guide/guide.html (last accessed 13 Jan. 2014).

1. THE DEOBANDIS: THE MARKET LEADERS

1. 'The Fiqh of Muslim Non-Muslim Interaction: A Detailed Explanation'. Available at: http://www.daruliftaa.com/node/4940?txt_QuestionID= (accessed 26 Jan. 2014).

2. Based on Apr. 2013 data collected and analysed by Mehmood Naqshbandi.

3. Dietrich Reetz, *Islam in the Public Sphere: Religious Groups in India 1900–1947*, New Delhi: Oxford University Press, 2006, pp. 126, 130.

4. Ibid., p. 251.

5. Charles Allen, *God's Terrorists*, London: Little, Brown and Company, 2006, p. 267.

6. Ibid., p. 268.

7. Reetz, *Islam in the Public Sphere*, p. 187.

8. Ibid., pp. 201, 231

9. Ibid., p. 154.

10. Ibid., p. 201.

11. Ibid., p. 197.

12. The JuI initially mobilised scholars from a range of religious backgrounds to campaign for the creation of a separate Muslim state. However, after partition, the party became the political party of Deobandi scholars in Pakistan. See ibid., p. 198.

13. Author interview with Islam Ali Shah, then secretary of JuB, 8 Aug. 2009.

14. Ibid.

15. Philip Lewis noted that a president of the JuB was a Sufi follower (*mureed*) of the principal of Bury Darul Uloom and that a vice president of the JuB taught part time at the Tablighi Jamaat's headquarters in Dewsbury. See his *Islamic Britain, Religion, Politics and Identity among British Muslims*, London: I.B. Tauris, 1994, p. 91.

16. A study of Deobandi seminaries in Britain found that most of the staff were Gujarati. Sophie Gilliat-Ray, 'Educating the Ulama: Centres of Islamic Religious Training in Britain', *Islam and Christian–Muslim Relations*, 17, 1 (Jan. 2006), pp. 55–76.

17. Author correspondence with Maulana Mushfiq Uddin, 6 Jan. 2013.

18. www.inter-islam.org—an amateur website dedicated to Sheikh Mohammad Zakariyya and his followers.

19. Author interview with Mushfiq Uddin, 21 Feb. 2010.

20. In 2008 faith schools were given the option of submitting to inspection by the Bridge Schools Inspectorate as an alternative to Ofsted.

21. Edna Fernandes, 'Inside the Muslim Eton: Special Report', *The Mail on Sunday*, 20 June 2010.

22. 'Admissions', Jamea Al Kauthar website. Archived web page: http://web.archive.org/web/20100623132521/http://www.jamea.co.uk/admissions.htm (last accessed 3 Feb. 2014).

23. Author interview, May 2010.

24. Author interview with Mushfiq Uddin, 21 Feb. 2010.

25. Ibid.

26. Report of Bridge Schools Inspectorate of Jamiatul-Ilm Wal-Huda UK School, Mar. 2010. The school came to national attention in 2003 when one of its pupils,

Sajid Badat, was arrested on terrorism charges. Badat subsequently pleaded guilty to plotting to blow up a US-bound plane. However, he had decided to back out of the plot by the time he became a pupil at the school.

27. Author interview with Maulana Rashid Ali Seth, 16 Apr. 2007. Maulana Rashid is the imam of the Zakaria Mosque in Bolton.

28. Author interview with Mushfiq Uddin, 21 Feb. 2010. At the time of the interview, Ebrahim College was in negotiations with Roehampton University about the possibility of gaining accreditation for the college's proposed BA in Islamic Sciences and Society.

29. Author interview with Sheikh Riyadh ul Haq, 9 Feb. 2014.

30. Andrew Norfolk, 'The homegrown cleric who loathes the British', *The Times*, 7 Sep. 2007.

31. Andrew Norfolk, 'The sermons. Extracts from the preachings of Riyadh ul-Haq', Leading article, *The Times*, 7 Sep. 2007.

32. *Panorama*, 'British Schools, Islamic Rules', BBC, 22 Nov. 2010.

33. Philip Lewis, *Young, British and Muslim*, London: Continuum, 2007, p. 91–92.

34. Author interview with Sheikh Riyadh ul Haq, 9 Feb. 2014.

35. The dossier, by Khan Bilal and entitled 'Gardens of Truth, the media portrayal of Shaykh Riyadh ul Haq', was still in draft form in Feb 2014. It was due for publication by Bilal Khan in April 2014.

36. Andrew Norfolk, 'Hardline takeover of British mosques', The Times, 7 Sep. 2007.

37. 'Muslims in Leicester: At Home in Europe', Open Society Institute/Policy Research Centre (2010). Latent hostility from black Africans towards those of Asian origin in Malawi, Tanzania, Kenya and Uganda became more overt following independence from Britain in the mid-1960s. The most extreme example of this hostility was the decision by the Ugandan dictator Idi Amin in 1972 to expel all Asians. In Kenya, Africanisation policies made it virtually impossible for Asian workers to obtain jobs in the civil service where once they had held most of the positions. Many ethnic Asian entrepreneurs in Kenya were forced to close their businesses when the government of Kenya refused to grant them trading licences and undermined their traditional role as middlemen by creating state-controlled import monopolies.

38. Derived from the publicly available list of MCB affiliates in 2009, mapped on to mosque affiliations given on the MuslimsInBritain.org website, www.muslimsinbritain.org. Data collected and analysed by Mehmood Naqshbandi, webmaster of MuslimsInBritain.org as of 4 Apr. 2013.

39. Author interview with Yousif al-Khoei, MINAB trustee, 21 July 2010.

40. Author conversation with Mushfiq Uddin, 31 Dec. 2012.

41. Author interview with Mushfiq Uddin, 21 Feb. 2010.

42. See website of Leicester-based alim Mufti Muhammed ibn Adam al-Kawthari: http://www.daruliftaa.com/node/5857 (last accessed 24 Jan 2014).

43. Author interview with Suleman Nagdi, 2 Aug. 2010.

44. Author interview with Kaushar Tai, 29 May 2010.

45. Fatwa published on 21 Aug. 2008 on http://darulifta-deoband.org/showuser-view.do?function=answerView&all=en&id=7077 (last accessed 24 Jan. 2014).

46. Author interview with Kaushar Tai, 29 May 2010. The mosque's homepage at that time carried a prominent appeal to women to donate their jewellery to help pay for the cost of the new building. Such donations, according to the website, could result in many blessings including a place in jannat (heaven). Archived webpage accessible via http://web.archive.org/web/20101001201640/http://www.masjidhidayah.co.uk/page8.htm (last accessed 5 Feb. 2014).

47. Author interview with anonymous Dewsbury resident, summer 2010.

48. Author interview with Ismail Patel, founder of Friends of Al Aqsa, 2 Aug. 2010.

49. Confidential cable written by Richard LeBaron, deputy chief of the US embassy in London. Passed by WikiLeaks to *The Daily Telegraph* and published on *The Telegraph* website on 3 Feb. 2011. Available at: http://www.telegraph.co.uk/news/wikileaks-files/uk-terrorism-wikileaks/8302239/EUR-SENIOR-ADVISOR-PANDITH-AND-SP-ADVISOR-COHENS-VISIT-TO-THE-UK-OCTOBER-9-14-2007.html (last accessed 5 Feb. 2014).

50. Reetz, *Islam in the Public Sphere*, pp. 196, 293.

51. From a discussion, 'The Rise of British Jihad', hosted by the Frontline Club, London, 30 Oct. 2008.

52. M. Mansur Ali and Sophie Gilliat-Ray, 'Muslim Chaplains: Working at the Interface of "Public" and "Private"', in Waqar I.U. Ahmade and Ziauddin Sardar (eds), *Muslims in Britain: Making Social and Political Space*, New York: Routledge, 2012.

53. Author interview with anonymous male from Deobandi background, 24 Nov. 2011.

54. According to the biographical details given on his website, www.daruliftaa.com, Mufti Muhammad ibn Adam al-Kawthari also studied under the late grand mufti of India Sheikh Mahmud al-Hasan Gangohi, as well as Sheikh Mufti Muhammad Taqi Usmani of Pakistan and various scholars in Syria. Taqi Usmani is frequently cited by Mufti Muhammed ibn Adam on his website as a source of reference.

55. www.daruliftaa.com (last accessed 26–8 Nov. 2010).

56. Derived from data collected and analysed by Mehmood Naqshbandi, webmaster of MuslimsInBritain.org as of 4 Apr. 2013.

57. 'Women Praying at the Mosque', www.daruliftaa.com, available at: http://www.daruliftaa.com/node/6128?txt_QuestionID= (last accessed 3 Feb. 2014).

58. Author interview with anonymous male from Deobandi background, 24 Nov. 2011.

59. Reetz, *Islam in the Public Sphere*, p. 306.

60. Author interview with Suleman Nagdi, 2 Aug. 2010.

61. David Hughes, 'Summit of the Faiths at No. 10 Eases Fears of a Religious War' *Daily Mail*, 9 Oct. 2001.

62. Author interview with Suleman Nagdi, 2 Aug. 2010.

63. Interview of Nigel Inkster conducted by Frank Gardner, 5 July 2008 for *Analysis*, BBC Radio 4 (extract unbroadcast).

64. Author interview with Islam Ali Shah, 8 Aug. 2009.

65. While HuM had ties to the Deobandi movement, there were similar groups with links to other Pakistani religious groups: for example, Lashkar-e-Taiba (LeT) had links to the Ahl-e-Hadith (Salafi) and Hizbul Mujahideen had connections to the Jamaat-e-Islami. See Mohammed Amir Rana, *A–Z of Jehadi Organizations of Pakistan*, Lahore: Marshal Books, 2006.

66. 'Harkat-ul-Mujahideen', Stanford University website, http://www.stanford.edu/group/mappingmilitants/cgi-bin/groups/view/219 (last accessed 13 Jan. 2014).

67. Adrian Levy and Cathy Scott-Clark, *The Meadow: Kashmir 1995—Where the Terror Began*, London: Harper Collins, 2012, p. 296, p. 50.

68. Ibid., p. 296.

69. Ibid., p. xxvi.

70. Interview with anonymous Gujarati Deobandi from one of the English towns in which Azhar preached.

71. Harinder Baweja, 'Maulana Masood Azhar: Jaish-e-Mohammed', in Harinder Baweja (ed.), *Most Wanted: Profiles of Terror*, New Delhi: The Lotus Collection, 2002, p. 52.

72. Ibid.

73. 'Birmingham Terrorist Planted Suicide Bomb in Kashmir', The Press Trust of India, 28 Dec. 2000.

74. Dean Nelson, Hasnain Ghulam and Abul Taher, 'The Radical with a Perfect Cover', *The Sunday Times*, 20 Aug. 2006.

75. Interview by the author with undercover journalist who wishes to remain anonymous.

76. Zia Haq, 'Terror is Anti-Islamic', *Hindustan Times*, 25 Feb. 2008.

77. Zia Haq, 'Darul Snubs Pak Demand for Fatwa', *Hindustan Times*, 15 Dec. 2008.

78. Sheikh Musa Admani was brought up in Kenya. He studied in India at Darul Uloom Sabeelur Rashad, Bangalore and Darul-Ulum Bharuch, Kantharia. His father was head of the Tablighi Jamaat in Africa.

79. *File on 4*, 'Islamic Radicalisation', BBC Radio 4, 14 Nov. 2006.

2. THE TABLIGHI JAMAAT: MISSIONARIES AND A MEGA MOSQUE

1. Author interview with Faruqe Master, 16 Apr. 2007.

2. Zacharias Pieri, *Tablighi Jamaat*, London: Lapido Media, 2012.

3. Author interview with 'Omar', 27 Apr. 2007.

4. 2011 Census.

5. The location of the TJ's international HQ is a moot point. Raiwind is an important hub for the movement. However, Nizamuddin in Delhi is where the movement's leadership is based.

6. Ilyas preached that until Muslims themselves were reformed, non-Muslims could find no appeal in Islam. Maulana Wahiduddin Khan, *Tabligh Movement*, New Delhi: Goodwood Books Pvt Ltd, 1986, p. 40.

7. Ibid., pp. 30–1.

8. Philip Lewis, *Islamic Britain: Religion, Politics and Identity among British Muslims*, London: I.B. Tauris, 2002, p. 91.

9. The most recent annual report at time of writing was for year ended 31 Dec. 2010.

10. Yoginder Sikand, 'The Origins and Growth of the Tablighi Jamaat in Britain', *Islam and Christian–Muslim Relations*, 9, 2 (1998), p. 180.

11. Source: Mehmood Naqshbandi, webmaser of www.MuslimsInBritain.org, 4 Apr. 2013.

12. Sikand, 'The Origins and Growth of the Tablighi Jamaat', pp. 190–1.

13. Pieri, *Tablighi Jamaat*, pp. 30–1.

14. Ibid., p. 12.

15. Duncan Gardham, 'Fears Raised over Fundamentalist Islamic Group Operating in Britain', *The Daily Telegraph*, 9 Sep. 2008.

16. 'Tablighi Jamaat Does Not Preach Jihad, Says Senior Muslim Leader', Indo-Asian News Service, 8 July 2007.

17. 'Evidence in Secretary of State for the Home Department v. AP', 12 Aug. 2008, cited in Raffaello Pantucci, *'We Love Death as You Love Life': Britain's Suburban Mujahedeen*, London: Hurst, forthcoming.

18. Sean O'Neill and Roger Boyes, 'Islamic Missionary Group Links Alleged Plotters; Terror Plot', *The Times*, 17 Aug. 2006; Sandra Laville, 'Terror Arrests: Suspects Linked to Hardline Islamic Group: July 7 Bombers "Visited Movements Mosque HQ": Muslims Want Inquiry into Radicalisation of the Young', *The Guardian*, 18 Aug. 2006; Paul Lewis, 'Inside the Islamic Group Accused by MI5 and FBI', *The Guardian*, 19 Aug. 2006; Dean Nelson, Hasnain Ghulam and Abul Taher, 'The Radical with a Perfect Cover; Airline Bomb Plot', *The Sunday Times*, 20 Aug. 2006.

19. Paul Lewis, 'Inside the Islamic Group Accused by MI5 and FBI', *The Guardian*, 19 Aug. 2006.

20. Susan Sachs, 'A Muslim Missionary Group Draws New Scrutiny in U.S.', *The New York Times*, 14 July 2003.

21. Research interview carried out by BBC journalist Cheryl Varley in April 2006.

22. Omar Nasiri, *Inside the Jihad*, New York: Basic Books, 2006, p. 112.

23. Ibid., p. 114.

24. 'I Knew Exactly What I Was Doing', Peter Herbert interviewed by Vikram Dodd, *The Guardian*, 24 Aug. 2006.

25. 'Koran and Country: Biography of a Bomber', BBC Radio 4, 17 Nov. 2005.

26. Ed Vulliamy, 'Special Report: The IT Man who Tried to Stop the 7/7 Bombers: Exclusive: Computer Expert Made DVDs and Encrypted Emails for Islamist Circle', *The Guardian*, 24 June 2006.

27. Pantucci, '*We Love Death as You Love Life*'.

28. Dean Nelson, Hasnain Ghulam and Abul Taher, 'The Radical with the Perfect Cover: Airline Bomb Plot', *The Sunday Times*, 20 Aug. 2006.

29. 'Judgment of Mr Justice Kerr in the case of Secretary of State for the Home Department v. AP', 12 Aug. 2008, cited by Pantucci, '*We Love Death as You Love Life*'.

30. Author interview with Mehboob Kantharia, 9 Dec. 2007.

31. Pieri, *Tablighi Jamaat*, p. 45. Pieri is quoting from *Heavenly Ornaments*, the key TJ text for women.

32. Sheikh Musa Admani speaking at 'The Rise of British Jihad', a discussion hosted by the Frontline Club, London, 30 Oct. 2008. The full talk can be viewed online at www.frontlineclub.com/fully_booked_-_media_talk_the_rise_of_the_british_jihad/ (last accessed 13 Jan. 2014).

33. Sikand, 'The Origins and Growth of the Tablighi Jamaat'.

34. Sikand is quoting from a tract written by Haji Ibrahim Yoosuf Bawa Rangooni in *Al Islam Bartanniya*, 2, 1 (Apr. 1996), Gloucester: Idara Isha'at al-Islam. Sikand describes Rangooni, an Islamic publisher based in Gloucester, as someone who 'relentlessly espouses tablighi causes in his writings' and who claimed to be close to TJ leaders in Britain.

35. Pieri, *Tablighi Jamaat*, p. 42.

36. Author interview, 9 Dec. 2007

37. Pieri, *Tablighi Jamaat*, pp. 33–4.

38. Author interview with Mehboob Kantharia, 9 Dec. 2007.

39. Yoginder Sikand, 'The Tablighi Jama'at and Politics: A Critical Re-Appraisal', *The Muslim World*, 96, 1 (Jan. 2006), pp. 175–95.

40. Hakim Khwaja Iqbal Ahmad Nadwi, 'Mai Bhi Hazir Tha Vahan', *Zinadagi-I Nau*, 4, 2 (Mar. 1986), p. 44, cited in Sikand, 'The Tablighi Jama'at and Politics', pp. 175–95.

41. Sikand, 'The Tablighi Jama'at and Politics', pp. 175–95.

42. Ibid.

43. Speech on 30 Mar. 1965, delivered at Raiwind, Pakistan. Text reproduced in Khan, *Tabligh Movement*, p. 51.

44. Author interview with Faruqe Master, 16 Apr. 2007.

45. Author interview with Abdul Khaliq Mian, 3 Apr. 2007.

46. Ibid.

47. Sikand, 'The Tablighi Jama'at and Politics', pp. 175–95.

48. Abdul Taher, 'Giant Mosque For 40,000 May Be Built at London Olympics', *The Sunday Times*, 27 Nov. 2005.

49. Author interview with Alan Craig, 19 Jan. 2013.

50. Jamie Doward, 'Battle to Block Massive Mosque: Project for 40,000 Worshippers "Has Links with Radical Islam"', *The Observer*, 24 Sep. 2006.

51. Author interview with Mehboob Kantharia, 9 Dec. 2007.

52. Abdul Taher, 'Giant Mosque For 40,000 May Be Built at London Olympics', *The Sunday Times*, 27 Nov. 2005.

53. In 2013, the largest mosque in the UK was the Suffa-tul-Islam Central Masjid, a Barelwi mosque in Bradford with a capacity of 8,000. Source: Mehmood Naqshbandi, webmaster of MuslimsInBritain.org

54. Abdul Taher, 'Giant Mosque For 40,000 May Be Built at London Olympics', *The Sunday Times*, 27 Nov. 2005.

55. Author interview with Abdul Khaliq Mian, 3 Apr. 2007.

56. Author interview with Alan Craig, 19 Jan. 2013.

57. Ibid.

58. 'Muslims Oppose Building of Huge Mosque', *The Evening Standard*, 27 Nov. 2006.

59. Author correspondence with Minhaj ul Quran spokesperson, Shahid Mursaleen, Apr. 2013.

60. Daniel Nilsson DeHanas and Zacharias P. Pieri, 'Olympic Proportions: The Expanding Scalar Politics of the London "Olympics Mega-Mosque" Controversy', *Sociology*, 45, 5 (Oct. 2011), pp. 798–814.

61. Author interview with Alan Craig, 19 Jan. 2013.

62. Ibid.

63. Pieri, *Tablighi Jamaat*, p. 56.

64. 'Application for Mosque at Abbey Mills Site Rejected', London Borough of Newham press release, 5 Dec. 2012.

65. Pieri, *Tablighi Jamaat*, p. 73.

66. Pieri's publisher, Lapido Media, made Craig's alternative conclusion available on its website: www.lapidomedia.com/node/1849 (last accessed 13 Jan. 2014). Pieri, *Tablighi Jamaat*, p. 73.

67. Pieri, *Tablighi Jamaat*, p. 73.

3. THE SALAFIS: 'DON'T CALL US WAHHABIS!'

1. Natana J. DeLong-Bas, *Wahhabi Islam: From Revival and Reform to Global Jihad*, London: I.B. Tauris, 2007, p. 24.

2. Interview of Abu Khadeejah of Salafi Publications conducted by journalist Amardeep Bassey, June 2008, for BBC Radio 4 (extract unbroadcast). Programme produced by author.

3. Mariam Abou Zahab, 'Salafism in Pakistan, The Ahl-e Hadith Movement', in Roel Meijer (ed.), *Global Salafism, Islam's New Religious Movement*, London: Hurst, 2009, p. 127.

4. Author conversation with Abu Khadeejah of Salafi Publications, Apr. 2008.

5. Quintan Wiktorowicz, 'Anatomy of the Salafi Movement', *Studies in Conflict and Terrorism*, 29, 3 (Apr.–May 2006), p. 209.

6. Also described as 'purists', 'politicos' and 'jihadis' in Wiktorowicz, 'Anatomy of the Salafi Movement', pp. 207–39.

7. Manwar Ali later became known as Abu Muntasir. It means father of Muntasir and it was the name he adopted when he went to perform jihad in Afghanistan.

8. Author interview with Abdur Raheem Green, 25 June 2010.

9. Author correspondence with former JIMAS activist Usama Hasan, Feb. 2013.

10. Around the same time LeT representatives addressed a meeting in Birmingham at the headquarters of the Ahl-e-Hadith, the main South Asian Salafi network in Britain. Source: author correspondence with Usama Hasan who attended the Birmingham meeting.

11. The scholar in question was Ibn Qayyim al-Jawziyyah. The account of this conference is based on the recollections of Abu Khadeejah, a former JIMAS member who attended it. Author interview 1 June 2008 and subsequent correspondence.

12. Interview of Abu Khadeejah of Salafi Publications conducted by journalist Amardeep Bassey, June 2008, for BBC Radio 4 (extract unbroadcast). Programme produced by author.

13. Author interview with Manwar Ali, 30 Dec. 2011.

14. Biography of Muhammad Suroor Zayn al-Abidin in Stéphane Lacroix, 'Between Revolution and Apoliticism: Nasir al-Din al-Albani and his Impact on the Shaping of Contemporary Salafism', in Meijer, *Global Salafism*.

15. Rabi's book was *The Methodology of the Prophets in Calling to Allaah*, published in English by al-Hidayah Publications, Birmingham, 1997.

16. Ali al Timimi was subsequently imprisoned for life under the post-9/11 US anti-terrorist legislation for encouraging Muslims in America to go to camps run by Lashkar-e-Taiba in order to train to fight against US troops in Afghanistan.

17. Interview with Usama Hasan conducted by journalist Amardeep Bassey, 18 June 2008 for 'Jihad UK', BBC Radio 4. Programme produced by the author.

18. 'Profile: Sheikh Abdullah al-Faisal', BBC News online, 25 May 2007.

19. Author interview with Usama Hasan, June 2008.

20. Interview with Usama Hasan conducted by journalist Amardeep Bassey, 18 June 2008 for 'Jihad UK', BBC Radio 4. (Extract unbroadcast.) Programme produced by author.

21. Author interview with Cosh Omar, 5 Oct. 2008.

22. Chapter on the UK by Yahya Birt and Sadiq Hamid in 'Studies into Violent Radicalisation; Lot 2, The Beliefs Ideologies and Narratives', study carried out by the Change Institute for the European Commission (Directorate General Justice, Freedom and Security), Feb. 2008, p. 64.

23. Ibid.

24. DeLong-Bas, *Wahhabi Islam*.

25. Author interview with Abu Khadeejah of Salafi Publications, 1 June 2008. Several leading people in his organisation attended the University of Medina.

26. Jonathan Birt, 'Wahhabism in the United Kingdom, Manifestations and Reactions', in Madawi Al-Rasheed (ed.), *Transnational Connections and the Arab Gulf*, London: Routledge, 2005, p. 171.

27. WAMY was founded by Muslim Brotherhood exiles based in Saudi Arabia.

28. Author interview with Abu Khadeejah, 1 June 2008.

29. Author interviews with Abdur Raheem Green, 25 June 2010 and Abu Khadeejah, 1 June 2008.

30. Lacroix, 'Between Revolution and Apoliticism', pp. 60–1.

31. Ibid., pp. 66–7.

32. Data supplied by Mehmood Naqshbandi, webmaster of MuslimsInBritain.org, Apr. 2013.

33. Author visits in Oct. 2005 and June 2008.

34. Author interview with Umm Abdullah, 1 June 2008.

35. Author interview with Abu Khadeejah, 1 June 2008.

36. DeLong-Bas, *Wahhabi Islam*, p. 149.

37. Author interview with Abu Khadeejah, 1 June 2008.

38. 'Divorce, Sharia Style', Channel 4, 3 Feb. 2007. The scholar giving this advice was Suhaib Hasan, father of Usama Hasan and previously the head of the Ahl-e-Hadith movement in Britain. If the second marriage was legally contracted abroad, it could be recognised in Britain.

39. However, this is not the practice in Saudi Arabia where the triple *talaq* is considered valid even if done in one session. See DeLong-Bas, *Wahhabi Islam*, pp. 172–3. Abu Khadeejah also contests Usama's interpretation of the correct mode of divorce.

40. Muslim scholars who follow a madhab—a traditional school of Islamic law.

41. Author interview with Usama Hasan, June 2008.

42. *Dispatches*, 'Undercover Mosque', Channel 4, 15 Jan. 2007. The preacher is known as Abu Usamah.

43. Author correspondence with Abu Khadeejah, Feb. 2013.

44. *Dispatches*, 'Undercover Mosque'. The preacher was Abu Usamah, the same preacher who was shown in the documentary describing women as 'deficient'.

45. Bobby Pathak, 'Britain's New Preachers of Hate', *The Mirror*, 11 Jan. 2007.

46. *Dispatches*, 'Undercover Mosque'. According a Christian member of the Birmingham interfaith network, Green Lane Mosque has become far more engaged with non-Muslim faith groups since the 2007 'Undercover Mosque' programme. Author interview with anonymous interfaith activist 22 Mar. 2011.

47. Author interview with Usama Hasan, June 2008.

48. Ibid.

49. Suhaib Hasan is a former president of the Ahl-e-Hadith's national umbrella body, the Markazi Jamiat Ahl-e-Hadith UK. His mosque in Leyton disaffiliated from the network in 2005 after he was ousted as president. However, in 2008 he was still cooperating with the organisation.

50. Author interview with Usama Hasan, June 2008.

51. Author interview with Abu Khadeejah, 1 June 2008.

52. Author interview with Usama Hasan, June 2008.

53. Ahl-e-Hadith UK website, http://www.ahlehadith.co.uk/branches/fulldetails.htm accessible via Wayback Machine http://archive.org/web/ (last accessed 13 Jan. 2014).

54. Visit by the author, 29 and 30 May 2010.

55. Author interview with Manwar Ali, 30 Dec. 2011.

56. He married the daughter of Professor Khurshid Ahmad, a vice president of the Jamaat-e-Islami.

57. Rowenna Davis, 'Imam is Threatened with Death after Delivering Lecture on Evolution', *The Guardian*, 7 Mar. 2011.

58. Author telephone interview with Usama Hasan, Oct. 2011.

59. This story was related by Usama Hasan in 'Jihad UK', BBC Radio 4, 8 Sep. 2008.

60. Stephen Tankel, *Storming the World Stage: The Story of Lashkar-e-Taiba*, London: Hurst, 2011, pp. 109–10.

61. Interview with Usama Hasan conducted by journalist Amardeep Bassey, 18 June 2008 for 'Jihad UK', BBC Radio 4. Programme produced by the author.

62. 'A Controversial Cleric', BBC News online, 11 Oct. 2001: http://news.bbc.co.uk/2/hi/uk_news/1593025.stm (last accessed 13 Jan. 2014).

63. Philip Johnston and Nigel Bunyan, 'Imam "Linked to Terror" Free to Stay in Britain', *The Daily Telegraph*, 30 Oct. 2002.

64. Eric Lichtblau, 'Scholar is Given Life Sentence in "Virginia Jihad" Case', *The New York Times*, 14 July 2005.

65. *Dispatches*, 'From Jail to Jihad', Channel 4 television, 16 June 2008.

66. Based on data supplied by Mehmood Naqshbandi, webmaster of MuslimsIn Britain.org, Apr. 2013.

67. Mehmood Naqshbandi correspondence with the author, Apr. 2013.

68. Ismail Einashe, 'Mo and Me', *Prospect Magazine*, Aug. 2012.

69. *Dispatches*, 'Undercover Mosque'.

70. Author interview with anonymous Salafi activist, 24 Jan. 2010.

71. Author telephone interview with Faisal Hanjra, then president of FOSIS, Nov. 2009.

72. Author correspondence with Mehmood Naqshbandi, Apr. 2013.

4. THE JAMAAT-E-ISLAMI: BRITISH ISLAM'S POLITICAL CLASS

1. Author interview with Zahid Parvez, general secretary of UKIM, 22 Mar. 2011. He said 'Officially we have thirty-eight, but a few others are under our control.' Mehmood Naqshbandi, webmaster of MuslimsInBritain.org, estimated that the total of UKIM and other 'Maududi inspired Islamic movement' mosques totalled fifty-one in Apr. 2013.

2. Sayyid Abdul A'la Mawdudi, *Let Us Be Muslims*, Khurram Murad (ed.), Leicester: The Islamic Foundation, 2004, pp. 300–1. The original Urdu text was first published in 1940.

3. Lorenzo Vidino, *The New Muslim Brotherhood in the West*, New York: Columbia University Press, 2010, p. 116. Maududi also addressed the UKIM conference in Aug. 1968 (report in *The Muslim*, Jan. 1969).

4. Author interview with Dr Zahid Parvez, UKIM general secretary, 22 Mar. 2011.

5. Gilles Kepel, *Allah in the West*, Cambridge: Polity, 1997, p. 132.

6. The Markfield Institute of Higher Education website: http://www.mihe.org.uk/cert-chaplaincy (accessed 25 Jan 2014).

7. Author interview with Zahid Parvez, 22 Mar. 2011.

8. Author interview with Omar Faruk, 4 July 2009.

9. Author interview with Zahid Parvez, 22 Mar. 2011.

10. Author interviews with former members Dilwar Hussain and Omar Faruk.

11. Based on information at www.MuslimsInBritain.org

12. Its only other significant branch is in Oldham, Lancashire, where it opened the purpose-built Oldham Muslim Centre in 2008.

13. See Andrew Gilligan, 'Islamic Radicals "Infiltrate" Labour; Investigation: Secular Groups Lose Out as Funding Switched', *The Sunday Telegraph*, 28 Feb. 2010.

14. Mehboob Kantharia, a non-Islamist and one of those involved in the consultations which led to the creation of the MCB. Interview with author 7 Dec. 2007.

15. The award of a knighthood to Iqbal Sacranie for 'services to the Muslim community, to charities and to community relations' was announced in June 2005.

16. Lorenzo Vidino, 'London's Frantic Quest for the Muslim Holy Grail: The Post 9/11 Evolution of the Relationship between Whitehall and the British Muslim Community', *Religion Compass*, 5, 4 (Apr. 2011), pp. 129–38.

17. Martin Bright, 'Radical Links of UK's "Moderate" Muslim Group', *The Observer*, 14 Aug. 2005.

18. *Panorama*, 'A Question of Leadership', broadcast on BBC 1, 21 Aug. 2005. Transcript available: http://news.bbc.co.uk/1/hi/programmes/panorama/4171950.stm (last accessed 5 Feb. 2014).

19. Ibid. The affiliate in question was the South Asian Salafi movement the Ahl-e-Hadith.

20. The MCB's media officer Inayat Bunglawala (quoted in Martin Bright, 'Radical

Links of UK's "Moderate" Muslim Group', *The Observer*, 14 Aug. 2005) said that Maududi's *Let Us Be Muslims* had brought him to practise Islam. Sacranie told *Panorama*, 'I have read many of his [Maududi's] books and I believe he is one of the scholars that I certainly feel is an inspiration to many of us.'

21. Martin Bright, 'When Progressives Treat with Reactionaries: The British State's Flirtation with Radical Islamism', Policy Exchange, July 2006.
22. *Dispatches*, 'Undercover Mosque', Channel 4, 15 Jan. 2007.
23. The preacher, Dr Ijaz Mian, was also filmed speaking at an Ahl-e-Hadith mosque in Derby.
24. Together with another former Hizb ut Tahrir member, Ed Husain founded an anti-Islamist think tank, The Quilliam Foundation.
25. Dominic Casciani, 'Minister Backs New Muslim Group', BBC News online, 16 July 2006.
26. Jamie Doward, 'British Muslim Leader Urged to Quit over Gaza', *The Observer*, 8 Mar. 2009.
27. Vikram Dodd, 'Government Suspends Links with Muslim Council of Britain over Gaza', *The Guardian*, 23 Mar. 2009. The MCB lifted its six-year boycott of Holocaust Memorial Day in Dec. 2007 but resumed the boycott in 2009 in protest at Israeli actions in Gaza. The boycott was dropped again the following year.
28. The titles by Maududi advertised in the 2011/12 catalogue were: *The First Principles of Islamic Economics; Islamic Civilizations: Sources and Basic Principles; Towards an Understanding of the Quran; Four Key Concepts of the Quran; Let Us Be Muslims; The Islamic Movement: Dynamics of Values, Power and Change*.
29. Kepel, *Allah in the West*, p. 132.
30. Archived web page entitled 'Imam Hasan Al-Banna on Jihad', dated 3 Jan. 2001. Available via Internet Archive Wayback Machine: http://web.archive.org/web/20010507002317/http://www.ymuk.net/articles/?action=disparticle&id=9 (last accessed 5 Feb. 2014).
31. Author interview with Dilwar Hussain, 29 July 2009.
32. Author interview with Abdul Hamid Qureshim, 20 Mar. 2011
33. *Dispatches*, 'Britain's Islamic Republic', Channel 4, 1 Mar. 2010.
34. Tom Harper, 'Muslim Leader on War Crimes Charge; EX-NHS Adviser Who Met Charles Denies Claims', *Evening Standard*, 2 May 2013.
35. Dr Munir Ahmed, an ISB president, is one of the few leaders in the network to have trained as a scholar. He spent over thirteen years studying under an Iraqi scholar based in Leeds.

5. THE MUSLIM BROTHERHOOD: THE ARAB ISLAMIST EXILES

1. Gilles Kepel, *The Roots of Radical Islam*, London: Saqi, 2005, pp. 46–57.

2. Author telephone conversation with Kamal Helbawy, Nov. 2009.

3. Author interview with Ashur Shamis, 4 Aug. 2009.

4. Ibid.

5. Author interview with Kamal Helbawy, 28 June 2009.

6. Recollection of Anas Altikriti, son of Usama Altikriti. Interview with author, 18 Aug. 2009.

7. Author interview with Ashur Shamis, 4 Aug. 2009.

8. Ibid.

9. Kamal Helbway interview with Frank Gardner, BBC security correspondent, recorded 11 Oct. 2005 for BBC Radio 4 programme 'How Islam Got Political', broadcast 10 Nov. 2005.

10. Author interview with Kamal Helbawy, 24 Mar. 2010.

11. Kamal Helbway interview with Frank Gardner, BBC security correspondent, recorded 11 Oct. 2005 for BBC Radio 4 programme 'How Islam Got Political', broadcast 10 Nov. 2005.

12. Author interview with Kamal Helbawy, 24 Mar. 2010.

13. Ibid.

14. Ibid.

15. Author interview with El Mahboub Abdel Salim, an aide to Hasan Turabi, 23 Aug. 2009.

16. Author interviews with former YMUK and ISB activist Omar Faruk and former ISB activist Ed Husain.

17. Author interview with Anas Altikriti, 18 Aug. 2009.

18. Ibid. A detailed account of these events is given by Robert Lambert, former Special Branch officer, in his book *Countering al-Qaeda in London: Police and Muslims in Partnership*, London: Hurst, 2011.

19. Dominic Kennedy and Richard Kerbaj, 'Sack Mohamed Ali Harrath, Scotland Yard Urged', *The Times*, 16 Dec. 2008.

20. *Panorama*, 'A Question of Leadership', BBC 1, 21 Aug. 2005. Transcript available at http://news.bbc.co.uk/1/hi/programmes/panorama/4171950.stm (last accessed 13 Jan. 2014).

21. They were also joined by a non-MAB member, Ismail Patel, a Deobandi who works for the campaigning group, Friends of al Aqsa.

22. Author interview with Said Ferjani, 13 Aug. 2009.

23. Ibid.

24. Author interview with Anas Altikriti, 18 Aug. 2009.

25. Ibid.

26. *Panorama*, 'Faith, Hate and Charity', BBC 1, 30 July 2006.

27. Author interview with Kamal Helbawy, 24 Mar. 2010.

28. Quoted in Senior British Islamist Praises Osama bin Laden, Quilliam Foundation press release, 4 May 2011. Explanation given during an author interview with Kamal Helbawy, 10 June 2013.

29. Stephen Glain, 'Sibling Rivalry', *The Majalla*, 21 May 2013; Stephen Glain, 'Liberal Islam's Poster Boy', *The Majalla*, 8 July 2013.

30. Author telephone conversation with Ashur Shamis, 8 Dec. 2011.

31. Of Al-Muntada Al-Islami mosque in London.

32. Accounts filed with the Charity Commission, 2008.

6. THE BARELWIS: SUFIS AND TRADITIONALISTS

1. Data supplied by Mehmood Naqshbandi, webmaster of MuslimsInBritain.org, Apr. 2013.

2. Written in Arabic and pronounced 'Ya Allah, Ya Rasoul Allah.'

3. Figures on mosque management based on author's calculations using data supplied by Mehmood Naqshbandi, webmaster of MuslimsInBritain.org, Apr. 2013.

4. Pnina Werbner, *Pilgrims of Love: The Anthropology of a Global Sufi Cult*, London: Hurst, 2004, is devoted to an in-depth study of the tariqa in Pakistan and the UK.

5. Ron Geaves, *The Sufis of Britain: An Exploration of Muslim Identity*, Cardiff: Cardiff Academic Press, 2000, p. 93.

6. Ibid., p. 42.

7. Author interview with Sheikh Muhammad Ramadan al Qadri—who runs the Farghana Institute, an MuQ mosque and study centre in the Whalley Range district of Manchester—7 June 2008. The sheikh stated that MuQ had around twenty-five scholars in the UK, all graduates of MuQ's own university in Pakistan.

8. For a sympathetic description of Tahir al Qadri's agenda see Muhammad Rafiq Habib, 'A Critical Analysis of the Ideology of Dr Muhammad Tahir-ul-Qadri with Special Reference to Islamic Revivalism', unpublished PhD thesis, Al-Maktoum College of Higher Education, University of Aberdeen, 2012.

9. Author interview with Sheikh Muhammad Ramadan al Qadri of al Farghana Institute, Manchester—a Minhaj ul Quran centre, 7 June 2008.

10. Accounts filed with the Charity Commission for year 2010/11.

11. Ibid.

12. Author visit 28 Feb. 2008.

13. Author interview with Sajad Ali, 11 Apr. 2008.

14. Ibid.

15. Author interview with Abu Khadeejah, 1 June 2008.

16. A slightly different translation of Imam Malik's words is cited by Geaves in *The Sufis of Britain*, p. 44: 'He who practices tasawwuf without learning sharia corrupts his faith, while he who learns sacred law without practising tasawwuf corrupts himself. Only he who combines the two proves true.' Geaves' source for this quotation is a work written by Haras Rafiq's spiritual guide, Sheikh Hisham Kabbani—*The Encyclopaedia of Islamic Doctrine*, Chicago: As-Sunna Foundation of America, Kazi Press, 1998.

17. Geaves, *The Sufis of Britain*, p. 35.
18. Ibid., pp. 152, 155.
19. Author interview with Sajad Ali, 11 Apr. 2008.
20. Ibid.
21. Author interview with Mas'ud Ahmed Khan, 10 May 2008.
22. Sheikh Nuh Ha Mim Keller, 'Is it Permissible for a Muslim to Believe that Allah is in the Sky in Literal Sense?', 1995. Originally published in Q News. Accessed via http://www.masud.co.uk/ISLAM/nuh/inthesky.htm (last accessed 13 Jan. 2014).
23. Mahmood Murad, 'Where is Allaah?', salafipublications.com, available at http://www.salafipublications.com/sps/sp.cfm?subsecID=AQD05&articleID=AQD050004&articlePages=1 (last accessed 13 Jan. 2014).
24. Author interview with Mas'ud Ahmed Khan, 10 May 2008.
25. Author correspondence with Mas'ud Ahmed Khan, Jan. 2012.
26. The term was coined by Yahya Birt.
27. See 'Why Muslims Follow Madhabs?' a lecture given in 1995 by Sheikh Nuh Ha Mim Keller on his 1995 UK tour. Available at http://masud.co.uk/ISLAM/nuh/madhhabstlk.htm (last accessed 13 Jan. 2014).
28. See Chapter 1. Deobandi scholar Maulana Mushfiq Uddin estimated in 2010 that the Deobandis had twenty-two Darul Ulooms in the UK.
29. The list was compiled by Jonathan (aka Yahya) Birt and was cited in Sophie Gilliat-Ray, 'Educating the Ulama: Centres of Islamic Religious Training in Britain', *Islam and Christian–Muslim Relations*, 17, 1 (Jan. 2006), pp. 55–76.
30. Author correspondence with Sheikh Ruzwan Mohammed, 8 Jan. 2013.
31. This account of the BMF's origins is based on the author's interview on 31 May 2008 with Hafiz Gul Mohammed, imam of the Fezane Madina Mosque in Peterborough and a teacher at Jamia al Karam School in Retford. Hafiz Gul moved temporarily to London to work on establishing the BMF in 2005.
32. Author interview with Haras Rafiq, 17 Apr. 2008.
33. Author interview with Hafiz Gul, 31 May 2008.
34. Author correspondence with Haras Rafiq, Jan. 2013.
35. Referred to by Paul Wolfowitz, deputy secretary of defence, in a speech entitled 'September 11th, One Year Later', at the Brookings Institution, Washington, DC, 5 Sep. 2002. Kabbani is a US citizen.
36. 'Uzbek Leader, Foreign Minister Meet Visiting US Islamic Leader', BBC Monitoring Central Asia Unit report of Uzbek radio broadcast, 10 Apr. 2001.
37. Simon Stjernholm, 'Sufi Politics in Britain: The Sufi Muslim Council and "the Silent Majority" of Muslims', *Journal of Islamic Law and Culture*, 12, 3 (Oct. 2010), pp. 215–26.
38. Ibid., pp. 223–5.
39. The exception to this pattern is perhaps Asif Mohammed Hanif, a British

Pakistani Muslim who carried out a suicide bombing attack on a bar in Tel Aviv in 2003. Hanif had been a dedicated member of the Hounslow branch of the Sufi group LightStudy before he carried out the attack which went directly against LightStudy's teachings. See Martin Bright and Fareena Alam, 'Making of a Martyr: From Pacifism to Jihad', *The Observer*, 4 May 2003.

40. Author interview with Hafiz Gul, 31 May 2008.

41. Ibid.

42. On this point, Hafiz Gul echoes the pronouncements of the late Salafi scholar Sheikh Muhammad Nasiruddin Al-Albani.

43. Author interview with Hafiz Gul, 31 May 2008.

44. Ibid.

45. Ibid.

46. Philip Lewis, *Islamic Britain: Religion, Politics and Identity among British Muslims*, London: I.B. Tauris, 1994, p. 167.

47. Author interview with Sajad Ali, 11 Apr. 2008.

48. Ibid.

49. Geaves, *The Sufis of Britain*, p. 152.

50. Martha Linden, 'Suicide Bombers "Heroes of Hellfire", Says Muslim Scholar', Press Association Mediapoint, 2 Mar. 2010.

51. Ron Geaves, 'Learning the Lessons from the Neo-Revivalist and Wahhabi Movement: The Counterattack of the New Sufi Movements in the UK', in Jamal Malik and John Hinnells (eds), *Sufism in the West*, London/New York: Routledge, 2006, pp. 153–5.

52. Habib, 'A Critical Analysis of the Ideology of Dr Muhammad Tahir-ul-Qadri'.

53. Author interview with Murtaza Pooya, 29 July 2010. Pooya spent thirteen years in al Qadri's political party: Pakistan Awami Tehreek.

54. Author interview with Sheikh Faiz ul Aqtab Siddiqi 3 Dec. 2007.

55. Ibid.

56. 'Mujadid of the 20th Century, Hazrat Allama Pir Muhammad Abdul Wahab Siddiqi (ra)—1942–1994', International Muslim Organisation, available at http://www.al-hijaz.co.uk/tareeqa/AWS_STORY_IMO.HTM (last accessed 6 Jan. 2012).

57. Private video recording of the opening of the Muslim Parliament on 4 Jan. 1992, cited in Lewis, *Islamic Britain*, p. 53.

58. 'Mujadid of the 20th Century'.

59. Innes Bowen, 'The End of One Law for All?' BBC News Interactive, 28 Nov. 2006.

60. The man was Liaqat Hussein, the assistant to the Bradford-based Barelwi sheikh, Pir Maroof. He told writer Malise Ruthven that he bought the book for burning. See Malise Ruthven, *A Satanic Affair*, London: Chatto & Windus, 1990, p. 103.

61. Waqar Gillani and Carlotta Gall, 'Pakistan Killing Bares Deep Societal Rift', *International Herald Tribune*, 6 Jan. 2011.

62. Carlotta Gall, Waqar Gillani and Salman Masood, 'Governor's Assassination Deepens the Divide in Pakistan', *New York Times*, 6 Jan. 2011.

63. When the BBC journalist Owen Bennett Jones visited the self-confessed assassin's home in 2012 he noted that one visitor who had signed the guestbook claimed to be representing a Barelwi Muslim organisation in the West Midlands.

64. 'Pakistan Clerics Say Slain Ex-Governor Did Not Commit Blasphemy', *The News* (Pakistan), 14 Oct. 2011 (via BBC Monitoring).

65. Author's own estimate based on figures given in official inspection reports of educational institutions.

7. THE SHIA 'TWELVERS': NAJAF IN BRENT

1. See Robin Wright and Peter Baker, 'Threat To Election From Iran: Leaders Warn Against Forming Religious State', *Washington Post*, 8 Dec. 2004.

2. Author interview with anonymous local Shia Muslim, summer 2009.

3. Author interview with Rebecca Masterton, 4 Aug. 2010.

4. Ibid.

5. Ibid.

6. 'Mapping the Global Muslim Population: A Report on the Sizes and Distribution of the World's Muslim Population', The Pew Forum on Religion and Public Life, Oct. 2009.

7. Mehmood Naqshbandi, who via his website MuslimsInBritain.org has collected the most extensive dataset on mosque affiliation in the UK, cautions that his data on Shia mosques and prayer facilities is not as authoritative as it is for other groups. He estimates that there are around sixty Shia Twelver mosques and centres in the UK. A senior Shia scholar in the UK, Syed Ali Raza Rizvi, estimates that there are ninety-nine to 100 Shia Twelver mosques and places of worship. The Shia tend to establish 'Islamic centres' rather than mosques for communal worship. This is to avoid certain Islamic restrictions which apply to mosques. For example, it is not religiously permissible to sell or demolish a mosque. Many of these centres are known as Hussainias as one of their purposes is to act as a gathering place to commemorate the martyrdom of Hussain, a grandson of the Prophet Muhammad revered by the Shia. Author interview with Syed Ali Raza Rizvi, president of the Majlis E Ulama E Shia Europe, 13 Jan. 2013. Rizvi says he knows of only five Shia mosques in the UK.

8. Author interview with Dr Saeed Bahmanpour, 26 July 2010.

9. Vali Nasr, *The Shia Revival: How Conflicts within Islam Will Shape the Future*, New York: W.W. Norton, 2007, pp. 126, 144.

10. Elvire Corboz, 'The al-Khoei Foundation and the Transnational Institutionalisation of Ayatollah al-Khu'i's Marjaiyya', in Lloyd Ridgeon (ed.), *Shi'i Islam and Identity: Religion, Politics and Change in the Global Muslim Community*, London: I.B. Tauris, 2012.

11. Yasin T. al-Jibouri, 'A Brief Biography of the Late Grand Ayatollah Abul-Qasim al-Khoei', available at: http://www.academia.edu/4745047/A_Brief_Biography_of_the_Late_Grand_Ayatollah_Abul-Qasim_al-Khoei_1_In_Memory_of_His_Late_Holiness_Grand_Ayatollah_Sayyid_Abul-Qasim_al-Khoei (last accessed 5 Feb. 2014).

12. Author interview with Yousif al-Khoei, 23 July 2010.

13. Ibid.

14. The other organisations which helped to set up MINAB were the Muslim Council of Britain, the Muslim Association of Britain and the British Muslim Forum.

15. Corboz, 'The al-Khoei Foundation', pp. 107–8.

16. The foundation is at 65 Brondesbury Park, London NW6.

17. Author interview with Yousif al-Khoei, 3 June 2013.

18. The foundation is at 75 Brondesbury Park. The premises were purchased for £875,000 in 2001 by Seyed Jawad Shahrestani. Shahrestani is a former trustee of the UK branch of the Imam Ali Foundation.

19. Author interview with Dr Sayed Fadhil Bahrululoom, founder and director of the Alulbayt Foundation, 21 July 2010.

20. In Aug. 2010 the director of the Alulbayt Foundation, Dr Sayed Fadhil Bahrululoom, and his colleague Sajad Jiyad were both on the four-member Validation Board for the Islam and CitizenShip Education Project.

21. 'Could I Stop Being A Muslim?' BBC Radio 4, 22 Apr. 2008. Programme produced by the author.

22. Author interview with anonymous former student of Dr al-Milani, June 2009.

23. Author interview with Shazim Hussayn, then principal of Al Mahdi Institute, 28 July 2010

24. According to Charity Commission records, in 2008 the college also received some funding from The Irshad Trust, the charity which is the main benefactor of the Islamic College of Advanced Studies.

25. Funding comes from Al-Mustafa International University in Qom. Author interview with Dr Bahmanpour, 26 July 2010.

26. Dr Bahmanpour was succeeded as principal in Dec. 2011 by Mohammad Jafar Elmi.

27. Author interview with Dr Saeed Bahmanpour, 26 July 2010.

28. Nasr, The Shia Revival, pp. 128–9.

29. Author interview with Dr Saeed Bahmanpour, 26 July 2010.

30. Correspondence with the author, June 2013.

31. Matthijs van den Bos, '"European Islam" in the Iranian Ettehadiyeh', in Ridgeon, Shi'i Islam and Identity, p. 66.

32. Author interview with Iraqi Shia scholar, July 2010.

33. Martin Fletcher, 'Iranian TV mouthpiece shut down by UK watchdog', The Times, 21 Jan. 2012.

34. Author visit to Idara-e-Jaaferiya, Tooting, 9 Jan. 2013.
35. Author interview with Syed Ali Raza Rizvi, 13 Jan. 2013.
36. Author interview at Tooting Idara, 9 January 2013.
37. Account of Shabbir Razvi, who is the son of one of the original Idara trustees and is writing a history of the Shia community of Britain. Author interview with Shabbir Razvi, 9 Jan. 2013.
38. The Muhammedi Trust relocated to Cricklewood in North West London in 2005.
39. Author interview with Syed Ali Raza Rizvi, 13 Jan. 2013
40. Ibid.
41. Author visit to Idara-e-Jaaferiya, Tooting, 9 Jan. 2013
42. Data provided by Mehmood Naqshbandi, webmaster of MuslimsinBritain.org, Apr. 2013.
43. Author interview with Syed Ali Raza Rizvi, 13 Jan. 2013.
44. The founders were followers of Grand Ayatollah Sayyid Muhsin al-Tabatabai al-Hakim. Source: Dr Sayed Khalil Tabatabai, a grandson of al-Hakim who assisted the Shia communities in London (author interview, Aug. 2010).
45. Corboz, 'The al-Khoei Foundation'.
46. Author interview with Mulla Mohammed Kassamali, 31 May 2008.
47. Author visit and interview with Abbas Ismail, Dec. 2010.
48. Author interview with Imranali Panjwani, 27 July 2010.
49. Al Rasul Al Akram Islamic Centre, Nairobi, Kenya.
50. Author interview with Abbas Ismail, Dec. 2010.
51. Author visit to the Shia Ithna'ashari Community of Middlesex centre at its premises, North Harrow Assembly Hall, 30 July 2010. None of the SICM members interviewed wished to be named in this book.
52. The imam was Shakyh Hasan Ali al-Taraiki, a graduate of Dr Fadhil al-Milani's International Colleges of Islamic Science in North London. Al-Taraki is based at the Al Abrar Foundation. Interview with author, 3 Aug. 2010.
53. Author interview with SICM executive committee member, 30 July 2010.
54. Abdulaziz Sachedina, 'What Happened in Najaf?', available at http://islam.uga.edu/sachedina_silencing.html (last accessed 13 Jan. 2014), plus author correspondence with Dr Abdulaziz Sachedina, Nov. 2011.
55. Author interview with senior SICM member, 30 July 2010.
56. Author interview with Ali Ismail, 30 July 2010.
57. Author visit to Dar Al Islam Foundation, 30 July 2010.
58. Author interview with Saeed Shehabi, 3 Aug. 2010.
59. Ibid.
60. The Lebanese Dawa Party was later disbanded. Some activists entered the secularist Amal party where they remained. Others broke away to found Hezbollah. Augustus Richard Norton, *Hezbollah: A Short History*, Princeton: Princeton University Press, 2007, pp. 31–2.

61. Laurence Louër, *Transnational Shia Politics: Religious and Political Networks in the Gulf*, London: Hurst, 2008, pp. 200, 85.

62. Ibid., p. 85. According to Louër, al-Sadr also recommended Hizb ut Tahrir as a model.

63. Author interview with Saeed Shehabi, 19 June 2013.

64. Ibid.

65. For a detailed account of the Kanoon Towhid, see van den Bos, '"European Islam" in the Iranian Ettehadiyeh'.

66. Author interview with Saeed Shehabi, 19 June 2013.

67. Author interview with Saeed Shehabi, 3 Aug. 2010.

68. Ibid.

69. Shehabi's co-editor was Laith Kubba, who later went on to be an adviser to Iraqi Prime Minister Ibrahim Jaaferi and to head the Middle East and North Africa programme at the US foundation the National Endowment for Democracy.

70. The imam is Sheikh Hasan Ali al-Taraiki. He is the same imam who regularly leads the prayers at the SICM in Harrow but does not support its liberal views.

71. Author interview with Saeed Shehabi, former MYA member, 3 Aug. 2010.

72. Ibid.

73. David Hughes, 'Summit of the Faiths at No 10 Eases Fears of a Religious War', *Daily Mail*, 9 Oct. 2001.

74. Author interview with Abbas Ismail of the World Federation, Dec. 2010.

75. Author interview with Saeed Shehabi, 3 Aug. 2010.

76. Robert Dreyfus, 'The Shia Fellas', *The American Prospect*, June 2007.

77. Author interview with Ali Ismail, 30 July 2010.

78. Grant says that as a UK citizen he decided on principle not to fight against British forces in Iraq. Author interview 28 June 2009.

79. Grant has an unusual background. Having initially converted from Christianity to Sunni Islam as a teenager, he came under the influence of the pro-al-Qaeda preacher Abu Hamza in the 1990s. When war broke out in Kosovo, Grant says that Abu Hamza arranged for him to fight with a jihadi group against the Serbs. Grant later converted to Shi'ism.

80. 'Shia Organisations Show their Displeasure towards the Muslim Council of Britain', Ahl ul Bayt News Agency, 1 July 2010.

81. Author interview with Yousif al-Khoei, June 2013.

82. Ruth Gledhill, Tamanna Ali and Omar Shahid, 'Jailed Radical's New Mosque Raises Fears of Sunni–Shia Conflict in Britain', *The Times*, 4 May 2013.

83. Human Rights Watch, 'World Report 2013: Pakistan', available at: http://www.hrw.org/world-report/2013/country-chapters/pakistan (last accessed 5 Feb. 2014).

84. 'Mosque Hall Blaze was Arson, Say Police', *Birmingham Post*, 6 Sep. 2004.

85. Author interview with Syed Ali Raza Rizvi, 13 Jan. 2013.

86. Ibid.
87. Speech given by Dr Sayyid Ali Murtaza Zaidi at the Islamic Centre of England, 'The Plight of the Shia in Pakistan', 30 Dec. 2012.
88. 'Written Evidence C. Christine Fair (Assistant Professor, Center for Peace and Security Studies, Georgetown University, Washington DC) to the US Senate Committee on Foreign Relations Inquiry into Al Qaeda, the Taliban and Other Extremist Groups in Afghanistan and Pakistan', 24 May 2011.
89. Speech given by Dr Sayyid Ali Murtaza Zaidi at the Islamic Centre of England, 'The Plight of the Shia in Pakistan', 30 Dec. 2012.
90. Viewable via web page archived in July 2013: http://web.archive.org/web/20130723011220/http://absoc.co.uk/?page_id=1038 (last accessed 5 Feb. 2014).

8. THE ISMAILIS: THE DAWOODI BOHRAS AND THE FOLLOWERS OF THE AGA KHAN

1. The figure of 10,000 is cited in Marc van Grondelle, *The Ismailis in the Colonial Era*, London: Hurst, 2009. The 50,000 figure comes from the Institute of Ismaili Studies—they estimate the total number of followers as being between 25,000 and 50,000—but with the caveat that the Ismailis do not carry out a census of their membership.
2. Farhad Daftary, *The Ismailis: Their History and Doctrines*, Cambridge: Cambridge University Press, 2007, pp. 248–52.
3. Grondelle, *The Ismailis in the Colonial Era*, pp. 11–12.
4. *The Ismailis: Their History and Doctrines*, p. 5.
5. 'Prince Karim Aga Khan IV and the Ismaili Sect of Shia Islam', broadcast in The World, Public Radio International, 26 July 2011.
6. Hakim Elnazarov and Sultonbek Aksakolov, 'The Nizari Ismailis of Central Asia in Modern Times: A Modern History of the Ismailis', in Farhad Daftary (ed.), *Continuity and Change in a Muslim Community*, London: I.B. Tauris/The Institute of Ismaili Studies, 2011, p. 62.
7. James Reginato, 'The Aga Khan's Earthly Kingdom', *Vanity Fair*, Feb. 2013.
8. The Aga Khan was addressing volunteers for the Indian Field Ambulance Corps in Oct. 1914. Grondelle, *The Ismailis in the Colonial Era*, pp. 33–5.
9. Correspondence with the author, Jan. 2013.
10. Daftary, *The Ismailis*, p. 496.
11. Ibid., p. 486.
12. Author interview with Shams Vellani of the Institute of Ismaili Studies, 29 Mar. 2011.
13. Ibid.
14. Correspondence with Shams Vellani of the Institute of Ismaili Studies, Jan. 2013.
15. A list of the locations of the UK jamatkhanas can be found online at http://ismaili.

net/heritage/jk_view2?filter0=&filter1=United+Kingdom (last accessed 13 Jan. 2014).

16. Author interview with an anonymous non-Ismaili previously employed in an Ismaili institution.

17. Author correspondence with Shams Vellani, Jan. 2013.

18. Author interview with Shams Vellani of the Institute of Ismaili Studies, 29 Mar. 2011.

19. Aga Khan Development Network (AKDN), 'An Ethical Framework', published on the Institute for Ismaili Studies website, available at http://www.iis.ac.uk/view_article.asp?ContentID=101094 (last accessed 13 Jan. 2014).

20. Author interview with an anonymous non-Ismaili previously employed in an Ismaili institution, Mar. 2011.

21. Reginato, 'The Aga Khan's Earthly Kingdom'.

22. Figures from the AKFED website: www.akdn.org/akfed (last accessed 25 Jan. 2014).

23. 'Aga Khan Development Network Initiates US$25 Million Kabul Hotel Project', AKDN press release, 20 Nov. 2002.

24. Abdul Waheed Wafa and Graham Bowley, 'The Taliban Says it Hit Kabul hotel; 6 are Killed', *The International Herald Tribune*, 15 Jan. 2008.

25. Jonah Blank, *Mullahs on the Mainframe: Islam and Modernity among the Daudi Bohras*, Chicago: University of Chicago Press, 2001, p. 13.

26. Author interview with Shabbir Abidali, 31 July 2010.

27. Daftary, *The Ismailis*, p. 260.

28. Al Dai Al-Fatimi, *Syedna Mohammed Burhanuddin: An Illustrated Biography*, London: Al-Jame'ah al-Saifiyah Trust, 2001, pp. 3–4.

29. Blank, *Mullahs on the Mainframe*, pp. 134–52.

30. Daftary, *The Ismailis*, p. 291.

31. Al-Fatimi, *Syedna Mohammed Burhanuddin*, p. 4.

32. Blank, *Mullahs on the Mainframe*, p. 184.

33. Author conversation with Bohra woman at Mohammedi Park Mosque Complex.

34. Correspondence with Adnan Abidali, Dec. 2012.

35. Blank, *Mullahs on the Mainframe*, p. 197.

36. Author interview with Shabbir Abidali, 31 July 2010.

37. Blank, *Mullahs on the Mainframe*, pp. 180–3.

38. 'Archbishop's visit to Dawoodi Bohra Mosque and Jain Temple', official website of Dr Rowan Williams, Friday 7 May 2010, available at http://rowanwilliams.archbishopofcanterbury.org/articles.php/989/archbishops-visit-to-dawoodi-bohra-mosque-and-jain-temple (last accessed 13 Jan. 2014).

39. Author interview with Adnan Abidali, 31 July 2010.

40. Author interview with Shabbir Abidali, 31 July 2010.

41. Ibid.
42. Ibid. Subsequent correspondence with Adnan Abidali.
43. Author visit June 2013.
44. Author interview with Haki Kapasi, 7 June 2013.
45. Author interview with Fazlehusein Hassanbhai Kapasi, 7 June 2013.
46. Author interview with Haki Kapasi, 7 June 2013.
47. Daftary, *The Ismailis*, p. 483.

INDEX

INDEX

INDEX

INDEX

INDEX

INDEX

INDEX

INDEX

INDEX

INDEX

INDEX

INDEX

INDEX

INDEX

INDEX

INDEX

INDEX

Obama administration 4
  State Department 27, 127
University of Central Asia 174
University of Central Lancashire 20
University of Gloucestershire 85
University of Medina, Saudi Arabia
  20, 65, 68
University of Wales 113
Urdu 18, 21, 34, 36, 68, 75, 86, 121, 137,
  145, 148, 149, 163
Uzbekistan 87, 127

Vanity Fair 168
Vellani, Dr Shams 169, 170, 172
Versi, Ahmed 158
Victoria, Queen of the United King-
  dom, Empress of India 169

Wahaj, Siraj 86
Wahhabism 4–5, 57–8, 67, 123, 124,
  126, 129, 162
  bida (innovation) 57, 124
  origins 57–9
  tawhid (oneness of God) 57
Wakefield Central Mosque 15
Wales 113
Wales, Sir Robin 55
Walsall, West Midlands 117
Walthamstow, London 79
Ware, John 2, 3, 91
Watford, Hertfordshire 150
West Yorkshire 79, 117, 118, 133, 175
Westminster, London 135
WikiLeaks 27
wilayat al-faqih (Guardianship of the
  Jurist) 139, 142, 155
Willesden, London 135, 137, 138, 143

Willesden Islamic College of
  Advanced Studies 142–3
Winter, Tim 123
women's rights 3, 12, 14–15, 27, 28–30,
  40, 46, 69–72, 97, 169, 173
World Assembly of Muslim Youth
  (WAMY) 69, 105, 158
World Federation of Khoja Shia
  Ithna'ashari Muslim Communities
  150, 151, 154, 159, 160
World War I 13, 169
wudu (ablutions) 30

X Factor 127

Yacoob, Salma 96
al-Yaqoubi, Sheikh Muhammad 124
Yasin, Khalid 80–1
Yasin, Sheikh Ahmed 91
Yemen 124, 125, 130, 177
Young Muslims Organisation
  (YMO) 88, 89, 93, 97–8
Young Muslims UK (YMUK) 86–7,
  95, 96, 107
  radio stations 86
Yousuf, Maulana Mohammad 49
YouTube 21–2, 148
Yusuf, Sheikh Hamza 86, 124

Zaidi, Dr Sayyid Ali Murtaza 162
Zakariya, Maulana Mohammed 16, 39,
  49, 51
Zanzibar 170
Zardari, Asif Ali 130
Zawiya, Birmingham 118–19
Zia-ul-Haq, Muhammad 84
zikr (meditation) 18, 116, 118–19
Zindapir, Sheikh 117